Teaching English through integrated education in lower primary school

Linguistic behaviour and executive control

WYDAWNICTWO
UNIWERSYTETU
ŁÓDZKIEGO

Anna Parr-Modrzejewska

Teaching English through integrated education in lower primary school

Linguistic behaviour and executive control

Łódź–Kraków 2015

Anna Parr-Modrzejewska – University of Lodz, Faculty of Filology, Institute of English Studies
171/173 Pomorska St., 90-236 Lodz
anna.parr@uni.lodz.pl

Published by Łódź University Press & Jagiellonian University Press

First edition, Łódź–Kraków 2015

ISBN 978-83-7969 513-3 – paperback Łódź University Press

ISBN 978-83-233-3922-9 – paperback Jagiellonian University Press

ISBN 978-83-7969-514-0 – electronic version Łódź University Press

ISBN 978-83-233-9203-3 – electronic version Jagiellonian University Press

Łódź University Press
8 Lindleya St., 90-131 Łódź
www.wydawnictwo.uni.lodz.pl
e-mail: ksiegarnia@uni.lodz.pl
phone +48 (42) 665 58 63, fax +48 (42) 665 58 62

Distribution outside Poland
Jagiellonian University Press
9/2 Michałowskiego St., 31-126 Kraków
phone +48 (12) 631 01 97, +48 (12) 663 23 81, fax +48 (12) 663 23 83
cell phone: +48 506 006 674, e-mail: sprzedaz@wuj.pl
Bank: PEKAO SA, IBAN PL 80 1240 4722 1111 0000 4856 3325
www.wuj.pl

To my brother with love

TABLE OF CONTENTS

INTRODUCTION

The first years of formal education are the most exciting ones. This is the time when children become pupils and there is a world of new experiences and knowledge open for them to explore. This is also the time when they undergo an intensive cognitive, as well as social and psychological development. The process of education in this sector is, thus, far from mere knowledge transfer that follows the core curriculum. Teachers of young learners need to be exceptionally sensitive and responsive to their students' needs in order not to destroy their natural curiosity and eagerness to learn. It is of utmost importance to remember that teachers do not teach their subjects in isolation but rather are responsible for a holistic development of the learners' construction of knowledge about the world. Approaching the process of formal instruction from this perspective, teachers acknowledge the learners' right to take partial control over their own learning and they react to their pupils' needs that are often motivated by the not yet fully developed cognitive skills.

Among a rich repertoire of cognitive abilities required for successful participation in formal educational context, executive functions seem to have attracted a lot of attention in various fields of research (e.g. Letho et al., 2003 – psychological perspective; Miyake et al., 2000 – neurological perspective; Sonuga-Barke et al., 2003 – dysfunctional development perspective). Executive functions are self-regularity capacities that include attention and inhibitory control, which are esential for school readiness and further educational success, including social and bahavioural adaptability, as well as academic achievement (cf. Liew and McTigue, 2010; Payton et al., 2008). The ability to control one's executive functions is a decisive factor not only in adademic success but in early socialisation porocess itself. Problems in this area are associated with numerous dysfunctions and atypical development in children including the ADHD syndrome (cf. Willcutt et al., 2005). Developing executive functions are responsible, among others, for the lengthening attention span in young learners which allows them to participate in formal education. Andrews-Espy et al. (2011: 41) found that a number of dysfunctional behaviours in young children are correlated with their executive control. The dysfunctions identified by the researchers to be related to the executive control capacity included hyperactive behaviours, attention problems, disinhibition behaviours and emotional dysregulation.

The level of executive functions development is determined by the pace and dynamics of developmental changes resulting from the biological maturation processes as well as by stimulation from the socio-cultural environment in which the child is raised (Brzezińska, 2000a; Smykowski, 2000). The process of gaining increasing control over one's executive functions should, thus, be considered not only from the point of view of internal biological factors but also in terms of external conditions including the socio-cultural and educational context of school. Although all typically developing children will eventually gain considerable control over their executive functions, it is interesting to observe how certain developmental conditions and educational practices interact with the process of cognitive growth in this area.

In Poland lower primary education is conducted in a content-integrated form of topic-based units that include all areas of early primary education. Formal instruction is conducted by one teacher (with the exception of religious education and in some cases physical education) who spends all days with the learners organising a variety of activities that are logically linked together by the topic of a day (and a week, in a broader perspective). Foreign language instruction, which has been obligatory in this sector since 2008, is most typically delivered by a specialist teacher who spends two didactic hours (per 45 min) with a given group a week. The specificity of such contact often limits the teacher's objectives to covering the content curriculum and ignoring all other elements of pupils' activity in a classroom. It seems that the structure of Polish lower primary education offers an ideal opportunity for introducing foreign language instruction in the form of bilingual education. The structure of such integration, as well as its possible effects on pupils' skills, merit investigation.

This book consists of five chapters, the first three of which contain the discussion of the relevant theoretical concepts and positions and the last two outline and discuss the findings of two studies of different character conducted on early primary students learning English as a foreign language. The development of young learners in all areas is the main concern of Chapter One, which attempts to explain childrens' behaviour through an in-depth analysis of maturation processes in different areas of development. It consists of two parts, the first of which aims to discuss the different perspectives on the description of developmental aspects in the literature. The second part concentrates on the physical, cognitive, linguistic, socio-emotional and moral dimensions of child devlopment with special emphasis on lower primary ages and executive functions that form the bases of cognitive maturation processes.

Chapter Two presents a summary of the various perspectives on the notion and typology of bilingualism. Different points of view are considered in looking at the issue as both an individual and societal phenomenon. The naturalistic contexts are described as the most common environments where bilingualism is present typically reflecting unequal power relations and leding to negative phenomena like language loss rather than positive enrichment. In each of the sections the elements that may be referred to the situation of the present study are highlighted. The most characteristic feature of bilingual discourse, codeswitching, is discussed in detail, as it forms the basis of the longitudinal observation based study that is the subject of Chapter Four.

Chapter Three discusses the issue of pedagogy and the approaches to teaching. It does not, however, offer a profound historical insight into the issue but rather focuses on possible theoretical backgrounds of the science of teaching. A post-method approach (Kumaravadivelu, 2006) is assumed as a current perspective on the metodology of teaching languages. Then four models of the new pedagogy are discussed, including Stern's (1992) Three Dimensional Framework, Allwright's (1991) Exploratory Practice Framework, Kumaravadivelu's (1992) Macrostrategic Framework and Brown's (2008) Principled Approach. Models of early primary education, with the focus on holistic and cross-curricular teaching, are also presented in this chapter. The last part of Chapter Three is devoted to the forms of bilingual education in general perspective, and their possible applications in Polish early primary education are discussed.

Finally, Chapters Four and Five report on the results of a study conducted in an early primary education context from two different perspectives. Chapter Four summarises a longitudinal (lasting 25 months) observation which aimed to describe the linguistic behaviours of discourse participants in different communicative situations in the classroom. The observed participants of the study are students of the first, second and the first half of the third grade in a public primary school no. 199 in Łódź, Poland who are taught English in accordance with a pedagogical innovation assuming its integration with all other subject areas taught by the same teacher. The chapter contains transcribed conversations that reveal a tendency for frequent codeswitching. The collected data is subject to *qualitative analysis*. The quoted examples also reveal students' motivation to develop the competence of the foreign language and take partial control of the learning process. The pupils' willingness to use the target language and pleasure in switching codes is reported in communicative situations that occur also outside teacher controlled tasks. Over thirty unique examples are analysed and discussed in this chapter giving possible justifications for the use of the foreign language in a given context.

Chapter Five describes a comparative study of the observed group as compared with a control group consisting of students from a parallel grade of the same school taught English in accordance with the general curriculum for languages at the first stage of formal education (two lessons per week) by a different, specialist teacher. Both groups use the same course books for English and for general early primary education which is taught in the form of integrated subjects in the case of study and control groups. The test has a quasi experimental character and focuses on the measurement of reaction times in a Stroop task administered in three different conditions: within language (in Polish), within language (in English) and across languages (English to Polish) The obtained data is subject to statistical analysis (with SPSS 20 statistical software) and the results are discussed.

All the findings and conclusions are summarised, and implications and suggestions for adjustments are made which may, if applied in early primary context, contribute to higher efficiency of foreign language teaching not only in the aspect of increased L2 competence, but a much broader dimension of an increased cognitive development in the form of executive control. The major conclusion of the study is that integration of English into general formal lower primary education, that results in a specific discourse structure, may positively correlate with executive functions' development and thus, prepare the learners better for further education in other areas.

***

With special thanks to 199 Primary School in Łódź and Agnieszka Jakubczak – an inspiring teacher who truly changes the world.

1. EARLY CHILDHOOD DEVELOPMENT

Children have naturally been members of societies for centuries. Yet, the attitude towards them has been changing under the influence of external conditions and the existing knowledge. In the first hunter-gatherer social structures it was economically justified to have few children and form nuclear families which developed strong emotional ties. In agrarian societies, which depended on farming for survival, it made sense to have a lot of children who quickly assumed adult responsibilities to contribute actively to the development of the community, thus increasing its chance for survival. They were, therefore, treated as miniature adults and their development and needs were largely neglected. In technological societies children ceased to be a necessity and became a luxury. The need to diversify workforce to cater for the increasing demands of society led to the emergence of schools, which in turn, lengthened the period of childhood.

Watson (2002) suggests that the history of child study can be divided into six phases. The initial lack of concern for children was followed by the belief that children are born evil. The third, pre-empirical phase, dominated by the influence of philosophy with the major contributions from Jean Jacques Rousseau and John Locke, was followed by observational research. Theoretical science focused on the development of competing ideas developed into contemporary diversity with a variety of theories, none of which wins popularity over the others.

The pre-industrial and industrial period in America and Europe was characterized by no concern for children. This was the time of high infant mortality and disregard for familial bonds. In England many children were used as cheap labour in coal mines as they were small enough to work in tight corridors. Deplorable living conditions and negligence led to high mortality in childhood. The society showed no understanding of the need to protect children and typically treated them as adults. One possible explanation for the lack of interest in children in those days may have been the fear of attachment seen as a bad emotional investment if so many of them would die. Needless to say, there was also no interest in exploring the mechanisms governing human development in the early years of life. The signs of interest in children are seen in the movement called „Sunday school" initiated by the Church and some practitioners of the time. The child came to be seen as evil, mainly due to the original sin, and in need of redemption.

During the Enlightenment people's view on children was influenced by philosophy. Two major philosophers presented two different world views which came to be the foundations of many further advancements in this field. John Locke's Empiricist theory claimed that all information available to people comes from empirical experience. Children are born without any prior knowledge, in a state referred to by him as *tabula rasa*. They can develop any skill and personality depending on the influences they will be subject to. There is endless possibility in any child, they are born with nothing except the potential of becoming anything. Therefore, the environment is supremely important. Locke's belief that children are born neutral and society models them is described as the ***mechanistic approach***. Humans are seen as machines (clockworks) composed of interchangeable components. They are passive, reactionary, stable mechanisms reacting only to outside stimuli. People internalize the world becoming its copies, reflections of reality in the same way in which symbols are copies of referents. Locke focused on individual differences. Rousseau, on the other hand, saw children as born good and then corrupted by society. He believed that children possess inborn capacities for optimal development into good and valuable adults. Social agents' role is to clear the obstacles and biases to let a child follow his natural course of development. Society is needed to channel the development. Children are not miniature adults and they are perfectly suitable for their given stage of development. Rousseau's concept is known as the ***organismic approach***, which focuses mainly on similarities between people at each stage of development, rather than on variation. Locke motivated further developments of interest in behaviourist theories and social development, while Rousseau inspired such figures as Piaget, Pestalozzi or Montessori, among others.

1.1. THEORIES OF DEVELOPMENT

The moment of birth marks the beginning of an incredible journey a child embarks on. A journey along which the child will change remarkably in all possible aspects of his existence. The inevitable development will tackle his physical, mental, emotional and cognitive abilities to eventually shape the child into a full-fledged individual. The notion of development, however, is theoretical in nature and as such may be differently interpreted by scientists focusing on different aspects. In the broadest sense the idea of development „implies systematic and successive changes over time in an organization" (Lerner, 2002: 16). Although this is a widely accepted definition, there is a lot of disagreement on the way it should be narrowed down to describe the process more precisely. The controversies are typically about the nature of changes that could be labelled developmental, as well as their source. The differences between those theories result from diverse worldviews of their creators. A worldview, as defined by Dale E. Goldhaber (2000), „represents a set of assumptions that a theory may draw upon to serve as the foundation of that theory's investigations" (in Salkind, 2002: 413). The author claims that there are three major worldviews that are adapted by a variety of theories of development, namely: *mechanistic*, *organismic* and *contextualist*. The main questions these theories aim to answer are whether development is predictable, whether we actively participate in the process, and whether development is universal. Within all these worldviews famous theories have been created.

1.1.1. The mechanistic worldview

Some scholars have adopted a rather convenient, from the experimental perspective, belief that behaviour and its change can be predicted and understood by systematic empirical research. Another belief of mechanistic scientists is that behaviour is caused by innate biological construct of an individual, determined by nature and called *material causes*, or external factors that an individual is exposed to, determined by nurture and termed *efficient causes*. The two extremes of the everlasting nature-nurture debate are exemplified within this worldview by Skinner's operant conditioning at one end, and Plomin's behaviour genetic model at the other.

Operant conditioning

Skinner's (1952) operant conditioning focuses on the relationship between behaviour and its consequence claiming that a given behaviour is more likely to repeat if it was followed by a positive consequence. Skinner experimented with stimulus-response-reinforcement chains that led to the establishment of fairly fixed behavioural patterns. He claimed that behaviour can be shaped in the process of operant conditioning where a primary reinforcer (innate, not learned like food, sexual gratification, etc.) is paired with a secondary reinforcer – stimulus learned through classical conditioning. There are two types of reinforcers: positive and negative. In the case of positive reinforcement, a subject is praised for engaging in a desirable activity and thus, infers that this particular action results in an occurrence of something positive. Negative reinforcement is created when engaging in a desirable activity results in terminating a negative stimulus.

Operant conditioning differs from its classical counterpart in that the response to stimulus is voluntary and targeted at gaining a reward. Skinner claimed that most human learning processes follow the operant conditioning mechanism and are, thus, controllable by alternations made to the environment. Although the claim about voluntary response is crucial in the theory, it seems questionable in the light of the experimental apparatus created by the scientist. Skinner's box is a soundproof cage that contains a lever and a conditioned animal. Pressing the lever brings reward but also in some of the experimental conditions allows the animal to avoid punishment in the form of an electric shock. While the attempt to get a reward or resign form it might easily be seen as free choice, the drive to evade electrocution does not seem so clearly voluntary. Skinner distinguished between positive and negative punishment. The former occurs when, as a result of a subject's engagement in some undesirable action, a negative stimulus is applied. The latter refers to a situation when under the same conditions a positive stimulus is taken away. The assumption is that in both cases reappearance of the same behaviour is less likely.

The difference between reinforcement and punishment is that reinforcement increases the likelihood of the reappearance of a desirable behaviour, while punishment decreases the likelihood of the reappearance of undesirable behaviour. Punishment does not erase the prior undesirable behaviour that may recover soon after the punishment is over. Therefore, it is believed to be less effective than reinforcement. When a new desired behaviour is the target, the subject needs to be rewarded for the more or less successful attempts on the way to reach it. Otherwise, he will soon stop trying as the goal will seem too remote to achieve and requiring him to reshape the whole prior behaviour and habit. Skinner believed that each learning process should be broken into several achievable stages whose completion should be rewarded to maintain the right level of motivation. This mechanism of gradual alternation is called shaping and is used by behaviourists to teach a subject a completely new behaviour. In terms of child development the theory offers explanation of how children's behaviour may be modified by reward and punishment.

It seems that punishment, whether positive or negative, is ineffective in that it does not completely eliminate the undesirable behaviour and may lead to psychological problems like low self-esteem or aggression. Reinforcement on the other hand, emphasizes the desirable behaviours that become more frequent than undesirable ones and if applied to those even remotely resembling the expected outcome at first should gradually lead to shaping the desirable result.

Skinner's general comment about human behaviour is that it is controlled and influenced by external factors rather than driven by some internal force. Although many people agree that the environment has a considerable impact on behaviour and psychological development, it is hard to accept Skinner's extreme standpoint. As Krapp (2005) explains:

> According to Skinner, each person is unique, but not because of choices the individual makes. Rather, personality arises from genetic makeup and the different experiences each person is exposed to during their lives. In addition, individuals remain under the influence of their environment throughout the lifespan, regardless of the degree of learning that has preceded. (416)

Skinner deprives humans of free will claiming that we are predetermined in our choices by the environment that shapes our behaviour. It seems, however, that the theory is self-contradictory in that it assumes that the changes in the environment are in fact caused by people on purpose. Thus, although the subjects in experimental conditions might have had limited or no control over their preconditioned behaviour, there was someone deliberately introducing the changes and thus imposing a desired behaviour. This manipulator does not seem preconditioned. However, in certain settings the situation may closely resemble Skinner's laboratory conditions. In a favourable manner school is such an environment, in which pro-social behaviour is praised and antisocial behaviour punished. From his mechanistic point of view he ruled out imagination and creativity claiming that a work of art is crafted in certain conditions by people with a defined set of experiences and thus is merely a reflection of environmental influences on the artist at that particular moment. Skinner conducted his experiments on animals and made an assumption that the same mechanisms as observed in the laboratory may be applied to humans with the same effect. It seems, however, that people are more complex beings with inner lives and possibly other cognitive abilities. While a rat will eagerly press a lever to avoid electrocution, a tortured soldier may refuse to betray his country despite the pain (cf. Chomsky, 1971).

One of the central concepts in Skinner's theory is the notion of control. Even though the subject is determined by the external conditions, he has to have the feeling of control within the limits imposed by the environment. In other words, he needs to see that the actions that are possible to take, influence the situation. Pushing a lever eliminates the unpleasant electric shock. Seligman and Maier (1967) found that dogs put in boxes where they were subjected to electrocution, learned quickly how to avoid the negative sensations be pressing a lever which terminated the flow of electric current. Dogs which were put in boxes with a non-functional lever, on the other hand, learned that whatever they did, they could not eliminate the painful sensation. When both groups were placed in boxes divided by a low partition into two compartments one of which caused electrocution and the other did not, it was found that the first group of dogs quickly jumped into the safe compartment while the second group did not even try to change their situation, concluding that it would be to no avail. The scientists found that when a subject does not have any control over his situation, he will soon give up trying and may develop depression. The phenomenon, known as *learned helplessness*, seems to apply to humans as well as animals. In his famous 1971 Stanford Prison Experiment, Zimbardo et al. (1973) divided randomly 24 carefully selected healthy psychology students with no emotional problems or prior criminal history into two groups: prisoners and guards. They were placed in a mock prison organized in the basement of Stanford University. The students who were assigned the role of prisoners were kept in their mock cells but the guards spent there only eight hours after which they went home. The experiment was planned for two weeks but had to be terminated after only six days. It turned out that the students assumed their roles so realistically that it became dangerous for their lives.

> Despite the fact that guards and prisoners were essentially free to engage in any form of interaction (positive or negative, supportive or affrontive, etc.), the characteristic nature of their encounters tended to be negative, hostile, affrontive and dehumanizing. Prisoners immediately adopted a generally passive response mode while guards assumed a very active initiative role in all interactions. (Huggins, Haritos-Fatouros, Zimbardo, 1973: 10)

The experiment was stopped because the subjects' distorted view or reality caused them to show antisocial behaviour. Levels of aggression between prisoners and guards were extremely high and the feelings of anxiety and stress evoked psychosomatic symptoms. The experiment showed the corruptive mechanisms of power that lead to abuse and turn normal, intelligent, good people into evil sadistic oppressors. It also supported Seligman's theory of learned helplessness. The harassed prisoners became so powerless that they seemed to have forgotten that the whole situation is fake and they can resign any time avoiding further negative treatment (Seligman and Maier, 1967).

Operant conditioning, though resembling dog training rather than human education, seems to be well grounded. Although people like to think of themselves as independent free thinkers, at least in extreme conditions, they willingly give up the privilege of self-control and let themselves be manipulated by the environment. It may not be easy to admit but people are prone to persuasion and external pressures. This feature of human nature is often employed in the mechanisms of propaganda and brainwashing to make people truly believe in a fake reality.

Behaviour genetic model

The belief that human behaviour is shaped solely by the experiences of the external world is challenged by the opposite standpoint. Behaviour geneticists claim that human nature is encoded in genes that are inherited from the parents and predetermine a child's future abilities and personality traits.

The behaviour genetic model employs elaborate statistical procedures to determine how much of a difference in behaviour in a given group of individuals depends on their inborn qualities and to what extent it can be explained through external factors. The most common subjects include twins and adopted children compared with their biological and adopted parents and relatives of different degrees of genetic relatedness. Researchers claim that genetic relatedness plays a significant role in a number of features such as intelligence and personality (Goldhaber, 2002). One of the central notions of the behaviour genetic model is the distinction between *phenotype* defined as „the observable characteristics of organisms in body structures and physiological and psychological functions" (Caprara and Cervone, 2000: 159), and genotype that is a set of genes, unique for each human being that predisposes people to perform these functions. Human behaviour may be predicted and explained through a set of fixed scientific laws that also apply to all other elements of nature. It is generally agreed that a lot of elements that determine the final construct of a human being are inherited.

> There is broad consensus of heritability over 70% (mostly additive) for general cognitive ability and IQ (…) There is much agreement on an average heritability of 50 % (about 30% of which is additive) for each of the Big Five Personality dimensions. (Caprara and Cervone, 2000: 163)

The Big Five Personality dimensions include *extraversion* (denoting warmth, positive emotions, assertiveness), *agreeableness* (including such features as trust, altruism, modesty), *conscientiousness* (meaning competence, order, dutifulness, self-discipline), *neuroticism* (described as anxiety, hostility, depression, vulnerability) and *openness* (involving fantasy, ideas, aesthetics, values) (Cattell, 1996).

Each child is naturally endowed with a mixture of these features, each of which is developed at a specific degree. As presented in Figure 1, a child may represent each of the two extremes of the traits but will more likely be a reflection of any of the degrees along the continuum.

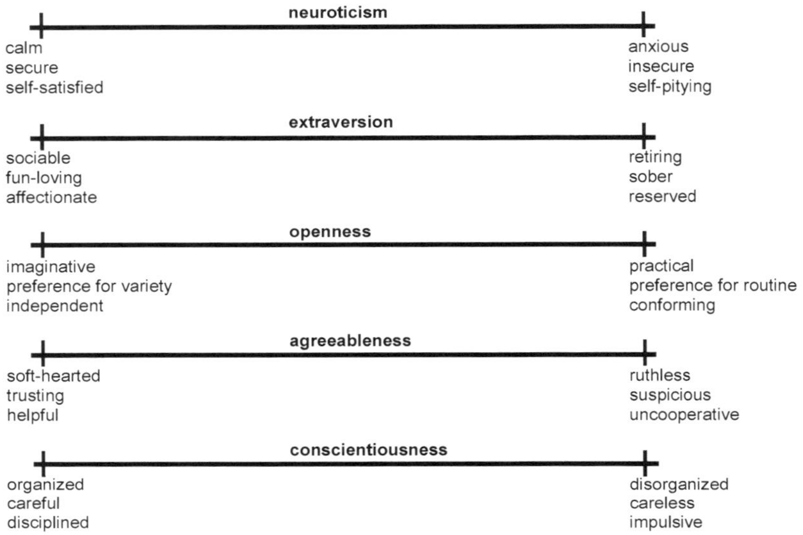

Figure 1. Big five personality traits

Source: Adapted from McCrae and Costa (1986: 1002)

Behavioural genetics posits that the child's genetic construct affects the environment he or she experiences. The way a child selects, modifies and interacts with the surroundings depends on his or her individual features inherited from the parents. It seems logical to assume that because the child exists in a given reality the interaction between the environment and the child will be bidirectional. The surroundings will obviously shape the child's idea of the world and its laws but the environment will not remain indifferent to the child's influence. People shape the world around them through their action in the same way in which the world models their behaviour and personality. Behavioural geneticists do not deny that the impact is mutual either. They distinguish between three types of correlation between biological properties and the environment: *passive*, *reactive* and *active*. Plomin (1994) defines them as follows:

Passive GE (genotype-environment) correlation occurs because children share heredity as well as environmental influences with members of their family… for example if musical ability is heritable (and this is not known), musically gifted children are likely to have musically gifted parents who provide them both with genes and environment conductive to the development of musical ability. Reactive or evocative GE correlation refers to the experiences of the child derived from reactions of other people to the child's genetic propensities. For example musically talented children may be picked out at school and given special opportunities. Active GE correlation occurs when individuals select to create environments that are correlated to their genetic propensities. For example, even if no one does anything about a child's musical talent, the child might gravitate toward musical environments (106-107).

The child is, thus, either the subject of influence from both his immediate surroundings and the outside world, or an active seeker for subjectively desirable influence (Fig. 2.) becoming a co-creator of the potential changes to his personality construct.

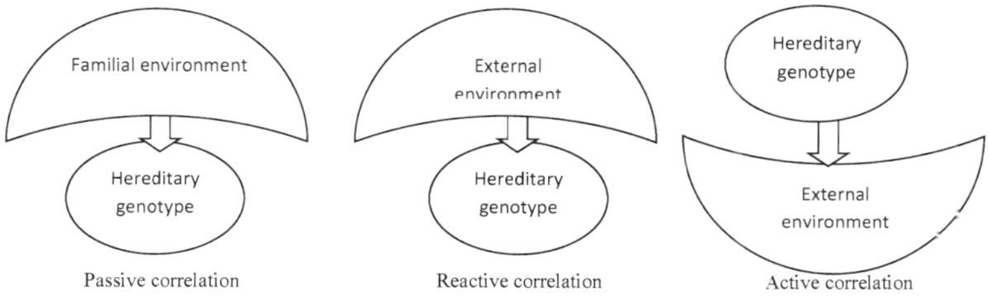

Figure 2. Three types of correlation between biological properties and the environment

Source: Adapted from Plomin (1994)

Mechanistic theories of development posit that it is either possible to fully control the progress of gaining competence including its rate and direction or that the outcomes of development are predictable and measurable. The complexity of human nature and its diverse character naturally caused scholars to consider the nature of development from a different, more multidimensional perspective.

1.1.2. The organismic worldview

The difficulty in determining whether the environment shapes the mind or the mind affects the environment is in deciding on the direction of causalty. Causalty is the relationship between two events where the second one, the effect, is a consequence of the first one, the cause. Aristotle distinguished between four main groups of causes. *Material causes* which are the elements from which the final outcome is constructed. *Efficient causes* are external entities constituting the original source of change. *Formal causes* determine the final shape of the end product and a *final cause* describes the purpose for which a given thing exists. Scholars who support the Organismic Worldview acknowledge efficient and material causes but focus on final and formal causes defined as „reflecting the organizational quality of all living systems" (Goldhaber, 2002: 414). Organismics believe in final causes; that is, they assume that a human is a more complex construct than the individual elements he consists of may suggest and that humans play an active part in self-creation. The representatives of this worldview include psychoanalysts Sigmund Freud and Erik Erikson, as well as cognitive scientist Jean Piaget.

Freud's theory of human development

Freud's (1905) work focused on adults whose contemporary behaviour had been preconditioned by early experiences. Traumatic childhood events determined their future life choices and so during therapeutical sessions his patients were helped to deal with those memories in order to become fully functional in their adult lives. Freud divided human development into a series of stages, each focusing on a different aspect closely related to biological existence. All stages are presented graphicaly in Figure 3.

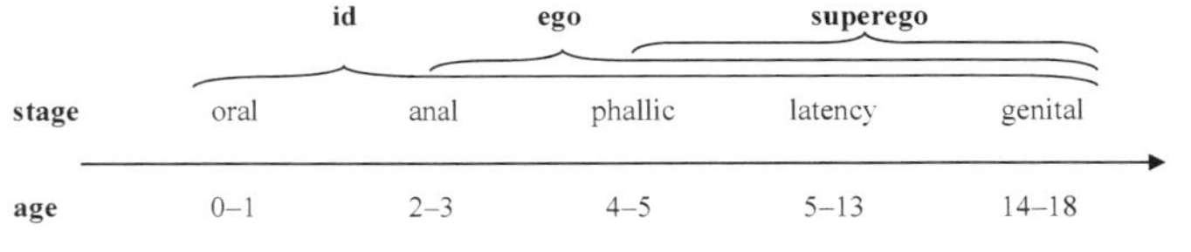

Figure 3. Freud's stages of human development

Source: Based on Freud (1905)

The first period recognized by Freud refers to the first year of a child's life and is called the *oral stage* as the child focuses on taking in both in biological (food) and psychological (experiences) sense. According to Freud, the operational part of a child's psyche in this period is the subconscious *id* whose function is to release tension and increase pleasure. At the age of two or three children progress to the *anal stage* during which retention and elimination become central. This is also the period when a child learns the first social norms and constraints.

This triggers the emergence of a partly conscious, partly unconscious *ego*, which supports the process of socialization. Pre-school children go through the *phallic stage*, associated with genitalia, during which sexual identity is discovered. At this stage the child initially sees the same-sex parent as a competitor and this conflict is resolved only by the emergence of a third psychological element – *superego*, which is fully conscious and informs the child of the expectations that the society has of them. Between the ages of five and thirteen children go through the *latency stage* in which they establish same sex friendships, build stronger bonds with the parents and strive to meet the expectations imposed on them by the school and society. In adolescence teenagers go through the *genital stage* during which focus is shifted back to the sexual sphere of their lives but this time efforts are directed at establishing an adult sexual relationship. Freud believed that the success of this relationship will depend on the experiences gained from all the previous stages.

Erikson's psychosocial tasks

Erikson (1950) divided human development into eight separate stages called *psychosocial tasks*. The first task of an infant is to develop a basic *sense of trust* through contact with his main caregivers. In the next stage toddlers develop the *sense of autonomy*. In the pre-school years children gain the *sense of initiative* which develops into the *sense of industry* by middle school. In order to successfully complete these four tasks, each of them needs to be fulfilled. Any problems in resolving previous tasks will result in restrictions in further development. Adolescents should form the *sense of identity* which forms the foundations for further establishment of the *sense of intimacy* in early adulthood. Fully mature adults develop the *sense of generativity* understood as concern for the next generation. The final stage of human development emerging towards the end of life is the *sense of ego integrity* marking the acceptance of all events that occurred during lifetime.

Each of these stages may also have a negative outcome (Erikson, 1950). If an infant is not provided with sufficient care and opportunity to build the first emotional bond, he will learn *mistrust* to other people and become withdrawn in the future. In the second stage, if toddlers are not encouraged to explore the world and praised for their small achievements, they will develop *shame and doubt* that will influence their self-esteem and self-attitude in their future lives. Later children who are punished for showing initiative will develop a sense of *guilt* over having personal desires, which may make them submissive in adolescence and adulthood. If they fail to establish a sense of identity in adolescence, they may experience *role confusion* and have problems with assuming responsibility in their adult lives. In the following stage well prepared young adults will readily enter relationships, while disrupted development will lead to *isolation* and inability to create meaningful ties with others. The opposite result of the generativity stage is *stagnation* when adults choose to be passive and self-interested. The last period of life in the worst scenario is dominated by a sense of *despair* when the predominant feeling of failure and regret fill the last days of life.

A summary of Erikson's stages is presented in Fig. 4 below.

Approximate Age	Stage	Description
First year	Trust vs. Mistrust	Infants learn to trust their needs will be met, or they learn to mistrust the world
2-3 years	Autonomny vs. Shame and Doubt	Children learn to do things and make choices for themselves, or they become doubtful of their own worth and abilities
4-5 years	Initiative vs. Guilt	Children learn to define personal goals and seek to fulfill them, or they develop a sense of guilt over having such personal desires.
6 years to puberty	Industry vs. Inferiority	Children develop a feeling of competence to learn things and to work on projects, or they develop a feeling of worthlessness
Adolescence	Identity vs. Role Confusion	Adolescents "find themselves"; they define themselves by choosing certain roles that suit them, or they become confused about what role is best for them
Early adulthood	Intimacy vs. Isolation	Young adults become able to enter into close, personal relationships (both intimate friendships and romantic relationships) with others, or they become self-centered and inactive
Middle age	Generativity vs. Stagnation	Adults become interested in efforts that aid the next generation (having children, working to help make the world a better place) or they become self-centered and inactive
Old age	Integrity vs. Despair	Older adults reflect on their lives, satisfied with what they have done, or they feel regret over what they have done or failed to do

Figure 4. Erikson's stages of development

Source: Allhousen (2002: 384)

The success at each stage of development depends on a positive outcome of the preceding stages. If anything goes wrong at any point on the way, it will adversely affect all future life, unless help is provided on time.

Piaget's model of human development

Unlike Erikson, who was mainly interested in human development in relation to other people, Jean Piaget (1969) focused more on a child's cognitive development. Piaget saw a child as an agent who strives to maintain equilibrium between himself and the environment by constructing meaning out of his experiences. New experiences shatter the balance and the child needs to reestablish either by drawing from previous experiences to make sense of the new one (*assimilation*) or by adjusting the existing knowledge to the new situation (*accommodation*). These two processes continuously reoccurring in the child's mind lead to cognitive reorganization, which in turn leads to development. The third process involved is *equilibration*, which has a more global character and helps to regain equilibrium after a number of local adjustments. Piaget divided development into four stages. The first two years of life fall into the *sensory-motor period* when meaning is drawn from sensory and motor interactions with people, objects and experiences. In the *pre-operational period*, lasting from two to five or even seven years, children gain a limited ability to act on the mental representations of objects, people and events. In this period children's linguistic ability increases rapidly together with engagement in pretend play as well as imitation and understanding of basic functional relationships. However, they are still unable to understand that other people do not see things from their perspective. Piaget called this feature of child behaviour *egocentric thought*. Children enter the *concrete operational period* between the ages of five and seven when they become capable of arranging, classifying and organizing information, understanding mathematical operations and acknowledging other people's points of view. The final stage of human development, the *formal operational period*, starts at adolescence and is characterized by the ability to apply logic to all real and hypothetical situations.

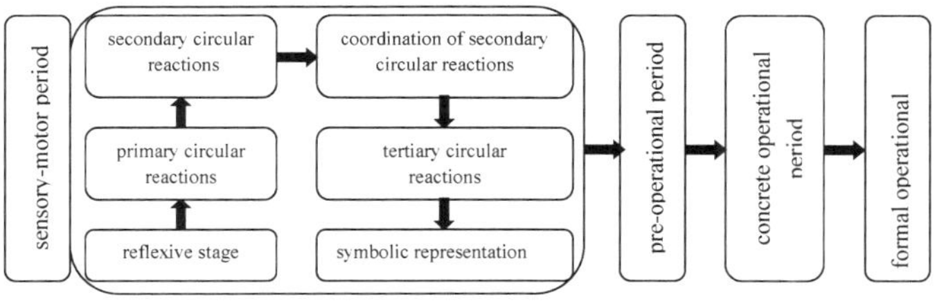

Figure 5. Piaget's model of cognitive development

Source: Based on Piaget (1969)

Figure 5. presents the model graphically as consisting of four distinct stages. The first, sensory-motor, period may further be divided into six stages (Wortham, 2000) starting with the *reflexive stage* in the first month of life, during which an infant is driven by its innate reflexive actions to explore the surrounding world. The following stage occurring between the first and fourth month of life – *primary cir-*

cular reactions – is characterized by the emergence of voluntary actions performed by the infant. In the third stage between the fourth and tenth month of life, known as *secondary circular reactions*, an infant becomes more involved in interactions with people and objects, initiates contact, and responds to external cues. The child experiences results of random actions and repeats them learning the cause and effect rule. The next stage, between ten and twelve months, requires the infant to *coordinate secondary circular reactions* when he looks for hidden objects and starts to understand simple words. This is also the time when he starts to understand that people and objects do not vanish entirely when they get out of sight. The fifth stage, *tertiary circular reactions*, occurs at the beginning of the second year of life and lasts until about six months, when the toddler actively explores the world and learns to understand time, space and causality. The last stage of the sensory-motor period is the *symbolic representation stage*, during which the toddler can mentally represent objects for imitative behaviour (e.g. get involved in pretend play).

A child's active interaction with his surroundings provides him with information that his brain may process to varying extent, depending on the stage of maturity. The experience gained in this way is, according to Piaget, more valuable and effective in developing a child's understanding of the world than an intentional interaction with an adult in a formal educational setting. Since it is children who have control over their own development which is additionally conditioned by biological and psychological readiness, attempts to externally modify the input are unjustified. As Laura Berk puts it, "if children are masters of their own learning, then adult efforts to teach them new skills before they indicate they are interested or ready are doomed to failure" (2001: 14).

Fodor *vs.* Pinker – debate over language development

While Piaget's theory maintains that subsequent stages of development are increasingly complex as a result of learning, Fodor (1975) argues that this increase in complexity is a result of maturation processes and learning only uses experience to draw on mental representations already available at a given stage of development. This concept is in line with the scholar's theory known as *extreme nativism*. It is generally agreed, among nativists and empiricists alike, that there are some basic elements of knowledge that are inborn and form the basis for all further development. Children are born with a capacity to understand the meaning of words and gradually master comprehension of language by analysing more complex elements through decomposition into simpler, innate concepts. As Pinker puts it, perhaps 'mother' is mentally represented as 'female parent', perhaps 'kill' is conceptualized as 'cause to be not alive'. These units are innate, or perhaps in turn are decomposable into even more elementary units that are innate (2007: 93).

Fodor, on the other hand claims that there are many words that cannot be decomposed into simpler units as definitions created in this way do not fully reflect the meaning. Thus, he claims that children are born with a lexicon perhaps as large as half a million items. The major criticism of this theory is evolutionary. It seems unlikely that certain concepts that Fodor claims to be innate have been created in pre-historic times and preserved until today, although they served no purpose to our ancestors. Another weakness pointed out by Pinker is that a definition of a word is not the same as its semantic representation.

A definition is a dictionary's explanation of the meaning of an English word using other English words, intended to be read by a whole person, applying the entirety of his or her intelligence and language skills. A semantic representation is a person's knowledge of the meaning of an English word in conceptual structure (the language of thought), processed by a system of the brain that manipulates chunks of conceptual structure and relates them to the sense. (2007: 100)

It follows that when a person is confronted with a word, he or she uses a number of internal systems to make sense of its meaning in this particular instance determined by external conditions like communicative situation, intentions of the speaker, his assumed attitude towards the topic and listener's expectations and experience. The actual meaning of the word per se is more basic and secondary to its communicative function. It seems that the problem lies in the unclear distinction between lexical items and concepts. While the analysis of encountered lexical items relies heavily on the conditions of their use, common cultural and social understanding of certain phenomena and definitions created by the users of this particular language, the concepts underlying the words have to be universal for all human beings to be considered as innate.

Therefore, it is reasonable to claim that it is not words that people inherit form past generations but basic concepts (like Pinker's analysis of verbs that uncovers the underlying meaning of 'motion', 'contact', 'cause and effect') that are employed in all languages to convey meaning. After all, the fact that Russian lacks the verb 'have' does not mean that Russians do not have the concept of possession. Contrary to Fodor's theory, they did not inherit a very important word but they do have an inborn concept of possession that allows them to express it through alternative linguistic means.

At the other extreme of the debate is the *radical pragmatics* view of how language comes into existence. Proponents of this view maintain that there are no mental representations of word meanings but "patterns of association among stereotypical events and their typical participants" (Pinker, 2007: 112). Thus, a listener bases his understanding of an utterance on prior experience and flexibly chooses the most probable message a speaker intends to convey in this particular situation. The argument comes from the interest in polysemy. Nearly all words have multiple meanings depending on the context. From the radical pragmatics point of view it is impossible to have one mental representation of a word if it can be used flexibly to convey a number of unrelated meanings. Pinker, on the other hand, claims that polysemic meanings are memorized as being conventional and characteristic of a given speech community. In his example the word *red* used to describe the colour of hair (that is clearly not red) is an English convention since other languages, like French (or Polish, for that matter) have separate words for it, like *roux* (or *rudy*). This makes this particular context-bound meaning of red specific for English and thus non-universal.

1.1.3. The contextualistic worldview

As opposed to the previously discussed positions, contextualists believe that development is not universal but depends on socio-temporal conditions. Fox (2008) defines this perspective as follows:

> Contextualism - philosophical worldview in which any event is interpreted as an ongoing act inseparable from its current and historical context and in which a radically functional approach to truth and meaning is adopted. The root metaphor of contextualism is the *act-in-context*, and the truth criterion of contextualism is *successful working* or *effective action*. (55).

The notions of root metaphor and truth criterion are adopted from Stehphen Pepper's model of a worldview structure. Pepper (1942) believed that an analyst who tries to define the complexity of the mechanisms ruling the world chooses a familiar concept to serve as an analogy (root metaphor) of the phenomenon in question. Once the link is made, the analyst compares the mechanisms operating in the familiar entity with those present in the subject of study to validate the analyses. The basic metaphor for this worldview is that of the world seen as a machine with numerous interrelated parts. Since the most important issue for contextualism is its utilitarian function, the truth criterion sees any analysis as valid when it produces effective action or leads to achieving a goal.

Contextualists (Fox, 2008) do not believe that development is universal but rather that it is determined by the historical times and social situation of the subject analysed. Since there are so many individual differences that contradict the claim about universality of development, it is justified to conclude that any individual progress is unique and shaped by external conditions. Another argument raised by contextualists is the inability to analyse development in isolation. Whoever is the subject of a study, he or she is not free form potential influence of the environment and thus it is unfeasible to eliminate additional variables and study his or her behaviour ignoring external factors. Since it is impossible to describe human development in isolation from any socio-cultural context, it makes sense to take its influence into consideration as a factor determining to some extent the developmental processes.

Vygotsky's cognitive-mediation theory

The chief representative of this worldview is Lev Vygotsky, who perceived development as a transition through a number of stages differing in the advancement of social engagement. He claims that development is organized along three dimensions: four levels in the organization of production (adopted from Marx), i.e. tools and practice, social relations, consciousness and language and self; motivation and relations between the inner and the outer worlds. Social knowledge is transmitted to the child through *shaping* (punishing and rewarding), *imitation of actions* and *meaning conveyed by signs* (Langford, 2005). Lev Vygotsky's cognitive-mediation theory rests on the assumption that human development occurs in cultural context, it is mediated by tools like language and is understood through individual and species historical development. Language is the property that distinguishes humans from all other species. Since it is the tool for creating culture, it is also a uniquely human property and so also history can replace biology as a defining criterion of human beings. Vygotsky's theory has three major components: the internalization of culture means, the interpersonal, or social, process of mediation and the idea that a child's knowledge is formed within the *zone of proximal development* (ZPD) (Taylor and MacKenney, 2008: 56).

The most renowned element of his theory is the ZPD, through which culture encoded in signs and symbols is passed down from generation to generation. It marks the gap between what an individual is able to do on his own and what he can do with the help of a more able person. Another element of the theory is the relationship between the knowledge existing in a given society (*intermental*) and the knowledge internalized by a learning individual (*intramental*). Vygotsky believed that all knowledge is initially acquired as social and then it is incorporated into an individual's cognitive system. As Taylor and MacKenny put it, the major claim of Vygotsky's theory of development is that "the natural development of children's bodies creates the biological conditions necessary to develop to higher psychological processes, while cultural factors create conditions by which the higher psychological processes may be realized" (2008: 56).

Rotter's social learning theory

Although biological maturation is necessary for development, it is culture that allows the child to reach higher levels of cognition that differ humans from other species (Taylor and MacKenny, 2008). A similar theory acknowledging the importance of biological processes is Julian Rotter's (1966) social learning, for which he formulated seven basic principles. First of all, the unit of investigation for the study of personality is the interaction of the individual and his or her meaningful environment. It emphasizes the importance of interaction as a means of gaining knowledge. The second principle claims that personality constructs do not depend on explanation for constructs in any other field. Rotter maintained that scientific concepts should be independent and consistent within the realm of social sciences. Behaviour, as described by personality constructs, takes place in space and time and should, therefore, be analysed in relation to those dimensions.

Behaviour that may be described usefully by personality constructs appears in organisms at particular levels or stages of complexity and development. A given selected behaviour has to be carefully positioned in a given moment of development and its analysis should take into consideration all variables operant at this particular moment of observation. General conclusions cannot be drawn from a single occurrence of behaviour disregarding all contextual and developmental conditions. Personality has unity. This relative stability does not, however, exclude variation in behaviour conditioned by external or internal factors. Behaviour as described by personality constructs has directionality and is said to be goal directed. All learned human actions are directed at achieving some goal whose importance is assessed on the basis of previous experience. The last principle posits that the occurrence of a person's behaviour is determined not only by the nature or importance of goals and reinforcements but also by the person's anticipation or expectancy of achieving these goals. Whether or not an attempt will be made to pursue a given goal depends on the perceived chances of success (Rotter, 1966, in Taylor and MacKenny, 2008).

Whatever the individual theories might be, contextualists-common ground is the belief that development is determined by the external conditions offered by the meaningful environment in which it takes place.

1.1.4. The present perspective

The modern view on development is still diverse with various researchers focusing on different areas of the child's early activity. However, there are some elements that all scholars agree with. Nowadays it seems justified to conclude that a child's development is affected by hereditary, biological features, his immediate surroundings including people and objects, community resources, cultural values and customs (Berk, 2001: 22). Development can be defined as "the process of change over time as a result of the interaction between environmental and genetic forces" (Brunson, 2002: 120). The change refers not only to growth or increase in certain features but also to the reorganization of qualities already possessed in order to progress to a higher level of complexity. Additionally, the definition recognizes the importance of both natural propensities of an organism and the environmental influence on its maturational processes. The nature versus nurture debate has changed its focus from attempting to establish the supremacy of one side to establishing a balance in which both of them influence human development. This discovery was aided by the computer-operated equipment made available only recently. Great technological advances allowed scientists to obtain reliable accounts of neural activity through brain imaging techniques.

The very nature of these mysterious processes that transform babies into adults has been the subject of many investigations, which resulted in a number of theories aiming to explain the complex phenomena of development. Although the data available nowadays is rich in various examples of developmental processes in individuals and groups, there are still many mysteries yet to be solved.

1.2. DOMAINS OF DEVELOPMENT

Throughout life, people change in many ways. Developmental research looks into various areas of human activity that are influenced by the development of physical and mental features. Physical development focuses on general growth and improvement in sensory-motor abilities. Cognitive aspect of maturation is debated in the area of intellectual skills including language, memory, learning and problem solving. Social development emphasizes the creation of interpersonal bonds and relationships with others. Advancements in the emotional domain allow individuals to express and correctly interpret other people's feelings, whereas moral development enables them to function well in the society. Rapid growth in all these areas takes place in early childhood and, in some cases, even before birth.

1.2.1. Physical development

Humans begin their physical development in the pre-birth period (Wortham, 2006). A future child starts its existence as a combination of two cells which rapidly proliferate to form a living organism. By the end of the prenatal period the child receives and responds to the limited external stimuli in the form of movement, sound and light. Even though the possibility of movement is severely constrained, the foetus practices a range of complicated movements preparing the muscles to function in the outside world. The speed of physical development in these nine prenatal months, transforming a crude group of cells into a masterpiece of natural engineering, is unparalleled to any other period of human life. Within the first year of life a child triples his body mass and learns a complex sequence of movements from sitting up straight to walking. The second year of life is a period when a child refines his motor skills, explores new possibilities of running, climbing and fine motor skills like picking up small elements and manipulating them. The progress is possible not only thanks to the innate abilities and maturation but also depends heavily on the environment as the source of experience. As Wortham puts it, "fine and gross motor development are controlled through biological maturation and stimulation and opportunities for physical activities" (2006: 77).

During the early primary years children become more dexterous developing their fine motor skills through arts and crafts activities gradually preparing for handwriting (Wortham, 2006). Physical activity improves their gross motor skills. Since children become easily fatigued by sitting at their desks, movement is a crucial element of the teaching process. This is the period of transition between concrete and abstract thinking and thus children need to engage actively in physical exploration of the world to be able to create mental representations of events, causes and results and to start reasoning. Hands-on experience, self-initiated project work, manipulative materials are important elements of early primary education.

1.2.2. Cognitive development

Brain development starts within weeks of conception and continues until the end of adolescence through a series of complex processes of neurulation, proliferation, synaptogenesis and myelination (Nelson et al., 2008).

In the first years of life the brain undergoes a dramatic growth which is connected with multiplication of neurons that interconnect with each other forming a network to support various cognitive functions. However, the development of connections between neurons is conditioned by the stimuli received through the child's interaction with the environment. If the stimulation is active, the network becomes impressive and ready to support more and more complex functions, otherwise the brain cells lose their connections and atrophy (Berk, 2001: 23).

The evidence is brought by researchers working with brain-impaired subjects. The brain is a fairly flexible organ in that it is able to adjust to the new situation in case of partial damage. Intact areas of the brain in injured patients show a natural ability to take over, to some extent, the functions supported by a damaged region. Joan Stiles (1998) managed to show that this process is much more effective when the injury takes place at an early age than in adulthood. In her study, brain damaged children, whose intact areas of cerebral cortex were adequately stimulated, showed little or no impairment by the age of five. At the age of eight to ten, various brain regions adopt particular functions and the initial plasticity declines. It is, therefore, essential that a child be exposed to enough external stimuli to reach his full genetic potential.

Memory

A crucial element of cognition is memory, which develops from birth moving from the pre-explicit to the explicit stage thanks to hippocampus maturation. During pre-school and elementary years multiple brain connections are developed to allow children to gain strategies for information retention and retrieval. It is essential for any organism's survival to be able to retain information gained from interaction with the outside world and retrieve it when necessary. Remembering that a given activity produces negative outcomes allows avoiding repetition of this activity. Thus, memory can be defined as "a general cognitive function for preserving information gained from interactions in the environment that are relevant to the organism's behavioural repertoire and continued successful functioning in that environment" (Nelson, 2005: 354). While some elements of this store are recognized as important for the rest of life, others are only useful for a short period of time.

For reasons of economy, information that is seen as irrelevant for the existence in a longer perspective it is stored only temporarily in order to allow for a successful completion of a given task at hand. This type of memory is referred to as *short term memory* (*STM*). Traditionally, its capacity has been studied through memory span tasks, which led to the conclusion that there exists a developmental difference between children and adults in the amount of information possible to store for immediate retrieval. Dempster (1981; in Schneider, 2002) reports that there is a clear developmental pattern of STM store showing that children at the age of two can store about two items of information, five-year-olds about four, seven-year-olds about five, nine-year-olds about six, while the adult's STM capacity is seven. However, the differences do not result from an increasing cognitive ability to remember as such but rather from the rising complexity of experiences and general knowledge development with age.

Schneider (2002) claims that memory span is domain specific and it depends on the familiarity of the items to be remembered. The example given by Schneider is that of a comparison of children expert chess players' memory span with that of adult novice chess players. The study showed that when given a task of remembering digits, adults outperformed children, but the latter did better at remembering chess moves (Schneider et al.1993; in Schneider, 2002: 253). This seems to suggest that experience, not age, is a factor in memory development. Professional taxi drivers will remember the names of streets in a new city better than pedestrians, musicians will remember the sequence of piano keys better than non-musicians, astronomers will outdo brick layers on remembering names of new constellations and so on, regardless of their age. On the other hand, age is a factor in experience. It could thus be claimed that, apart from very domain-specific tasks, in real life situations children have to develop their STM capacity to match that of adults in storing telephone numbers, addresses, instructions, etc. It also seems justified to claim that the effectiveness of remembering items of information depends heavily on factors other than maturation and familiarity such as relevance, motivation, and attention. Information that is of interest to the child and has a potential application in his reality of the given time of life will be more likely remembered than that of little or no interest, even though it may objectively be important for his educational development.

Short term memory stores items of information for immediate use. It is essential for effective functioning. That is why brain injuries that result in STM loss leave patients unable to function appropriately in a society. It is impossible to do the simplest tasks, to talk to someone because the sentences heard and uttered are immediately forgotten and then repeated over and over again much to the patient's and his interlocutor's frustration. The loss of STM also confines the person to his house as the decision to go anywhere is immediately forgotten together with the directions of how to get there. Patients may have vivid and detailed memories of their past life prior to injury but no recollection of events that happened on a given day.

Long term memory (LTM), on the other hand stores information for later retrieval. It has been proposed that there are two types of (LTM), *explicit* or *declarative* and *implicit* or *non-declarative*. The former is accessible for deliberate recollection of information and is divided into *episodic*, which stores the memories of events and *semantic*, which holds language, concepts and rules. The latter is used for storing non-conscious knowledge like skills and habits (Schneider, 2002). Episodic memory may also take different forms depending on the level of maturity. The earliest evidence of memory occurs in early infancy in the form of *perceptual representations*. It allows a new-born child to recognize simple regularities that are available through senses like familiar faces of significant others and prosody of language (languages) spoken in the immediate environment. *Event representations*, on the other hand, allow children to form basic expectations as a result of repeated action like in the peek-a-boo game which leads to forming *scripts* of action sequences that form a given activity (Nelson, 2005: 374). *Procedural memory* is also in operation in the first six months of life. It stores the information about motor actions occurring in specific contexts repeatedly. They may include such events as kicking a hanging toy to produce music.

The second year of life is dominated by imitation of observed actions and the type of memory developed during this period is referred to as *mimetic memory*. It relies on remembering a series of activities performed by someone else in order to reproduce them later. This kind of memory stores the image of events but lacks the commentary or description that requires higher level of linguistic complexity. On the other hand, mimetic memory is also responsible for the first words that are produced through the imitation of adult utterances. The imitation, however, is imprecise and often unintelligible and serves as an exercise for future improvement of the corrupted lexical items. Between the ages of two and five children are exposed to extensive storytelling that they both listen to and engage in to gradually develop in terms of vocabulary, structures and narrative construction. Once a child becomes able to retell past events in terms of time, space, cause and effect relations, at around three to five years of age, a new type of system referred to as *narrative representations* emerges that typically develops into *autobiographical memory* apparent through narratives of oneself engaged in social interactions that are usually fostered by the onset of formal education at around the age of five (Nelson, 2005).

Imagination and reasoning

In the preoperational period children can use symbolism and pretend (Wortham, 2006). They are able to engage in pretend play but see things from their egocentric point of view and can focus on one characteristic at a time. Between the ages two and four symbolic thought emerges. Children become able to imagine objects and events that are not there and represent them in the form of art. They also believe that inanimate objects are alive or capable of action. Interaction with peers is made difficult by the egocentric perspective, which makes the child believe that other people share his thoughts and feelings and he is unable to relate to other children's point of view.

Between the ages of four and seven children go through the intuitive thought substage, which marks the beginning of simple reasoning. Reasoning itself is a complex cognitive ability that "entails operating on internal, cognitive representations of segments of the world, the goal being to yield decisions and actions that are adaptive in the person's environment" (Halford and Andrews, 2006: 557). An important tool of reasoning is analogy understood as mapping form source to target defined as networks of relations. It seems that even very young children are able to make analogies that allow them to identify new problems that they are presented with as partially familiar on the basis of prior experience with similar situations. Perhaps it is no surprise that the ability to make analogies occurs so early in life as is seems to have been a powerful survival strategy. From the perspective of evolution, being able to recognize potentially life-threatening circumstances on the basis of comparison to earlier experiences of similar conditions might have been a prerequisite for survival of the species.

Abstract thinking

Cognitive representations are images of the real world that are, however, symbolic in nature rather than constituting a mirror image of reality delivered to the mind through senses. The symbols refer to semantic entities and thus create a network of interrelated elements encoding in a simplified way the complexity of the outside world. The system of symbols is governed by certain principles that allow for creating novel representations through combination of particular symbols. Fodor and Pylyshyn (1988; in Halford and Andrews, 2006) identified two such characteristics of symbolic systems, *compositionality* and *systematicity*. The former refers to the fact that when symbols are put together, their meaning remains the same. This may be true for simple compositions in literal meaning.

In a collocation "a cup of tea" the semantic reference is still to the object of cup and substance of tea. However, this principle excludes a plethora of compositions that are fixed collocations, metaphors, idiomatic expressions and figurative uses whose meaning is not the sum of the meanings of particular symbolic representations. In the phrase "it is not my cup of tea" comprehension cannot rely on symbolic reference to semantic entities. The meaning of the phrase depends heavily on the context, prior experience of having heard it spoken in a similar situation and analogy made between those two instances. The literal interpretation is possible in an actual situation of a tea party where the referents remain "cup" and "tea". The figurative meaning, however, has nothing to do with either of them.

On the other hand, since such compositions have been coined in particular situations in the past and entered the language as fixed units of meaning, they might have initially referred to the original semantic representations. The stories of how and in what circumstances a given phrase came to being can be traced in etymological dictionaries but, even if known, they will remain anecdotal for language users who will normally pay little attention to why a given phrase is used to express sense that could not be inferred from its elements. These compositions are also tightly connected with the history and culture of a given speech community and as such pose a considerable difficulty in intercultural communication. If the theory of compositionality is to be universal, it refers only to the most basic use of unambiguous, literal usage of language that can be interpreted the same regardless of the cultural and linguistic background of the interlocutors. Bearing in mind the fact that language is heavily influenced by the heritage and contemporary culture of any society, it seems rather unlikely that there is any composition that is totally transparent, evoking the same semantic associations in all humans.

The principle of systematicity posits that examples of language can be generalized on the basis of form. The meaning of novel sentences can be decoded through structural analogy with sentences already heard. Some representations are subsymbolic in that they do not have the properties of symbols but are still important for creating cognitive representations.

A key process in children's cognitive development is categorization. Categories are not built on the basis of assigning certain attributes but around prototypes or most frequently occurring examples of given sets and correlations between them. Thus a novel element is assigned to an existing category through comparison of its attributes with its prototypical representatives. It is possible that once a category comprises more elements, a basic theory can be formed and new candidates will be tested against it. Halford and Andrews claim that prototypes are not compositional, as the typical cognitive representations of the separate elements of a given composition do not necessarily combine. In their example the prototypical representation of a dog (or 'happy') may not retain its shape in a phrase 'happy dog' (2006: 562).

The development of cognition depends on maturational changes of the brain structure (Quartz and Sejnowski, 1997) and acquisition of knowledge. The developing brain offers more capacity and better conditions for cognitive functions which re spurred by experience. The first instances of thinking occur in infants in the form of prototypes and perceptual categories. These are followed by conceptual categories that allow for inductive inferences and precede categorical inductions in young children. Symbolic cognitive processes are activated around the end of the first year of life and depend on the representation of relations observed repeatedly in context in the real world. At first the child may be able to categorise objects into collections but true classification is impossible because it is inconsistent. Since the child can focus on only one characteristic at a time (a feature called *centration*), he may start classifying objects into a group of green ones but then move on to creating a collection of similar shapes regardless of colour.

The next step in developing complexity of reasoning is relating the previously created categories with each other. As Halford and Andrews (2006) explain:

> Relating classes hierarchically greatly enhances an individual's inferential capabilities. For example, knowing that a newly encountered entity is an animal allows us to infer properties that are characteristic of animals (e.g., it eats, breathes, moves around), and knowing it is also a fish enables us to infer attributes common to fish (has gills, lives only in water) and the likely absence of other properties (has feathers, flies, barks) (572).

It would, thus, be logical to expect that once children have created and enriched certain categories consistently and accurately, it should not be difficult for them to organise those categories in hierarchies or analyse a minor one as being a part of a major category. It has, however, been shown as early as 1964 (Piaget and Inhelder1964, as well as others, Halford, 1993; Brainerd et al., 1990) that children below the age of seven or even six are unable to recognize the relation of inclusion between categories. The example of a task cited by Halford and Andrews is that of apples being a subcategory of fruit together with bananas. It has been argued that the reason for such interpretation is underdeveloped inclusion reasoning. However, it has also been claimed that children tend to make a comparison between the two categories presented to them rather than a third one. Thus they compared category 'apples' with 'bananas' not 'fruit'. It seems that also other explanations are possible.

First, since the children tested lived either in the USA or Europe, they may identify apples as prototypical examples of the category fruit. Therefore, they may primarily associate the concept of 'fruit' with that of 'apple' treating all other types of fruit as secondary examples of the category. Another explanation offered by the authors is that children at this level of cognitive development function better in real categories than in abstract ones. Given two real categories of apples and bananas they automatically make a comparison between the objects they can see, rather than consider a third, abstract category. The first comparison is a binary relation (*there are more apples than bananas*), whereas the other is more complex, ternary relation which requires the realization of the fact that apples are fruit and bananas are fruit so together there are more of them than apples alone. There seems to be one more difficulty in completing this task successfully. The categories of apples and bananas have a number of tangible elements that can be counted but the category of fruit, being an abstract addition to the problem, is at the time of introduction empty. The problem may, thus, be not children's deficiency in categorization skills but inability to fill abstract notions with symbolic representations or real semantic referents (Halford and Andrews, 2006).

Advanced concept development

Children undergo a rapid development in concept creation between the ages of two and five when their abstract thinking and imagination refines (Wortham, 2006). This is the time when storytelling and drama increase children's interest in future reading and writing. Interest in role plays increases interaction with peers through which learning emerges in the form of new knowledge acquired from better able peers and socialization. Natural curiosity fosters the exploration of natural environment and helps a child to develop through creative activities like art and drama. Between the ages of five and eight children move from the preoperational period to concrete operations. This is also the time of greatest individual variety. Some children can perform Piaget's conservation tasks as early as at the age of four, while some have to wait until much later. In most countries this is the period when children start formal primary education (in Poland at the age of 6). The transition to the concrete operational stage changes the quality of thinking. Unlike the previous stage when children rely on perceptions to analyse experiences, this period offers logical thinking and mental operations. This advancement leads to improvement in memory and lengthening of attention span.

Further development in logical thinking leads to the ability of considering problems and solving them mentally, though they are limited to familiar means.

Concrete operational children understand that thought in multidirectional, selective and focused. Flavell and Hartman (2004) found that children at this stage understand that two individuals may have different mental interpretations of the same experiences (in Wortham, 2006). They are also able to use mental strategies to learn new information like rehearsal for memorizing. They also show a metacognitive ability, which allows them to make up jokes and play games that require strategic planning. The development of social skills allows children to work in small groups, as their cognitive abilities are mature enough to let them understand the thoughts of others and incorporate them in the process of exploring the world.

1.2.3. Linguistic development

Any normal child will eventually develop the language of his immediate surroundings and it may be any language regardless of its complexity in grammar system or phonology. A newly born infant possesses a unique capacity of being ready to master and code made available to him provided that the exposure is sufficient. Language is a uniquely human characteristic and develops in a series of steps (Hirsh-Pasek and Golinkoff, 2002). As far as exposure to language is concerned, even unborn children experience the somewhat muddled sound of voices. The first attempts at production of speech-like sounds occur when the infant reaches approximately 8 weeks of age (Hoff and Shatz, 2007). These first vocalisations known as coos are elicited by social interaction and signify content or happiness. Linguistically, coos sound like long vowel sounds that develop with age into strings of different vowels vocalised in different combinations. Between 16 and 30 weeks of age infants go through an expansion stage (Oller, 1980) characterised by producing a variety of consonant-like and vowel-like sounds of increasing complexity. Around the age of six to nine months, infants start to develop their early speech into a form called canonical or reduplicated babbling (Oller, 2000). During this stage the first true syllables are produced that typically consist of consonant-vowel combinations, which are reduplicated multiple times to form long strings. While babbling seems to be universal for all children, since even hearing impaired children produce single babble clusters, the ability to produce canonical babble distinguishes hearing from deaf children (Hoff, 2009). Deaf children born to deaf parents are reported to babble with their hands (Hirsh-Pasek and Golinkoff, 2002: 228).

The pre-linguistic stage is also characterized by the development of gestures like pointing or grunting which dramatically increase communication and attract attention of the caregivers. The first words appear around the age of thirteen months typically starting with terms describing the child's caregivers. The following elements entering the early lexicon are usually body parts and proper names. At the age of sixteen months children use on average fifty words which mainly denote objects and people in the immediate surroundings. The following period is characterized by a rapid vocabulary expansion with children capable of acquiring as many as nine new words a day and being able to use them reasonably well in context after having encountered them only once. This is also the time which marks the onset of grammar with children creating word combinations typically including two words. As Hirsh-Pasek and Golinkoff point out, the communicative aims expressed with those combinations are universal, i.e. regardless of the language or culture "children ask for more of something (e.g. 'More milk'), reject things (e.g. 'no bottle'), notice things (e.g. 'Look kitty'), or comment on the fact that something disappeared (e.g. 'Allgone milk')" (2002: 229).

Modern insights into early language development tend to focus more on comprehension than production. It seems that children in their pre-linguistic period are perfectly capable of understanding a few vocabulary items long before they are able and ready to utter them. It has been shown that children who are read the same poem over and over again during the last months in their mothers' wombs react to it differently soon after birth than to a new poem. They also react differently to the voices of the parents and strangers and distinguish between their own language and foreign speech at the age of two days (Hirsh-Pasek and Golinkoff, 2002: 230). Children all over the world go through roughly the same stages of language development even if the input they receive consists of two or more linguistic codes. Second language development follows the same pattern as L1 if it is acquired in natural conditions, i.e. in a bilingual environment.

Modern approaches to teaching foreign languages in monolingual formal education shift towards creating learning conditions resembling natural acquisition, real communication need (CLL) and incorporating the language in everyday routine (CLIL). The early lexicon consists primarily of nouns that have concrete tangible referents rather than other categories that are inherently more abstract and complex. Gentner and Boroditsky (2001) affirm that early acquisition of words follows a continuum starting with cognitive and finishing with linguistic dominance. Lexemes at the cognitive end are those that have concrete referents in the real world, while the other extreme is reserved for those lexical items that denote relations between other linguistic elements in the lexicon like conjunctions and determiners. Poulin-Dubois and Graham (2007) point out that this noun bias may not be universal and may result from the structure of the English SVO word order and characteristics of early input that favours nouns. The authors, thus, find it possible that SOV languages, which do not put nouns in salient positions, would produce counter results. However, it seems unlikely that any infant striving to communicate with his immediate surroundings would rely on abstract and semantically complex categories like verbs.

The basic function of language needed for effective reduced communication is referential. It is difficult to imagine that a child would focus on an invisible verb in the presence of tangible nouns that it refers to which denote objects that can be pointed at to form the most basic form of prelinguistic communication. Another issue is that it is equally difficult to establish beyond doubt that a child refers to an object limiting its meaning only to the noun itself. For instance when a baby says *bottle*, depending on the context it may mean *this is a bottle* or *give me a bottle*. Taking into consideration the pragmatic fact of a strong association between bottle and feeding, the latter message becomes more plausible. Perhaps a child extends the semantic meaning of *bottle* to the whole concept of *give me a bottle with milk because I am hungry*. Gil Diesendruck maintains that the noun bias is fostered by the type of input received by an infant in the form of caregiver speech.

> In sum, the "input proposal" suggests that not only the rate but also the manner by which children acquire words are significantly affected by the way their parents talk to them. The emphasis on parents as the source of the constraints makes this an exogenous mechanism, even if, eventually, children internalize the biases detected in the input. The fact that the constraining factor is linguistic input makes this a highly lexical-specific account. (2007: 261).

Regardless of language background, parents elicit familiar names of objects from their children while novel names are provided, thus allowing children to form an assumption that each object has one name to refer to it (Gentner and Boroditsky, 2001). Since an infant has a limited repertoire of words available for communication that is insufficient compared with the wealth of everyday experience, he may be well expected to acquire the lexical items that are of primary importance to him regardless of their category. A child who has siblings will be likely to use a possessive pronoun *my* to refer to the objects of desire that may otherwise be shared. The use of this particular word may ensure practical advantage through effective communication. While basic nouns may be privileged through extensive input, certain verbs or even phrases that have a utilitarian force may be internalized earlier than other nouns. For instance a child may learn the verb 'give' before many simple nouns because it serves his purposes well. It is also common for children in early language acquisition to use a phrase *what is this?* in order to gain more lexical counterparts of unfamiliar referents. The importance of input at this stage is reflected in the phenomenon of creating non-existent names for referents that are nevertheless accepted by the caregiver and thus understood only by him. The child-created words are then used more or less consistently and, unless the infant is told otherwise, they seem to enter his lexicon. A similar phenomenon is observed between siblings, especially twins who seem to create a language that is only mutually understandable by them, constituting a type of second language in bilingual L1 acquisition.

Lexical development

Children are not identical and they will typically differ in the rate and pattern of vocabulary acquisition. However, even taking individual differences into consideration, the expansion rate of early lexicon is impressive. Bialystok (2001: 25) lists the word number per day ratios proposed by some researchers in the field which range from Anglin's (1993) 5 words per day during the school years through Clark's (1995) 10 words per day in the first six years of life and only slightly fewer up to the age of seventeen, to Pinker's (1994) one word per every two hours of life from the second year of life till adolescence.

In an attempt to explain the mechanism of word acquisition Golinkoff, Mervis and Hirsh-Pasek (1994) proposed a system of six lexical principles graphically represented in Figure 6.

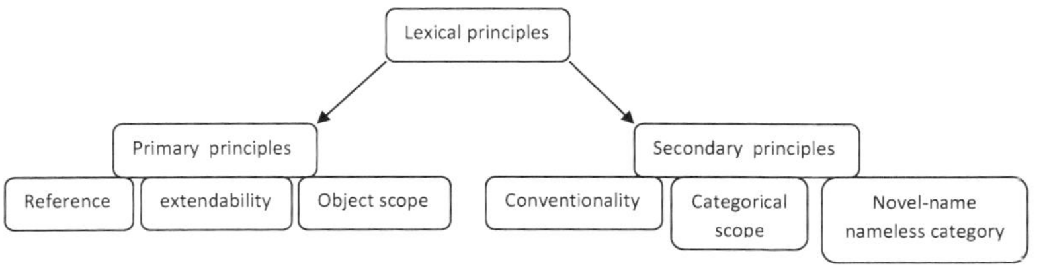

Figure 6. Golinkoff's et al. system of lexical principles

Source: Based on Golinkoff et al. (1994)

The first operating principles are: *reference*, *extendibility* and *object scope*. The first one states that words stand for objects that exist in reality. The second one means that words extend beyond an individual object initially referred to with a given name and encompass all objects that share characteristic features of the original referent. The last one allows children to understand that words refer to objects and uttering an object name will direct the listener's attention to this particular entity. The other set of principles is secondary to the first one and consists of *conventionality*, *categorical scope* and *novel-name nameless category*. The first one shows a child's understanding of the arbitrariness of language in that one object is referred to by standard, expected words. The second principle means that words are extended on the basis of taxonomic similarity. This recognition allows children to categorise words into grammatical sets and figure out which of them go together and in what order. The last principle explains that new words are used to denote objects that do not as yet have its own names. Although the above constraints are logical in that they organize the otherwise chaotic process of lexical acquisition, they seem oversimplified.

While the reference principle (Golinkoff et al., 1994) seems logical, it does not explain how children learn other categories than nouns whose referents are not visible or rely on more complex understanding of relationship. The extendibility principle, which relies on extending meaning onto similar entities, on the other hand, does not account for a common phenomenon of recognizing that certain names refer to unique referents and are not extendible, even though there may be similar entities in the surroundings. For example, it is common for children to extend the word 'mommy' to refer to any woman at roughly the same age but it is unlikely to function the other way round, i.e. to call the mother 'woman'. The principle of object scope seems to ignore all the words that do not refer to objects. The last principle, novel-name nameless category, restricts the lexicon to the one-referent one-word rule. It does not explain how children acquire synonyms or lexical items in more than one language. In a natural bilingual (or, in fact, multilingual) environment a child will easily acquire multiple names for the same object and extend them in accordance with other principles understanding that all the words denote the same set of characteristics.

Grammar development

Ages two and three are spent on further development of grammar with gradual increase in the number of words and complexity of utterances (Damon and Learner, 2008). Children exposed to sufficient input infer grammar rules from the language samples gathered and apply them to newly formed sentences as well as check their acceptability. This experimentation with grammar may lead to an apparent regression when previously proper structures assume an aberrant form due to overgeneralization (e.g. English past forms of irregular verbs initially acquired as fixed become ill structured as a result of regular past formation rule to finally return to the correct form in a cycle *went – goed – went*). A four-year-old child's language is developed to the extent which allows him to engage in fully communicative interaction with an adult or peer. The child is able to produce the sounds of a language spoken in a given community, knows enough vocabulary to talk about things of his interest, applies grammar rules well in most cases but there is still one important thing to master. The fourth year of life is devoted to developing sociolinguistic skills, which will allow the child to decipher what a speaker really means, understand that language has more functions than only the referential one and that people using language perform a variety of speech acts which require a certain reaction from the speaker who is expected to act accordingly.

It is remarkable that such a sophisticated process is mastered by an immature mind. A possible explanation of this phenomenon is one offered by Noam Chomsky in the form of *Universal Grammar* theory. Universal Grammar (UG) is a set of "abstract principles that comprise a child's innate knowledge of language and that guide L1 acquisition" (Ellis, 1997: 144). These inborn linguistic guidelines aid the acquisition of proper pronunciation and grammar and avoid creating "impossible" rules that are prohibited by UG. There is no agreement as to the way in which people access Universal Grammar but there are four contradictory positions. We may assume that people have *complete access* to UG and they are able to achieve native speaker proficiency in any language (first or other) at any time in their lives. This view rejects the existence of a *critical period* that is assumed to be the time in which the first language has to be acquired and after which the acquisition will be incomplete.

The evidence supporting the critical period hypothesis comes from language-deprived individuals who, for various reasons, were not exposed sufficiently to linguistic input until puberty and are unable to learn the language beyond rough communicative competence. If complete access to UG was possible, they would have no problem learning the language or any other languages additionally, regardless of when the education started. In fact, it seems that there are some people who never lose access to UG. However, concerning the countless second and foreign language learners who strive to gain competence in L2 often with little success, complete access to UG seems rather over-optimistic.

At the other extreme lies the belief that after puberty people have *no access* to Universal Grammar (Ellis, 1997). A child needs to master language before the access is lost and adult L2 learners have to depend on learning strategies and will normally not reach a full competence in a foreign language. This position, however, does not exclude the possibility of becoming multilingual if the exposure to the additional languages is experienced in childhood when there is still access to UG. The evidence supporting this view comes from experiment results concerning linguistic abilities of immigrants whose grammar and pronunciation is the better, the younger they were on arrival. Another possibility is that once children have mastered their mother tongue they lose access to those elements of universal grammar that are not operant in this language, that is they only have *partial access* to UG. It is claimed that learning L2 people have access to those principles of UG which are the same as for their first language but with instruction and the help of learning strategies they are able to switch to the new code. The final possibility is *dual access*, which grants both the access to UG and the use of learning strategies regardless of the time of acquisition. This position assumes that the application of learning strategies may interfere with the UG principles, which may result in producing "impossible" mistakes normally blocked by UG. Successful L2 acquisition results from relying on UG rather than learning strategies (Ellis, 1997: 69).

Semantic development

Alternatively, it can be assumed that central to the concept of language is its symbolic nature (Tomasello, 2008) and all linguistic items in an utterance are there to convey meaning rather than follow a complex pattern of grammatical interrelations. Theories adopting this viewpoint are referred to as *cognitive functional linguistics* or *usage-based linguistics*. In terms of language development this approach offers a different explanation of the transition from single lexical items to complex utterances. Tomasello (2008) presents this approach in the following way:

> According to the usage-based theory, there is no such thing as universal grammar and so the theoretical problem of how a child links it to a particular language does not exist. It is a single-process theory of language acquisition, in the sense that children are thought to acquire the more regular and rule-based constructions of a language in the same way they acquire the more arbitrary and idiosyncratic constructions: They learn them. (265).

Early in development children acquire concrete words, complex expressions and mixed constructions in which only one element is changeable thus allowing the utterance to be modified (Tomasello, 2008). This limitation is seen as evidence for lack of abstract categories and schemas of adult grammar that are learned gradually with age. Although there is a significant gap between child and adult language structure, the child has to constantly analyse the complex input using general cognitive processes available to him at the time. These processes are intention-reading on the one hand and pattern-finding on the other. While the former focus on the comprehension of the communicative function of an utterance, the latter concentrate on its structure at a more abstract level, which adds to the understanding of the language system through analogy and schema formation.

Once children have absorbed enough lexical items and evidence of their proper use in adult utterances, they use the words available in their lexicons and the rules they inferred from language samples provided to build novel, creative constructions. The first utterances of single lexical items accompanied by appropriate intonation are referred to by Tomasello (2008) as *holophrases* and are defined as conveying a communicative intention. According to the author in question, regardless of their mother tongue, children use holophrases for a number of reasons: to request objects or indicate their existence (*teddy*, depending on the intonation may mean *look there is teddy* or *give* me teddy. In inflecting languages the distinction is also marked by the form of the noun that makes the intention clear, e.g. Polish *[patrz,] miś* vs. *[daj] misia*[1]); to request or describe the reoccurrence of something (*more*, *again*, *another*); request or describe events including objects (e.g. using prepositions of place); request or describe the actions performed by people (using action verbs); comment on the location of objects and people; ask basic questions (e.g. *where-go?*); attribute property to an object (e.g. dirty, wet); use performatives in social situations (e.g. *hi*, *thank you*) (Tomasello, 2008: 268). An interesting comment made by Tomasello is that the fact that children start with single linguistic items (words of holophrases) may result from their limited focus on adult utterances or inability to process more than one item at a time. Both of these explanations are cognitive in nature. In the first case it means that children concentrate on analysing only a fragment of an adult's utterance including the element of interest or desired intention.

It seems possible that form a complex sentence uttered by a caregiver (e.g. *We are going to eat some soup now*) that is followed by the desired outcome, a child focuses only on one part that seems most important (e.g. *soup*). Wishing to get the same result the child may then try to reproduce the same utterance but, perhaps due to memory constraints, will only be able to say the word seen as bearing the most weight of the meaning (e.g. *soup!*). In the other case the child can only process one language item in a longer adult utterance. It seems unlikely, though, that the child chooses to focus on randomly selected items of a longer string and they happen to be the ones carrying communicative intention. Perhaps the child identifies the important word in an utterance by statistical analysis of its occurrence in linguistic input received. Thus, high frequency words are omitted as not charac-

[1] [look] (Nom) bear vs. [give me] (Acc) bear

teristic for a given communicative intention and items that are unique are ascribed the intended function. As in the example above, words like *we*, *are*, *going to*, *some* and *now* may be identified as more or less irrelevant to the change in reality experienced by the child, unlike *soup* which is the centre of interest. It is also possible that the whole structure has been heard numerous times with only one element changing (e.g. *We are going to eat some porridge now*, *we are going to eat some apple now*, etc.). The child learns that by manipulating one element he can express his preference that is followed by reward. Following the rule of the economy of language, children will utter only the word that is significant for the communicative intention. The verb could also be identified as important and chosen to convey meaning but it leaves too much room for speculation if it is not strictly connected to the situational context (e.g. *eat!* but what? porridge, soup, apple?). The noun, on the other hand, leaves little or no doubt as to the communicative intention as there is not much one could want to do with soup other than eat it.

It seems, however, that there might be another reason for this single word period in a child's linguistic development, a more social and interactional one. At this period of life the interactions a child engages in are largely if not solely with his primary caregiver, usually the mother. The characteristics of caregiver speech include repetition and elaboration of the basic utterances of a child. The nature of interaction is highly predictable and the communication built between the interlocutors becomes intuitive. Therefore, there is no actual need for a child to construct utterances more sophisticated than single words. In fact, some children create non-existing words to refer to a number of objects or activities which are recognized by the caregiver as meaningful. With time a child starts to interact with other adults and finds that his imaginary lexemes are not comprehensible at all and single word utterances are not clear enough to convey communicative intention and so the child modifies his speech to incorporate more items. The two-word period begins at about 18 months of age and the utterances are composed of concrete items rather than abstract categories.

Further language development

Language development is one of the most complex tasks accomplished by children of all cultural and linguistic backgrounds. Regardless of the mother tongue, the cognitive processes involved follow the same pattern of gaining complicated skills to produce a fully proficient user of a given language. Tomasello (2008) proposes the following collection of skills necessary to accomplish the task of linguistic development:

> To become competent users of natural language, children must, at the very least, be able to comprehend communicative intentions as expressed in utterances; segment communicative intentions and ongoing speech and so extract individual words from these utterances; create linguistic schemas with slots; mark syntactic roles in item-based constructions; form abstract constructions across these schemas via analogy; perform distributional analyses to form paradigmatic categories; learn to take their current listener's perspective into account in both forming and choosing appropriately among conventional nominal and clausal constructions; learn to comprehend and express different modalities and negation (speaker attitude); acquire competence with complex constructions containing two or more predicates; learn to manage conversations and narratives, keeping track of referents over long stretches of discourse; cut and paste together stored linguistic units to produce particular utterances appropriate to the current communicative context; and on and on (292).

Mastering a language is a formidable task indeed and the fact that children as young as six achieve enough competence in a language to be considered proficient speakers is remarkable. Perhaps the path to perfection is a rough one and requires a lot of effort to analyse external input and incorporate it in the inner language system, as it is viewed by usage-based linguists, or a natural process of creative art involving bits and pieces of real language and the rules of universal grammar. Whichever of the above models is true, it seems that a child raised in an environment where more than one language is spoken, will develop a higher level of competence than an adult person faced with the same task. Thus it is justified to introduce languages as fields for exploration for a young mind at the onset of formal education.

In the early primary years children expand and refine the already possessed linguistic knowledge (Wortham, 2006). Thanks to metacognitive ability, they are also able to think about language, which allows them to understand jokes based on linguistic ambiguity. This is also the time when many children are exposed to an additional language. In countries where more than one language is spoken in the society, children raised in one language meet the other languages in a school setting. Also immigrant children in a dominant language society experience a change or at lease addition of a linguistic code. In many monolingual countries (including Poland) foreign language learning is promoted through formal instruction from the very beginning of early primary education. One way or another, at this level of development young learners are exposed to at least one new language.

A crucial moment of a child's linguistic development is the emergence of literacy. In the field of early literacy there has been a shift from the previously predominant belief that reading and writing develop in steps from story making through invented spelling to improvement aided by exposure to the written word in the real world (Wortham, 2006: 105). In the USA a National Reading Panel was established to review the existing literature concerning literacy teaching and in a report published in 2000 it stated that "the research conducted to date strongly supports the concept that explicitly and systematically teaching children to manipulate phonemes significantly improves children's reading and spelling abilities" (in Wortham, 2006: 105). However, there is a body of opposing opinions. Pressley (2001) claims that the Panel did not take into consideration home teaching, impact of certain TV programs or some elements of the whole-language teaching instruction. The author believes that effective literacy programs should combine both explicit focus on language and exposure to written language in the environment.

1.2.4. Social-Emotional development

Contemporary view on emotion emphasizes the active participation of the agent and what he is trying to achieve, thus showing a functionalist nature. From this perspective emotion can be defined as "*the person's attempt or readiness to establish, maintain, or change the relation between the person and her or his changing circumstances, on matters of significance to that person*" (Campos, Frankel, & Camras, 2004: 378).

Early emotional development

Not surprisingly, the infant develops the strongest emotional bond with his primary caregiver (Wortham, 2006). Typically, attachment is developed with the mother even before birth and remains strong throughout life. The early emotional experiences have an immense impact on the future development of the child, his self-esteem, attitude towards other people, success or failure. A child is also born with a temperament which is at the beginning only a pattern of moods and responsiveness but will develop into a personality. An infant may represent one of three basic types of temperament: *easy*, *difficult*, *slow-to-warm-up*. Easy children are usually positive, calm and predictable, while difficult ones can be described as easily distracted, typically negative and unpredictable. Slow-to-warm-up children are not happy with novelty but grow to accept it with time (Chess and Thomas1977; in: Wortham, 2006: 78).

In the first two years children learn to interact with their peers. The nature of these contacts depends on the attachment history. Positive emotional ties with caregivers allow children to respond properly to other children's distress, which they are able to do around the age of eighteen months. It is also suggested that emotions experienced in the early years may influence intelligence and emotional health (Erikson, 1963; in Wortham, 2006).

The affective bonds between a toddler and his significant adults and peers form the basis for future social relationships (Wortham, 2006). In the first year of life the child establishes contact with his immediate surroundings through a developing linguistic competence and smiling at familiar faces. At the same time he may show distrust for strangers and awareness of separation from his caregivers. Newly acquired motor skills give the toddler more independence in social contacts as he may more readily initiate interaction and finish it through physical withdrawal. The interesting achievement at this stage is the development of the sense of self. This is often reflected in language in the form of switch form referring to himself by the name (e.g. *Kenny sleep*) to using a personal pronoun (e.g. *I sleep*).

Early social development

Between the ages of two and five a child gradually learns how to become a member of a social group. In order to enter a social structure children must learn a collection of rules. This process of acquiring the regulations of social interaction is generally referred to as socialization. It is understood as "a process in which an individual's standards, skills, motives, attitudes, and behaviours change to conform to those regarded as desirable and appropriate for his or her present and future role in society" (Parke and Buriel, 2008: 95). Parents play the main role in this period but peers are also important agents in the process since children at the age of two gradually start to transfer from solitary play to interaction. Cooperation and sharing are learnt through trial and error and positive/negative feedback from the environment. The more time children spend with peers who are not family members in a nursery or later primary school environment, the more rules of social behaviour they acquire and the more complex relationships they engage in. Piaget (1969) divided the assimilation of social rules and values into three steps starting with *rhythms*, acquisition of social routines and activities at a very early stage of life. The next step, *regulations*, involves rules internalized through interactions with others. The final step is becoming an element of social structures that Piaget referred to as *groupings* (p. 56).

Similarly, Robert Hinde (1987) distinguishes between three successive levels of peer relations complexity: interactions, relationships and groups. Two-year-olds tend to play in one sand pit completely ignoring other children in the playground even if they sit just beside them. During the first active contact stage children engage in simple interactions that are initially limited to exchange of names. It seems that this introduction ritual serves as a means of befriending a stranger and increasing the feeling of security. After all, adults often have a friendly chat with a co-passenger on a bus all the way home without getting to know his name. Obviously more complex interactions will include cooperation, competition, withdrawal and a myriad other types of behaviour. The research interest seems to be on childhood behavioural tendencies of moving towards, against and away from others (Rubin et al., 2008). The focus of observation is, thus, degrees of sociability, aggression and withdrawal. The next, more sophisticated level of contact with peers is relationships defined by the authors as "the meanings, expectations, and emotions that derive from a succession of interactions between two individuals known to each other" (2008: 143). Unlike interactions with strangers, these contacts are determined by the past experiences and future hopes connected with the development of the relationship. The dominant type of relationship with peers at this age will usually be a dyad. The uniqueness of this type of contact lies in its fragility. Unlike in larger social constructs (e.g. class, team, family), it takes one person to terminate the relationship. The subconscious understanding of this rule gives rise to stronger emotional investment, attachment and commitment to keep the relationship running. Typical relationships built at this stage of life are same sex friendships relying on reciprocity of affection. The fact that girls prefer to stick to other girls and boys engage in pretend wars with their male companions seems to result from shared interests and passions and lack of understanding for the opposite sex behaviours. Later on it depends on solidarity in views on life different between genders and the opportunity to discuss contacts with the opposite sex and be understood. With time, interest shifts from engagement in all male or all female relationships to a romantic involvement with the opposite sex. Even then, however, friendships will largely remain single sex.

The most complex social construct is a *group* understood as "a collection of interacting individuals who have some degree of reciprocal influence over one another" (Rubin et al., 2008: 143). Every group has an inner code of behaviour and norms that distinguish it from other groups. It also has a hierarchical structure typically with a leader at the top. Research interest in the case of groups focuses, thus, on the relationships within a group and the nature of contacts between different groups. From the point of view of early primary years it seems justified to treat a class as a group. However, far from being a homogenous environment, it is especially at the beginning a collection of individuals from various backgrounds and with different experiences at the early stage of socialization. Children spend most of their time at school observing, learning and co-creating the social scaffolding of a group. In this context there seems to be a difference between a group and a team (Hamer, 1994). A group is a selection of people put together randomly for formal reasons. A team is bound together by common aims and motivations. While members of groups tend to work individually and against each other, team is characterized by cooperation and support. A team is also the social structure where one can openly air one's views without the risk of being criticized or punished, team members are encouraged to pursue their own interests and be creative without the limitations of other members or curriculum.

Any classroom starts as a group and in optimal conditions with the help of the teacher should transform into a team which provides a proper environment for development at cognitive, social and emotional levels. Groups praise conformism while teams support individuality, independence and creativity. Although it seems obvious that a perfect school should provide the optimal conditions for personal development, it is doubtful whether such a supportive environment provides the students with appropriate tools to deal with problems in the outside world. People in real life situations rarely build social groups which are free from competition, envy, conflicts, enmities, value individuality and so on. A coherent group with strong emotional ties among its members serves as a safe haven in the hostile world outside the comfort of family. Group members share not only interests and hobbies but also secrets and opinions about other children outside the team. According to Rubin et al. (2008),

> Gossip, at this age, reaffirms children's membership in important same-sex social groups and reveals, to its constituent members, the core attitudes, beliefs, and behaviours comprising the basis for inclusion in or exclusion from these groups. Thus, gossip may play a role in fostering friendship closeness and in promulgating children's social reputations. (149).

Obviously, children gossip about those who do not belong to the group and it usually reflects hostile attitude towards the subject of rumour. Gossiping asserts group identity and serves a unifying purpose against common enemy.

Bandura's Social Learning Theory

Whatever the type of contact (interaction, relationship or group) and its nature (amiable, neutral, aggressive), the child's developing understanding of social norms is affected and modeled as a result. In his social-cognitive theory of child development Albert Bandura (1989) stresses the importance of observation and modeling. The theory claimed that a person's actions are determined by a combination of the outer world and the inner beliefs, thoughts and feelings (Krapp,

2005). In his experiments with an inflatable character called Bobo doll Bandura observed children's behaviour towards the dummy after watching aggressive behaviour. The results showed that subjects who saw violence towards the doll on a recording were more likely to imitate it when given a chance to play with it. This behaviour turned out to be also influenced by the result – reward strengthened the behaviour, while punishment had the opposite result. This was true not only in the case of real outcome but also the perceived result. However, the imitation is not passive but it entails an active process of choosing certain behaviours. It involves four different actions: attention, retention, motor reproduction and motivation. People are, however, self-controlled and can decide to take or abort action on the basis of a mental analysis of potential consequences.

An important element of Bandura's (1989) social-cognitive theory is what he calls *self-efficacy* and defines as "people's beliefs about their capability to produce desired results through their own action" (Krapp, 2005: 46). This capacity differentiates people in terms of their reaction to difficulty. High self-efficacy helps people perceive difficult tasks as challenges to be met, set challenging goals and recover from failures with increased determination to succeed. People with low self-efficacy, on the other hand, perceive challenges as threats to be avoided. Obstacles and difficulties easily kill their spirit and they find it difficult to restore self-confidence after failure. Faced with a challenge they tend to focus on their weaknesses and possibility of failure rather than considering available solutions. It seems logical to observe that people's actions are driven more by their beliefs about the world than the actual state of reality. Bandura (1989) claimed that the power of self-efficacy is great because it influences major psychological processes. In terms of cognitive processes, high self-efficacy allows to imagine success and stay focused in the face of pressures and setbacks. Motivational processes are adversely affected by low self-efficacy, which makes people avoid a challenge for fear of not having sufficient abilities to achieve.

People's perception of their ability to cope is also important for affective processes. Those who have a positive image of possible outcomes of their efforts are less likely to be stressed, anxious and depressed. In a wider perspective self-efficacy influences selection processes in terms of the quantity and quality of environments available for choice. Bandura (1989) found that those with high self-efficacy consider a wider range of career paths and determination in planning how to achieve the dream position. The concept of self-efficacy is not fixed. It develops through time in stages which are, however, not obligatory for everyone and merely reflect common situations that are likely to shape one's level of the capacity. Infancy is the period of gradual development of the concept of self and understanding of the action – reaction relationship. During this time and early childhood children experiment with the control they exert over their immediate surroundings. At the same time children start to interact with peers whose influence is second only to that of parents in terms of strength (and later gains priority). Peer group serves as a point of reference against which a child compares his abilities and thus builds self-efficacy. At school it is further increased or decreased as a result of influences from classmates and teachers.

Adolescence marks the transition from childhood carelessness to the adult world that requires responsibility for one's actions and taking important decisions that will shape the future life. Early adulthood is a test for the firmness of self-image when a number of crucial tasks like marriage, parenthood, career are to be faced. Ill-equipped individuals may become prone to self-doubt and depression. Later on, when people become settled in their jobs and experienced in the chosen field of professional career, the conditions are favourable for increased self-efficacy. However, competition from younger, more up-to-date specialists may be a threat that forces to increase competences at which those with high self-efficacy are more likely to succeed. In the late adulthood the perception of self as able and apt helps to remain active and sociable in the last years of life.

School as a socializing environment

The onset of formal schooling marks an important moment in a child's life. Even if the child attended a pre-school program, entering obligatory primary education is a milestone in his social and emotional development. As Rubin et al. (2008) put it,

> The school-age years represent a dramatic shift in social context for most children in Western cultures. During this time, the proportion of social interaction that involves peers increases. The peer group also grows in size, and peer interaction becomes less closely supervised by adults. (149).

At this stage of life achievement and social acceptance gain importance for children who strive to build their first relationships outside their immediate family environment. They are also expected to perform well in a number of tasks that are a part of the formal educational process and they will be judged by their teachers and peers. The importance of sense of achievement and success in social contacts should not be underestimated as these factors form the child's understanding of himself as a member of a social group. Children who have had positive experience will have high self-esteem, be more open and willing to take risks and establish new social contacts easily. Failure at this age may lead to low self-esteem, withdrawal, disruptive or even antisocial behaviour that will be difficult to change later on (Card et al., 2002). Social contacts in childhood are dominated by play that become gradually more sophisticated in the following sequence: solitary play (the child plays alone), onlooking (the child observer other playing but does not join in), parallel play (the child plays next to other children but not with them), associative play (the child plays together with other children), cooperative play (playing together assuming roles).

Early primary school is also the time for first friendships. This period favours same sex friendships which are based on demographical, social or academic similarities. Children tend to make friends with peers who behave in a similar way and also influence each other in a way that likens them to each other with time. In the course of social and emotional development, friendship plays a key role. As Card et al. (2002) explain, "having friends during childhood predicts having romantic relationships in adolescence and feelings of self-worth in adulthood, having supportive friendships predicts academic achievement during school transitions, and having protective friends can reduce peer victimization" (378).

Entering formal schooling children come under the influence of additional socializing agents – teachers and peers (Gonzalez, 2008). Until then the only people responsible for teaching pro-social behaviour were the immediate caregivers. Early primary teachers become very strong role models whose influence on children often exceeds that of their parents. School itself is the most powerful socializing institution. There seem to be two major reasons for that, namely the length of time spent at school and the character of the environment. Once a child starts school, he spends there over fifty percent of each day (or even more if he participated in extracurricular activities). It is at school that children experience all sorts of problems, feelings, successes and failures that they need to react to in certain socially acceptable ways. The other reason is the construct of school as a congruent environment which reflects the structure of society with all its rules and divisions. It is a small laboratory of life where a child can experiment with different behaviours to see the result and modify them to adjust to the requirements. He can also identify his place in a group, find his most suitable role and learn the mechanisms of relationships in a social structure bigger and often more hostile than a family. This is a very complex and intricate environment where only a fraction of learning takes place in subject areas taught explicitly in classrooms. All the most important elements of education do not concern the content material taught during lessons but what is included in the 'hidden curriculum' understood as a means through which a society recreates itself in the next generation.

1.2.5. Moral development

As defined by Salkind, morality is "the level of agreement or disagreement with a system of moral rules or standards of right and wrong" (2002: 276). It seems that the definition is too broad considering the variety between cultures and religions that determine to a large extent the way of thinking in social groups. The problem is the relativity of values. It appears justified to assume that there are many different systems of moral values governing societies around the world. The generalization may result from thinking locally about "the morality of western countries" or "American values" being the only possible sets of norms and disregarding at the same time the variety of systems prevailing among, for instance, various African tribes. Thus, the point of reference for morality should be the system of values that is functioning in the social group one is a part of. On the other hand, as the basic social structure one belongs to is family, the morality shown in behaviour may be a reflection of family values that may potentially be in conflict with those of the rest of society. Whatever morality a person displays, it is the end product of the acquisition of moral values gained through socialization at home, school and in the real world.

Kolberg's stages of moral development

The most prominent scholar working in the field of moral development was Lawrence Kohlberg, whose cognitive structural approach emerged in the sixties of the previous century (Krapp, 2005). Kohlberg's (1984) work focuses on a child's development in moral reasoning and the changes in thinking with regard to morality. In contrast to the Freudian approach treating a child as a passive recipient of morality presented to them by adults, cognitive developmentalists treat a child as a conscious being able to think about moral issues independently of the direct influence of the environment. As other developmental psychologists, Kohlberg saw development as a process divided into stages. He believed that people develop their morality in a sequence of three levels with two stages at each one, as illustarted in Figure 7.

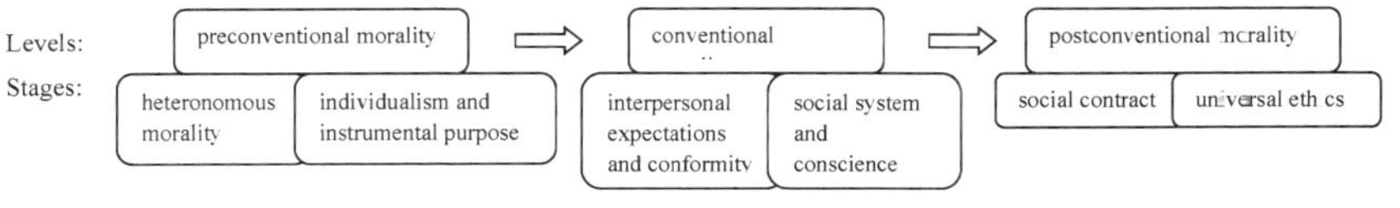

Figure 7. Kohlberg's model of moral development

Source: Based on Kohlberg (1984)

Level one referred to as *preconventional morality*, includes the stages of *heteronomous morality* (or the punishment-and-obedience orientation) and *individualism and instrumental purpose* (or the instrumental-relativist orientation) (Krapp, 2005: 262). The former concerns the avoidance of infringement of laws, which is supported by fear of punishment and obedience for its own sake. It is based on the acceptance of superiority of authorities. The child at this stage having an egocentric view of the world cannot take other peoples' perspectives into consideration and focuses on the physical rather than psychological side of actions. The latter stage is characterised by attempts to achieve self-satisfaction and fulfillment while allowing others to do the same. Fairness and reciprocity are central at this stage and children start to recognize that sometimes there is a conflict between one's interests and needs. The second level of development, known as *conventional morality*, is divided into the stage of *interpersonal expectations and conformity* (or the "good boy, good girl" orientation), when the need to please people from the immediate environment by meeting their expectations arises and gains importance as a means for building trust, loyalty and gratitude in relationships, and the stage of *social system and conscience* (or the "law-and-order" orientation) when the feeling of responsibility for the undertaken duties emerges together with the willingness to contribute to the society. At this stage the motivation to do what is right comes from the need to act in accordance to one's conscience and ensure the functioning of the society. A child at this level of moral development understands personal relationships as elements of a larger network of interdependencies in the society.

The final level of *postconventional* or *principled morality* includes stage five: *social contract* (or legalistic orientation) and stage six: *universal ethical* (or principle orientation). At the fifth stage of development comes the awareness of the multiplicity of perspectives and opinions within a society and the moral principle to avoid violation of other people's rights. It is also at this time that people realize that rights and values exist prior to social contracts and relationships. Stage six marks the moment of choice of ethical principles to follow and the recognition of existence of universal moral principles and declaration of personal commitment to them.

While Kohlberg (1984) believed that the stages are naturally age related, they are not age dependent meaning that in any group of peers there will be children who are at a lower and higher level of moral maturity. The same, however, can be said about all other spheres of development. While the theories attempt to define a typical route and progression of matriculation, there are bound to be individual differences between children concerning one or more of the fields. In other words, it seems justified to assume that a group of children at the same age and roughly at the same developmental stage will show increased maturity in some fields in comparison with peers while at the same time they may show a lower stage of progression in other sphere of development.

Kohlberg's (1984) theory excluded the possibility of skipping stages on the way and regressing to a previous stage once a higher level has been achieved. However, the research conducted by his team in the last years of his life seemed to contradict this assumption. The transition from a lower to a higher stage of development requires a shift in moral reasoning. At any stage moral decisions can be taken only within cognitive limits of this stage. At some turning points, however, children are met with situations that contradict their mental representation of a society and they have to readjust their reasoning to incorporate that new encounter. Kohlberg called this process *equilibration* and believed that it serves as a propeller of moral development. Teachers could aid this process in three different ways: through the presentation and discussion of moral dilemmas, the establishment of alternative schools called by Kohlberg *just communities* and exposure to moral reasoning above one's current stage – a concept much in line with Vygotsky's ZPD.

As a result of his studies, Kohlberg created a list of rules that should govern a model program for moral development through group membership (in Krapp, 2005: 265):

– The student's social identity should be defined by the group, and the group should define normative standards of appropriate behaviour.
– The group should discipline its members–informally at first, and then by the group as a whole if necessary.
– The members should become emotionally attached to the group, and to other members of the group, both as individuals and because they share a common social identity.
– Group members should be expected to develop a sense of collective responsibility, such that each member recognizes that he or she is in a sense responsible for the behaviour of the others.
– Discussions of values and value conflicts should be conducted to promote the group's improvement as a social unit as well as serve the moral development of individual members.
– The educator's role should include introducing the group to the values of the larger society as well as facilitating moral discussions and decisions within the group.

Kohlberg claimed that there is one morality and justice as a moral principle is universally held across all societies regardless of religion and education. Moral education is a process in which modeling of children's understanding of values leads to an increase of justice in the society as a whole. The individual dimension of moral development, thus, is paired with a corporate impact on the world. This puts an immense strain and responsibility on educators who, through teaching individuals, contribute to the development of societies. As all theories, Kohlberg's moral development came under criticism from other scholars working in the field. Carol Gilligan (1982), for example, attacked his bias in basing the stages on case studies that included privileged male members of western society excluding at the same time women, races other than white Caucasian, sexual minorities, people with disabilities or poverty stricken.

Similar criticism was voiced by Kegan and Lamb (1987), who believed that the division into stages is too heavily reliant on verbal abilities. The authors claimed that it is possible to assume that a child below the age of four, contrary to Kohlberg's belief that he has no moral reasoning at all, is not able to fully verbalise his thoughts to reflect his actual moral maturity. The same could be claimed in the case of an underprivileged adult who will score worse on the scale not because of lower moral development but due to language deprivation. A more recent development of the theory made by Thomas Lickona (1993) adds to Kohlberg's original idea that a good character has the knowledge of what is good the aspect of desiring and doing the good. In his view moral action requites the three qualities in listening, communicating and cooperating. Kohlberg's theory also caused controversy in the social and religious areas and was criticized for imprecision and flaws in psychometric tests. Nevertheless, it served as an important achievement in terms of drawing attention to the issue of moral development and the possibility to influence it from the outside. The theory had its practical applications in the form of the previously mentioned alternative schools and prison programs, both based on the idea of justice and democracy as the tools for socialization and resocialization. Whatever justified criticism the theory was subjected to, it remains admirable that it made the attempt to produce real tangible outcomes for the benefit of all society, a virtue that not all theories have.

Bandura's moral justification

Bandura's (1989) social-cognitive theory has also contributed to the understanding of morality. His studies of aggression led him to become interested in people's attempts to justify their own immoral actions. Bandura claimed that people set their own moral standards which they try to adhere to most of the times for fear of feeling guilty. When they break the rules they often look for justification and explanation of their behaviour. Bandura (1989) found a few typical tricks for this moral disengagement. *Moral justification* is a mental process that allows the perpetrator to believe that although the action was improper, it served a good case. People also use *euphemistic labelling* to discuss their immoral behaviour making it sound less harmless than it was in reality. A common means of moral disengagement is *advantageous comparison*, when the perpetrator belittles his actions by comparing them to worse behaviour. *Displacement of responsibility* shifts the focus from the actual agent to another person (usually superior) who had indirect control over the activity. A similar mode of reasoning is referred to as *diffusion of responsibility* where an individual's fault is blamed on a number of co-perpetrators. Alternatively, the *attribution of blame* may fall on the victim as one deserving immoral treatment. The agent may also think of the harm done by his actions as minimal or non-existing, thus presenting *disregard or distortion of consequences*. In contrast, the consequences may not be belittled but the affected may be treated as inferior, not worthy of better treatment in a mental process referred to as *dehumanization*. Although Bandura did not ascribe any of the tricks to particular levels of development, it seems that some are more likely to occur earlier, some later, and some characteristic of sociopathic or psychopathic behaviour. While pre-school and early primary children will tend to diffuse responsibility and attribute blame to the victim, they will not normally use moral justification as it suggests a more complex cognitive ability that is available to them. Similarly, it could be claimed that although older individuals could easily displace responsibility or disregard consequences, they would not normally dehumanize the victim of their behaviour, which seems rather extreme and reminds of such atrocities as the Holocaust that no one could justify morally.

Obviously, all development is subject to individual differences. Some children may develop rapidly in cognitive abilities and be thus perceived as exceptionally gifted while at the same time lacking the emotional maturity characteristic of their age. A three-year-old child capable of reading is not necessarily a prodigy and care should be taken to ensure that his development in other areas is also supported. For the future well-being in all spheres of life it is important to maintain balance between the various fields of development in early childhood.

2. MULTIPLE FACES OF BILINGUALISM

Bilingualism takes different forms and degrees and is in itself a complex social, psychological and linguistic construct. We may look at this issue from various perspectives but the most common distinction is that of an individual and societal dimension. When two languages come in contact they will inevitably have influence on the structure of speech. This impact may be mutual but probably more often it is one-directional with the stronger language affecting the weaker. Apart from linguistic changes, bilingualism exerts a deep impact on an individual's psychological construct, social life, cognitive development and economic status. In a more global perspective, it influences the structure of society, relationships within one community and between communities.

Bilingualism causes constant frictions and may lead to conflicts or prevent them. There are cognitive, social, practical and psychological advantages reported together with parental, cultural, educational and politico-ideological fears. It may, in short, be seen as a very positive phenomenon or a destructive power. This chapter aims to look critically at the very definition of bilingualism and review its typology. Linguistic outcomes of bilingualism like lexical borrowings and codeswitching will be discussed taking into consideration both, their reasons and outcomes. It is estimated that from half to two-thirds of people around the world speak at least two languages (Baker, 2001: 8). While learning an additional language is a part of obligatory education in many countries and millions of people strive to gain competence in at least one other language, bilingualism is very often perceived as an anomaly rather than norm. In many countries where the tensions between languages are great, the ability to command two languages (or rather the ability to speak the minority, less prestigious language) may be shameful and kept secret (*covert bilingualism*). This chapter does not, by any means, attempt to thoroughly analyse all intricacies of the complex phenomenon of bilingualism, nor does it claim to support either of the conflicting views. Rather, it serves as a short summary of the ongoing discussions with some comments on the nature of the phenomenon.

2.1. MULTIPLE PERSPECTIVES

Bilingualism can be broadly understood as an ability to use two (or more) languages. The problem in constructing one viable definition lies in the multitude of perspectives and subjectivity of interpretations. The literature on the subject is rich in a whole range of definitions and typologies, which help to describe a specific case of bilingualism, becoming at the same time a tool for political manipulations. It can be assumed that there exists a wide spectrum of bilingualism with minimal and maximal points at its extremes and numerous sideways in between. Let us consider the two extreme cases. Bloomfield's definition of bilingualism, stating that it is a "native-like control of two languages" (1933), would be placed at the maximal point of the spectrum (in Butler and Hakuta, 2006: 116). The other extreme, on the other hand, would be occupied by Diebold's (1961) *incipient bilingualism*, which incorporates people with minimal second language competence into the category of bilinguals (in Li Wei, 2005). The problem with the first definition is not only that it is too strict and exclusive, but more importantly, too imprecise.

Since language differs from person to person depending on their social status, educational background, occupation, etc., it would be hard to establish the exact meaning of 'native-like'. Should a bilingual's competence in one of his or her languages be compared against that of a highly educated middle-class monolingual office worker, thus excluding all bilinguals whose competence may be identical with that of working class monolingual factory workers? Would that mean that language-deprived monolinguals are not users of their own mother tongue? Another problem is that of the term 'control', which is a rather unclear notion that may refer to the oral and/or written abilities, passive and/or active command, phonological and/or sociolinguistic competence, etc. The other case is, by contrast, too inclusive. Such understanding of bilingualism would lead to including practically everyone who has learned some phrases in another language for example for touristic reasons.

Adopting this view would result in putting nearly the whole world population into the category of bilingualism or even stating, like Edwards, that "Everyone is bilingual. That is, there is no one in the world (no adult, anyway) who does not know at least a few words in languages other than the maternal variety" (2006: 7). Other definitions of bilingualism tend to lean towards one extreme or the other. Weinreich (1953), for example, thought of bilingualism as an ability to use two languages alternatively and Haugen (1953) claimed that anyone who can produce complete and meaningful utterances in another language can be referred to as bilingual (in Romaine, 1995: 11). It can be assumed with reasonable certainty that no one definition of bilingualism will ever be decided upon as the only appropriate version to describe this complex phenomenon. The understanding of bilingualism will always depend on the perspective adapted by a researcher looking into a particular case of bilingualism or a political body investigating the linguistic composition of a given community. The fact that the notion of bilingualism is so relative and its limits so unclear, seems to be both inspiring and rather problematic. First of all, one can choose nearly any context where language is used and explore the interrelations between its various varieties from a multitude of perspectives since nearly no language use is entirely homogenous and isolated from the contact with other varieties. On the other hand, however, bilingualism may serve as a powerful tool for political manipulation especially when the languages in contact differ in power. Baker suggests that in countries where there is one indigenous language (like Irish in Ireland), "a government may wish to maximize its count of bilinguals. A high count may indicate government success in language planning" (2001: 6).

The difficulty to identify with either of the extreme understandings of bilingualism and inability to fully accept any of the ones in between, often leads authors to come up with their own definitions for the sake of a given discussion which they state at the beginning of their papers so that the reader knows what perspective is adopted. Whether or not a given *ad hoc* definition will prevail in the literature or in a given author's attitude is not certain.

It does, however, help to understand the discussion led from the pre-stated point of view. Butler and Hakuta, for example, state that "bilingualism can be defined as psychological and social states of individuals or groups of people that result from interactions via language in which two or more linguistic codes (including dialects) are used for communication" (2006: 115). The focus of this definition shifts from the understanding of language as a set of rules and lexical items to its primarily communicative function. Secondly, it acknowledges extra linguistic features of bilingualism as a psychological and social phenomenon. Thirdly, it includes both individual and social versions into one notion of bilingualism.

Another example of creating a definition to serve a temporary purpose is one given by Judith Kroll and Paola Dussias who inform the reader that "for the purpose of our review, we assume a broad definition of bilingualism. We take anyone who actively uses two languages at some level of proficiency to be bilingual" (2006: 169). Again this is not a fully precise definition. By choosing to incorporate active users of a language the authors exclude those who can only understand it but do not state what they mean by 'actively'. Does it include being competent in all four language skills across all domains? Similarly, 'some level of proficiency' is not a strictly defined criterion. Is it enough to, say, be able to ask for directions in the street or would one need to produce a well-structured inauguration speech to be included in this category?

In the same publication Ingrid Piller and Aneta Pavlenko state that their definition of bilingualism "is an inclusive one, and we consider the use of two or more languages on a regular basis, irrespective of proficiency and age of acquisition as a bilingual practice" (2006: 489). Here the problem focuses on the relativity of the notion 'regular'. Does a person attending an evening language course twice a week count? Finally, the example of a definition offered by Nkonko Kamwangamalu reflects the need of creating a temporary description to serve the current needs of the author when he openly states: "In this chapter the term bilingualism is used to encompass both the individuals who are fluent in two languages only and those whose linguistic repertoire consists of three or more languages (2006: 726).

This definition created for the sake of a single chapter broadens the idea of bilingualism to address the ability to use more than two languages, an approach adopted by other authors as well (see Mackey, 1968; Ferguson, 1972; Myers-Scotton, 2002). To be fair, Kamwangamalu also quotes Skutnabb-Kangas (1981: 81) who noticed that "there are as many definitions of bilingualism as there are scholars investigating it, with every researcher using the kind of definition that best suits their particular area of inquiry" (2006: 726).

2.1.1. Balanced *vs.* unbalanced

Bilingualism comes in a number of types that are determined by a perspective adopted by the researcher. One idea is to divide bilinguals into those who can both comprehend and produce the language and those who have only a passive competence. The latter case is referred to by Hockett (1958: 16) as *semibilingualism* (Edwards, 2006: 10). When a person has both a passive and active command of at least two languages, the question which emerges is that of degree. To what extent is this particular individual competent in these languages? The ideal bilingual is often described as having equal competence in both languages thus presenting a type of bilingualism referred to as *balanced*. It is, however, difficult to imagine a person who is equally able (and willing) to express himself or herself in both languages across all domains, in all real life situations. In fact, bilingualism is very often the effect of particular circumstances and necessity rather than conscious choice. Many bilinguals have the command of other languages because they were forced, in one way or another, to communicate with others, be it at work or public institutions, in a different language than that spoken at home. Thus, it is reasonable to assume that they will have a different repertoire of vocabulary, grammar structures or even sociolinguistic competences appropriate for particular communicative situations, which will not necessarily be represented in both languages. A Polish-English bilingual computer scientist working in an American company may be perfectly able to communicate complex ideas connected with his professional field in English but unable to render the same in Polish.

An example given by Harding-Esch (2003) describes a situation when an English-French bilingual boy explains in French (home language) to his mother how to use a tube of glue. Lack of practice in speaking about one domain (school) in the language appropriate for another (home) results in codeswitching when he says:

Tu dévisses le bouchon… comme ça… et tu **squirt**. (you unscrew the cup… like this… and you squirt) (63).

Fishman (1971) claims that a person equally competent in two or more languages in all situations is a rarity (in Baker, 2001: 7). Another problem with the idealized concept of balanced bilingualism is that it assumes equal competence in all four language skills. This is difficult especially in countries with more than one official language or where differences between languages of various groups are big like in India, in the case of indigenous languages (especially when there is no written form) or wherever literacy in one or both languages is low. Bilingual teachers interviewed by Sidhu and Mills may be competent in three or more languages but their abilities in particular skills will vary, as one of the teachers admits: "I can speak and understand Punjabi, but I can't read and write it" (2002: 137). It seems, therefore, that it is much more common to meet a person whose bilingual competence is not identical in two languages and can thus be referred to as *unbalanced* or *dominant* (Peal and Lambert, 1962; in Butler and Hakuta, 2006).

It would seem reasonable to assume that the dominant language is the mother tongue but research shows that it is a more complex matter. Lieberson (1969: 291) defines the mother tongue as the "language usually spoken in the individual's home in his early childhood, although not necessarily used by him at present" (in Romaine, 1995: 19). This, however seems quite confusing taking into consideration cases where the childhood language differs from that of either of the parent's as in the example, quoted by Romaine (1995: 20) after Malherbe (1969: 45), of white infants in South Africa who acquire Zulu from their nannies before they start to speak English or Afrikaans. The author also raises the question of the term *mother tongue* itself pointing out that it suggests that a language is passed down from one's mother, whereas in some bilingual communities the primary language is that of one's father.

Another approach to defining the mother tongue is defining it on the basis of competence. One's mother tongue would, therefore, be the one which one knows best. However, it is possible to imagine a situation when one's language of community and schooling is better developed than that used at home but emotional attachment is placed with the latter. It is, thus, safer and more popular among researchers to use terms like *first language* or *community language* (Romaine, 1995: 19–20).

Butler and Hakuta point to the controversy over yet another term used in relation to bilingualism, namely *semilingualism* coined by Hansegard (1972) and widely debated henceforth (2006: 132). Initially the term referred to a failure in reaching a 'native-like' competence in either of the languages in the process of becoming bilingual. Bloomfield's (1927) report on the speech of a Menomini Indian in North America, quoted in Romaine (1995), exemplifies this attitude when the scholar notes that "White Thunder, a man around 40, speaks less English than Menomini, and that is a strong indictment, for his Menomini is atrocious" and states that the speaker 'may be said to speak no language at all" (6).

Romaine also points out that a similar term *double semilingualism* has emerged as a result of a debate about bilingualism in the Scandinavian context (1995: 261). The author states that both these terms are "defined with reference to some idealised and rather narrow notion of full competence in one language or another" (1995: 262). Butler and Hakuta quote Cummins (2000) who admits that "the term has no explanatory or predictive value but is rather a restatement of the equally ill-defined notion of 'limited proficiency' in two languages" (2006: 131).

2.1.2. Compound *vs.* coordinate and subordinate

Another dimension of bilingualism is that of its mental representation. The question here is whether the separate languages in a bilingual's brain are independent or interdependent. Baker (2001: 143-144) quotes Kolers' (1963) separate storage hypothesis which claims that the two languages are stored separately and the only channel of communication is that of translation between the systems. A shared storage hypothesis, on the other hand, claims that there is one memory store with two separate input and output channels. This distinction is reflected in Weinreich's (1953; in Butler and Hakuta, 2006) model of *compound*, *coordinate* and *subordinate* types of bilingualism. In compound bilingualism it is believed that there exists one meaning unit to which two linguistic codes refer. Romaine points out that it is characteristic for people who learn the languages "in the same context, where they are used concurrently, so that there is a fused representation of the languages in the brain" (1995: 79). Baker suggests that this type of bilingualism is often connected with an early age of bilingual acquisition (2001: 144). Coordinate bilingualism, on the other hand, occurs when one acquires the languages in separate environments (e.g. school vs. home) and the two systems refer to separate mental representations. A subordinate bilingual is believed to have one set of mental representations established by his or her dominant language, and the weaker language items are interpreted through the first language. In other words, in coordinate and compound types of bilingualism words in both languages are tied to their concepts (be it the same set or two separate ones), whereas in the subordinate type a word in a weaker language is tied to a word in the dominant language which only then evokes the concept.

2.1.3. Simultaneous *vs.* successive

If we take the age of acquisition as the point of focus in typology of bilingualism, it is possible to divide it into *simultaneous* and *successive*. The former refers to a situation when one is exposed to both languages early in life. "Early' is not a clear notion and it varies from researcher to researcher sometimes trying to fit in other theories like the "critical period hypothesis". Edwards concludes that it can refer to individuals who have been exposed to 'more than one variety from the onset of speech or, at least, from a very young age (some commentators have suggested age three or four as a rather arbitrary cut-off)" (2006: 11-12). The pace of child development in all aspects is a very individual matter and language is no exception. It is, therefore, difficult to draw any clear line between simultaneous and successive types of bilingualism if the latter occurs in relatively early childhood.

2.1.4. Primary *vs.* secondary

Another distinction, also connected with the age of acquisition, is that between *primary* and *secondary* bilingualism. The former is defined as a "dual competence acquired naturally, through contextual demands" and the latter is "one where systematic and formal instruction has occurred" (Edwards, 2006: 11). It seems that what is understood by this dichotomy is that primary bilingualism is characteristic for a situation, where the language of the home differs from that of the country of residence or where there are more than one languages used widely in one country. It would also be assumed that the exposure to both languages is simultaneous and early. Secondary bilingualism is thought of as a situation where the second language is learned at school, the implication being that the exposure is limited to classroom environment, and that it occurs after the first language acquisition (successive and late). The terms 'primary' and 'secondary' may imply that in the former case there is no language competence in any language prior to dual exposure while the latter may suggest that the exposure to the second language occurs when there already exists some competence in L1.

However, it is possible to imagine a situation when a fully competent L1 speaker is exposed to another language only in a situational context without formal education (e.g. because the language has no tradition of formal instruction). Such a person would then have to be classified as a primary bilingual despite his or her prior competence in L1.

2.1.5. Bilingualism *vs.* bilinguality and diglossia

The above described types of bilingualism refer more to the individual perspective than to the social dimension of the issue and are as such all a part of what Hamers and Blanc (2000) called *bilinguality* as opposed to *social bilingualism*, also referred to as *societal*, *collective* or *diglossia* (Ek, 2008: 749). Bilinguility, as described by Hamers (1981), is "the psychological state of an individual who has access to more than one linguistic code as a means of social communication; the degrees of access will vary along a number of dimensions which are psychological, cognitive, psycholinguistic, social psychological, social, sociological, sociolinguistic, sociocultural and linguistic" (in Hamers and Blanc, 2000: 6). Ferguson's (1972) initial definition of diglossia was a 'specific relationship between two or more varieties of the same language in use in a speech community in different functions' (in Romaine, 1995: 33). Later the term was broadened to enclose the use of two or more different languages in a variety of contexts.

These contexts are situated within certain domains which are abstract notions referring "to a sphere of activity representing a combination of specific times, settings and role relationships" (Romaine, 1995: 30). Romaine reports Fishman, Cooper and Ma's (1971) findings which led them to establish a list of five domains: family, friendship, religion, employment and education (1995: 30). Obviously, not all of them are equally prestigious and consequently the languages used in each of them differ in status. In diglossic distribution there is a high and low variety ascribed to corresponding functions establishing the position of a given language in a society.

Romaine presents some of the typical contexts which seem to come in pairs of related domains but different prestige. For example, a university lecture is conducted in the high variety, whereas a conversation with family is held in the low. Similarly, a news broadcast will be delivered in the high variety while a radio soap opera will be rendered in the low (1995: 33). Ferguson (1972; in Romaine, 1995: 34) came up with nine different dimensions which differentiate the high variety from the low i.e. function, prestige, literary heritage, acquisition standardization, stability, grammar, lexicon and phonology. Fishman (1980; in Romaine, 1995) offers examples of the relationship patterns between the high and the low varieties. One situation may be that the high variety will be perceived as classical and the low as vernacular while they are genetically related (e.g. Arabic, Sanskrit and Hindi) or unrelated (e.g. textual Hebrew and Yiddish). Another situation refers to two varieties where the high is used as a written and formal spoken language while the low is vernacular while they are genetically related (e.g. Urdu and spoken Panjabi) or unrelated (e.g. Spanish and Guaraní in Paraguay). There are situations where two languages serve as the high variety, like French and Classical Arabic in Tunisia, while Tunisian Arabic constitutes the the low variety. This is referred to as *triglossia* (Romaine, 1995: 35). It is also possible that any one language serves as the high or the low variety depending on the other languages it comes in contact with. Such *broad diglossia* (Fasold, 1984; in Romaine, 1995: 35) occurs when a language has a the higher status in comparison with local vernaculars, but the lower than the superposed variety. *Polyglossia* (Platt1977 in Romaine, 1995: 35), on the other hand, occurs where there are several language codes in use and they are distributed according to domains (e.g. in Malaysia where Mandarin Chinese is considered the high variety, although it is not used extensively in any domain, Bahasa Malay serving as the high variety, a low variety of Malay and English).

In contrast to bilingualism, diglossia is a stable arrangement which comes into being under certain conditions. For societal bilingualism to occur there must be "a sizeable body of literature in a language closely related to (or even identical with) the natural language of the community and this literature embodies some of the fundamental values of the group. Another precondition for diglossia obtains when literacy in the community is limited to a small elite" (Romaine, 1995: 36).

Naturally, the literate members of the community will have the ability to function in both varieties, which will make them bilingual while those deprived of access to the written (and possibly high) variety will remain monolingual. In fact,

Fishman (1967) claims that "the relationship between individual bilingualism and societal diglossia is not necessary or causal one" (Romaine, 1995: 36). Although the majority of people in the world are more or less bilingual, it is possible to imagine a country (or community) where neither bilingualism nor diglossia occurs. These are countries with very little immigration and few, if any, indigenous minorities. Diglossia without bilingualism results from a situation where two language communities coexist in the same area as one political entity but there is resistance on the part of the citizens to learn the language of the other group. Probably in this case there is little interdependence between the communities and thus the need to communicate in the other language is not strong. It may also be assumed that in such circumstances there is no evident disproportion in power relation or prestige between the two coexisting languages although tensions may occur (e.g. Canada). Possibly the most common situation is the opposite: bilingualism without diglossia. The community as a whole has one official language but its members may be bilingual. There are a number of circumstances in which this combination will occur, naturally often leading to language shift. One such setting is a country invaded by a linguistically alien community that is dominant and will aim to eradicate the indigenous language or its higher status itself will encourage the acquisition of the dominant language. One may also imagine a shift in the opposite direction when the immigrants' status is lower than that of the indigenous community and the newcomers will be forced to learn the majority language. Either way, bilingualism without diglossia seems to be a transitional stage leading to language shift in the next generations, if not in the first one. However, it also seems possible to imagine a situation in which a large group of a community becomes bilingual out of choice and without a threat to its first language.

The added language may serve as an aid in trade, exchange of services, business contacts for people living in border areas or countries with strong relations with other communities. This situation does not necessarily refer to a certain elite but it rather concerns common people who have frequent contacts with users of another language which may have no power advantage over their mother tongue (e.g. countries relying on tourism). Another reason for becoming bilingual without losing the first language is acquiring a lingua franca, which is often perceived as more elitist. This function in Europe used to be fulfilled first by Latin and then by French. These languages were seen as media of high culture and science, and as such were only learnt and used by the privileged members of European communities. The modern lingua franca, however, seems to occupy a different position in the contemporary world. English is an expansive language that has become the additional code of communication for many people across the world. It has dominated certain spheres of life that may be perceived as international domains such as the Internet, international air traffic, scientific publications, technology and entertainment. I would claim that bilingualism with the use of English as the second language is not as elitist as Latin and French used to be. Even though in many countries English is seen as imperialist and eradicating indigenous varieties, there are numerous communities which willingly choose to add it to their linguistic repertoires without losing their first languages. Whether this, nonetheless, poses a threat to these languages is unclear. There is little doubt that this added language will have influence on a community's mother tongue or its culture as a whole. It may also affect the individuals' perception of self and the world in general.

Perhaps in the long run this popularity of English that we so gladly welcome today will sneak into the first language culture and alter it, just as it would in the case of circumstantial bilingualism, and slowly but gradually lead to language shift. Whether the societies which today pride themselves on promoting bilingualism with English are heading for ultimate language loss in the future remains to be seen.

2.2. MULTIPLE POWER RELATIONS

Language is a means of communication and as such requires an individual to come in contact with other people (directly or indirectly) in order to use it. These people will have to understand each other for the communication to be effective. Language is therefore an inherent feature of a community and is thus affected by the process it undergoes. The study of bilingualism is interested in looking at languages in contact in an individual but also, more globally, in society.

2.2.1. Additive *vs.* subtractive

This contact between communities which have developed different languages and cultures can be friendly and equally beneficial for both language communities but more often there is a clash between these languages, one of which assumes a superior position. The resulting bilingualism is then not a free choice but rather a means of survival for those whose first language has a lower status in the speech community. This perspective has led to the division between *additive* and *subtractive* forms of bilingualism (Lambert, 1977; in Romaine, 1995: 117). An additive form of bilingualism occurs when the second language is acquired without the loss of the first language. Baker suggests that when in a given society two different languages are clearly ascribed to separate domains it is more likely that the more positive, additive form of bilingualism will result. The author states that "the learning of a majority second language may undermine a person's minority first language and culture thus creating a subtractive situation" (Baker, 2001: 59).

2.2.2. Folk *vs.* elite

It seems the power relationship pointed out by Baker between 'majority' and 'minority' languages is very often, but not always, true. These terms refer to the numbers of speakers using a given language in a society. Considering the situation, for example, in South Africa it may be concluded that L1 English speakers learning Afrikaans would be an instance of additive bilingualism, although they may be in a minority. It may be assumed that the more important factor than the numbers of speakers is the actual power relation between the languages. It may, therefore, be more accurate to define the dichotomy between additive and subtractive bilingualism by referring to the more powerful languages as 'dominant', 'stronger', 'superposed' or perhaps even 'expansive'.

This division is connected with Fishman's (1977) idea of *elite* and *folk* bilingualism based on different social status of languages in contact. The former is characteristic of L1 speakers of the dominant language who also have a command of a different language as an additional advantage. Myers-Scotton understands elites as people holding political power who will often use language policies to block access to official positions by linguistic groups they do not favour. She refers to the resulting situation as *elite closure*, which is "a type of social mobilization strategy by which those persons in power establish or maintain their powers and privileges via linguistic choices" (1993; in Myers-Scotton, 2002: 35). Harding-Esch and Riley interpret *elite* in a different way and express doubts concerned with the term itself, which suggest that those speakers are "both small in number and rich" (Harding-Esch, 2003: 24). The authors point out that nowadays bilingual families resulting from marriages of people from different European countries represent a wide spectrum of educational background, social status and financial situation. Their study showed that the fact of being somehow privileged does not solve their linguistic problems like maintaining two languages in the family when the additional language is not taught at school or is taught at a basic level.

Folk bilingualism, on the other hand, is characteristic for language minority groups "who have to become bilingual involuntarily, in order to survive" (Tosi, 1982; in: Harding-Esch, 2003: 24). In the case of immigrants, the motivation to become proficient in the majority language may develop into the need for complete switch from L1 to L2. A clear pattern of language shift may be observed in families where the first generation of immigrants has only a limited command of L2, the second is typically bilingual and the third has a limited, if any, command of their ancestors' L1. As Edwards puts it, "collective bilingualism is relatively permanent unlike the impermanent, transitional variety common in many immigrant contexts in which, in fact, bilingualism is a generational waystation on the road between two unilingualisms" (2006: 20).

Mackey (2006) describes this transition as a process consisting of consecutive steps which starts with what he calls the *incipient* phase when a second-generation immigrant experiences first contact with a new language of work. This is followed by the *progressive* phase in which he will be on his way to gain better proficiency in the new language than his parents. Next, the new language will become incorporated into his life outside workplace, which marks the *integral* phase. At this point he will have a roughly equal (though possibly imperfect) command of both languages, i.e. will pass for a bilingual. Having reached this, possibly most desirable, point of considerable balance he will move on to the *regressive* stage losing the language of his ancestors in favour of the new more useful (and often prestigious) one. Finally, he will find himself in the *residual* phase of his bilinguality "with a smattering of [his] ancestral tongue, its grammar imperfect and its use incidental" (2006: 614). As a result of the situation, the immigrant finds himself in, he develops bilingualism which is unstable and prone to loss due to the unequal power relation between the dominant new language and the ancestral speech that has a lower social status. In fact, the use of L1 by groups of immigrants may be frowned upon by the majority language users who will typically "perceive bilingualism as divergence from the norm of 'open communication'. That is, speaking a 'foreign language' may be considered an unwelcome sign of out-group allegiance" (Myers-Scotton, 2002: 40).

Inability (and often unwillingness) to understand the foreign language by the dominant language users leads them to treat any such exchange with suspicion and see it as a plot against those who are excluded (though voluntarily) from the discussion. Such assumptions affect the relationships between monolingual communities within the same society causing frictions and encouraging minority language users to quickly become bilingual and finally to drop their L1s in order to belong to the dominant community.

2.2.3. Elective *vs.* circumstantial

A similar idea to folk bilingualism, reduced with time to its residual form as a result of social pressure, is expressed by Valdez and Figueroa (1994) as *elective* and *circumstantial* bilingualism. Elective bilingualism occurs when dominant language speakers choose to acquire an additional language. This may, and very often is, the language of the ethnic minority whose command is hoped to help in maintaining balance between the groups coexisting in the same area and to promote some understanding of the minority language culture, perhaps ideally leading to biculturalism. The additional language may also be the one holding cultural heritage of the community that is dying and requires revival to avoid extinction. Another motivation to become bilingual voluntarily is of psychological nature. Myers-Scotton points out that "exposure to outside lifestyles causes individuals and entire groups to change their interpretations of their own world. That is, becoming bilingual can be part of a change in how individuals perceive and express themselves" (2002: 38). It seems that people choose to become bilingual not only for utilitarian reasons. Knowing English may be useful for any factory worker around the world in the event of a rather unlikely encounter with an English-speaking visitor. However, having no competence in this language will not influence his professional career to any significant extent.

On the other hand, this worker may have a positive association with English as a language of the modern world, open-mindedness, endless opportunities and will perceive anyone who has a command of this language as possessing the same qualities that the language itself stands for. Myers-Scotton, quoting Kulick (1992), gives an example of using Tok Pisin in Papua New Guinea, which is "associated with the sociable, cooperative side of a person. In contrast, the other side of personhood – what villagers call *hed* – is associated with the individualistic, selfish, and unbending side of personhood" (2002: 39). While the former is perceived by the villagers themselves as more desirable than the latter, the choice of language is threatening the vernacular, although there seem to be no external pressures to eradicate it but rather an internal psychological drive to opt for Tok Pisin. Circumstantial bilinguals usually come from minority language groups and are forced by the circumstances to acquire the dominant language in order to function in the society.

It seems that compulsory education offers an interesting case of this dimension of bilingualism. In most primary and secondary schools in Europe, for example, a foreign language is an obligatory subject. Although sometimes it is possible to choose between two or three languages, it is still impossible to decide not to learn a foreign language at all. It is, to be sure, of the elitist, additive, elective type but, nonetheless, it is thrust upon the dominant language speakers. In many cases this additional language may also be perceived as having a higher prestige in the world than the dominant language in the community. For example, in many European countries the foreign language learnt at school will inevitably be English which may be perceived as having a higher status than the mother tongue even if the society is almost homogenous linguistically. The reason for this is perhaps the fact that in a wider, world perspective, English may be perceived as a dominant language, the command of which is necessary for everyone to survive in the global village.

Such an assumption would place native English speakers in the elite and allow them to be the only group to have the privilege of becoming additive, elective bilinguals. It seems that L1 English speakers may have a similar point of view taking into consideration the fact that they are rarely interested in learning foreign languages.

2.2.4. Bicultural *vs.* monocultural and deculturated

Language imperialism and colonisation have also contributed to another distinction, namely that of *endogenous* and *exogenous* bilinguality. The former is developed in a social environment where both speech communities are present. The latter type is characteristic of countries with colonial heritage where one language belongs to the speech community and the other is used "as an official [language], institutionalized but has no speech community in the political entity using it officially" (Hamers and Blanc, 2000: 29).

Hamers and Blanc (2000) have also looked at the issue of bilingualism from the perspective of cultural identity and made a distinction between *bicultural*, *monocultural* and *deculturated* bilingualism. Biculturalism may be defined as "the ability to effectively navigate day-to-day life in two different social groups and to do so with the anticipated result of being accepted by the cultural group that is not one's own" (Smith, 2008: 65). This implies that a bilingual has the knowledge of understanding of socio-cultural rules at least at the level of basic communication and that he or she has the intention to be accepted in the non-native environment. Since language is an inherent element of culture, one needs to be bilingual at least in the minimal meaning of this word to become bicultural. It is, however, easy to imagine a situation when one is bilingual (even highly proficient in both languages) but not bicultural.

If being bicultural requires willingness to be accepted by the L2 culture or even to identify with it, many people who become fairly proficient in languages through formal instruction for occupational reasons, for example, may not be called bicultural. It may be assumed that many of those who have an instrumental motivation to learn a language, may not want to be a part of their target language culture (although they may have extensive knowledge about it) or even resist it, especially if they are made to learn the language (e.g. French in England, Russian in communist Poland). At the ether extreme one may decide to fully integrate with the L2 culture rejecting at the same time one's mother-tongue culture, thus remaining monocultural but shifting one's affiliations to the second language reality. This type of bilingualism (or rather bilinguality) is referred to by Hamers and Blanc as L2 acculturated as it leads to the identification with L2 culture with the rejection of one's mother tongue cultural membership (2000: 26).

The third possibility occurs when one renounces one's first language culture without adapting that connected with L2, thus becoming deculturated (Berry, 1980). On a more global level, biculturalism is a situation in a country where there are two different, officially recognized cultures (e.g. New Zealand, Hawaii, Belgium) (Smith, 2008: 66). Here too it is possible to imagine that in a (even officially) bilingual country, biculturalism is not present. In Canada there are often frictions between French and English speakers who, far from trying to identify with the other culture, choose to emphasise the differences and keep the two cultures in contrast if not conflict. This hostility is reflected in Heller's (1992: 123) example of an anglophone man in Canada who is looking for a room where a French test is taking place.

The logical assumption is that this man has at least an elementary command of French required to take a test in this language. However, he deliberately chooses to speak English to the receptionist in a provincial government office, to distance himself from the French environment:

MAN: Could you tell me where the French test is?
RECEPTIONIST: *Pardon?*
MAN: Could you tell me where the French test is?
RECEPTIONIST: *En français?* (in French?)
MAN: I have the right to be addressed in English by the government of Québec according to Bill 101
RECEPTIONIST: *Qu'est-ce qu'il dit?* (What's he saying) (1995: 168).

The breakdown of communication here is due to the unwillingness on the part of the man (or perhaps of both interlocutors) to adjust the language code to that of the other speaker. It seems unlikely that the man could not formulate his initial question in French, or that the receptionist did not understand it in English (even if s/he did not understand the other utterance). The lack of understanding occurred on a cultural level rather than linguistic.

2.3. MULTIPLE CIRCUMSTANCES

People become bilingual for various reasons, most of which have sadly nothing to do with a genuine desire to learn another language for the sheer beauty of its sound. Li Wei provides a number of possible situations which place people in contact with other languages. The first on the list, perhaps not surprisingly, is politics, by which he means military actions resulting in colonisation (e.g. India, where local languages were suppressed by English), annexation (e.g. the Soviet Union where Russian was introduced as an obligatory language at school), resettlement (e.g. former Yugoslavia) and federation (e.g. Switzerland) (2005: 3). Myers-Scotton offers more global examples of linguistic imperialism, namely the popularisation of Latin in Europe by the Roman Empire, Arabic in the Middle East as a result of Muslim invasions or Spanish in Central and South America (2001: 31). Natural disasters like famine, floods or volcanic eruptions may force people to migrate and settle in a different place, which will almost inevitably entail acquiring a new language. A more common reason for migration, however, is the desire to improve one's socio-economic situation. A third possibility is forced migration, as in the case of slavery or caused by war in the native country. In the case of migration the developed bilingualism is almost always one-directional, that is the newcomers have to learn the dominant language to survive in the host country. In the past the lower social status of immigrants (caused by their inability to communicate in the dominant language), limited access to language classes and generally scarce contact with model native speakers caused them to develop simplified versions of the target language that evolved into creoles.

Li Wei also mentions religion as an incentive to acquire a new language in order to live in a country of religious significance or as a necessity in the case of the need to leave one's country for religious reasons (e.g. Russians in Israel) (2005: 3). Both Myers-Scotton and Li Wei point to ethnic awareness or culture as reasons for becoming bilingual in a situation when a community living in a dominant language society wishes to maintain their heritage. If such a community consists of mainly second or third generation immigrants, the (sort of backward) development of bilingualism may take a form of language revival with the aim of preserving the ancestral speech. Yet another factor promoting bilingualism is education. In certain situations the knowledge of a major language may be the only way to access knowledge otherwise beyond reach (as it is in the case of languages that have no written forms). Li Wei gives an example of Latin in the Middle Ages as the language of the educated. Nowadays, the majority of scientific papers are available in English only, which promotes worldwide acquisition of this language across all fields of knowledge. Similarly, technology is a powerful drive in the global spread of English. As Li Wei puts it, "The availability of information and communication technologies (ICT), such as the internet, has led to a further expansion of the use of English across the world", although the majority of users speak English as an additional language. The last factor mentioned by Myers-Scotton is living in a border area. Having close neighbours speaking a different language motivates bilingualism for practical reasons like trade, social contacts or avoiding conflicts. Sometimes the people will learn each other's languages. The author gives an example of such a situation of areas populated by many language groups in Africa and South America where "many persons learn as many as three or four of their neighbours' languages" (2001: 31).

However, probably even more often the bilingualism is one-directional with the less powerful, numerous or economically developed community learning the language of the other.

2.4. MULTIPLE EFFECTS ON LANGUAGE

Whatever the motivations for bilingualism, there are a number of interesting effects of it on language, people and culture. When languages come in contact with each other, be it in a society or in an individual, a number of interesting phenomena occur. When a person (or a whole group of people) speaking one language starts acquiring another language (for whatever reason), the very fact that he already has a command of a language will inevitably influence the new one. This effect L1 exerts on L2 is sometimes referred to as *language interference*. However, this term suggests that it has negative consequences, which is not always true. A more neutral term *transfer* is more appropriate as it can be both positive (when L1 facilitates the development of L2 by providing e.g. similar grammar rules) and negative (when following L1 structure leads to errors in L2). Language transfer may also lead to overuse or avoidance of certain structures based on their occurrence in L1.

Crucial in the development of bilingualism are social and psychological processes. Giles's *accommodation* theory, for instance, may help to understand how a speaker's willingness to identify with the native speakers of the other language community influences the degree of bilingualism. Another theory applicable to languages in contact is that of Schumann's *acculturation* theory (1978), which claims that social (and psychological) distance from the target language community determines the degree of competence and may lead to fossilization (in Ellis, 1997: 29). The result is a simplified target language referred to as a *pidgin*. For the next generation the pidgin may evolve into a *creole*, a language which "is spoken natively by a whole speech community, often one whose ancestors were displaced geographically so that their ties with their original language and sociocultural identity were partly broken" (Holm, 1988: 6).

2.4.1. Lexical borrowings

Lüdi describes bilingual speech as "a mode of speaking where rules and norms are activated that overlap single languages and govern the harmonic i.e. the 'grammatical' mixing of elements from different languages" (2003: 175). One of the most natural consequences of bilingualism is lexical borrowing. Myers-Scotton points out that typically borrowing is one-directional: "L1 speakers of the less prestigious group (however prestige is conceived of) take into their language words from the L1 of the more prestigious language" (2002: 41).

Once a lexical item is borrowed and embedded into the recipient language, it becomes a part of it and one can predict with considerable certainty that it will tend to reoccur in the speech of the recipient language users. Myers-Scotton states that there are two types of content morphemes that can be borrowed: cultural borrowings, which are words connected with new objects and concepts that are introduced into the recipient language culture together with their names. The other case, core borrowings, is when the borrowed words duplicate already existing names of objects and concepts. While the former enter the recipient language rapidly, the latter are introduced gradually and, according to the author, result from codeswitching (2002: 41). When a speaker forms a message in one language (the *matrix language*) and comes to a point where he needs a word that he either does not know, that is not accessible for him at the time of speaking or this language does not have a word that would allow the speaker to fully express his intentions, he may fill this gap with a word coming from another language (the *embedded language*). Easy as it may seem, using more than one linguistic code in the same utterance is governed by rather strict and complex set of rules. Such filling of lexical gaps (*nonce borrowing*) is possible "only if the lemma of the embedded language word matches the slot provided by the matrix language" (Lüdi, 2003: 175). In such a case the utterance will be formed in the matrix language with only incidental appearance of single lexemes of the embedded language.

However, if the word triggers syntactic properties that are not compatible with those of the matrix language, the switch will comprise not only this single lexical item, but will be stretched to a longer fragment of the utterance creating an *embedded language island* (Lüdi, 2003: 176). Not all language mixing, especially at the word level, may be described as codeswitching. While codeswitching may have numerous extralinguistic functions, changing a language of an utterance to render a single word may result from incomplete competence in L2 and serve as a communicative strategy based on filling a lexical gap with a word of the speaker's L1 (or any other language he knows) in the hope that it will be understood by the recipient.

This phenomenon is referred to by Lüdi as *translinguistic wording* and is defined as a "conscious use of single words or longer sequences in L1 (or any other language likely to be understood by the native speaker of L2) as a form of rescue device" (2003: 176). This definition suggests that the interaction happens between a non-native and native users of a language. It seems reasonable, however, to extend this definition to include conversations between non-native users of a language in which the exchange takes place. In such situations it seems more likely that the negotiation of meaning based on the interpretation of a lexical item rendered in a language different from the matrix will be successful, as the linguistic repertoire of the interlocutors (and possibly their metalinguistic knowledge) may help them understand the word through comparison to other languages they know. To exemplify the difference between translinguistic wording and codeswitching, Lüdi quotes a conversation between a non-native speaker (NNS) of French (L1 German) with a native speaker (NS) of this language taken from Victor Saudan's corpus:

NNS: et il a un petit moteur oui. oui. qui tire le cocon il y a la **vorrichtung** il y a de grands **mast** de **stahl** *(and there is a little motor yes that pulls the cocoon and there is the device there are tall masts of steel)*
NS: oui donc *(yes)*
NNS: avec de des… bottes **oder eine Schiene** *(with… boots [manifestly wrong word, self-correction in German] isn't it a rail/or rather a rail/)*
NS: un rail *(a rail)* (2003: 180).

In the first turn the embedded language words (German) appear naturally with no hesitation on the part of the speaker and are understood by the addressee who reacts with a positive minimal feedback. The structure 'mast de stahl' follows the grammar of the matrix language - French (object+de+material), although the lexical items come from the embedded language – German. It is worth noting that, for this interaction to be successful, the NS of French needs to have considerable command of German. The second turn shows a different situation. The NNS lacks the word in the matrix language but instead of switching to German immediately, he hesitates and uses the wrong word before rendering the missing lexeme in the embedded language.

The reason for this behaviour may be that the intended French word is not totally unknown to the NNS but rather unavailable for him at the moment of speaking. Hesitation and using the wrong word as a place holder may indicate that the speaker is looking through his mental lexicon in search for this word, which he may have a recollection of knowing, but is unable to find it quickly enough to avoid communication breakdown. Instead, he chooses to switch to German in the hope that his interlocutor will understand the intended meaning. The NS interprets this change of linguistic code as a call for help and provides the orthonym which is repeated by the NNS before the conversation continues. It might be argued that the fact that the NNS so readily accepts the word proposed by the NS indicates that the NNS knew the word and hearing it made him recollect the lexeme, thus confirming the intended meaning. Alternatively, it may also be interpreted in the light of the relationship between the speakers. If the NS is recognised by the NNS as a competent user of both French and German (e.g. his language tutor), the translation is readily accepted as unquestionable truth rendered by a more knowledgeable interlocutor. Otherwise, the NNS would probably try to confirm the meaning by using additional strategies of negotiation to make sure that the French word is exactly what he meant.

Lüdi claims that codeswitching and translinguistic wording are placed along a continuum whose extremes are marked by an exolingual situation at one pole and endolingual at the other. The exolingual situation is characterised by an unequal competence of the interlocutors, while the endolingual situation features a "symmetrical interaction between two equally competent native speakers" (2003: 177). The author claims that translinguistic wording will be placed closer to the exolingual end of the continuum (and will be more typical of monolingual mode), while codeswitching will be more frequent in an endolingual situation (and will be more typical of a bilingual mode).

2.4.2. The nature of code swiching

Since it is rare that two languages of bilinguals are used across all language domains, they will typically compartmentalize the varieties restricting the use of each language to a given sphere of life (e.g. home language and workplace language, community langue and official language). Thus, bilinguals will switch from one language to the other depending on the domain they are talking about. Myers-Scotton mentions also two other possibilities: bilinguals code switch within a given domain and the same language may not be a preferred choice for all people taking part in a given interaction. Zentella (1997) recalls a study of Spanish-English bilinguals in New York City. The dyad mentioned in the text between daughter Lolita and mother Lourdes is perfectly comprehensible for both of them, although they use different codes, which are mutually known but not preferred for this particular conversation.

Mother: Sube ya mismo que van a ser las diez *come up right away because it's going to be ten o'clock*Lolita: I'm going with um este (um) Ana. She's coming up at ten – she's leaving at ten [struggles to put a sweater on]Mother: Pero quítate eso *but take it off*Lolita: Wait. I have to leave it on. I have to go like this and Ana's gonna put it all over again (1997: 63).

Lolita's persistence to use English in a home setting may be ascribed to her need to identify with the American society, which she stresses later on by saying "I'm not Puerto Rican, I'm American". Her mother's consistent use of Spanish, on the other hand, may reflect her attempt for language maintenance.

Codeswitching is one of the major phenomena accompanying bilingualism. Adding a language offers speakers a unique opportunity to change linguistic codes to achieve various effects. Codeswiching may be defined as "the use of two or more varieties in the same conversation" (Myers-Scotton, 2002: 44).

Structurally, codeswitching may appear between sentences (*intersentential*) or within a sentence (*intrasentential*, sometimes called *code mixing*). An intrasentential switch may be evoked by a word associated by the speaker with the other languge – a phenomenon known as *triggering*. An example given by Harding-Esch is that of a fourteen-year-old girl talking about a woman walking her dog: "I saw Mme Laurent *qui* was out with Cocky". The name Laurent is French and evokes an association with this language, thus the utterance is continued in French before it comes back to English. Harding-Esch claims that triggering is mechanical and unconscious, which explains the rapid return to the matrix language (2003: 64).

Myers-Scotton claims that codeswitching is a conscious process that serves as a social tool to either "comment on the speaker's perception of self" or "on his/her perception of the tenor of the ongoing interaction, its participants, its topics, etc." (2002: 45).

Although codeswitching seems to play a rather complex and sophisticated role, it is typically perceived as negative, hence the pejorative terms of language mixtures such as Spanglish (Spanish and English), Wenglish (Welsh and English), Franglais (French and English), Tex-Mex (Texan Mexican), etc. However, a fair number of studies (cf. Myers-Scotton, 2002; Romaine, 1995; Shin and Milroy, 2000) show that codeswitching is a positive phenomenon that expands a speaker's repertoire of communicative strategies and allows him to fully express himself with the best choice of linguistic elements at hand.

2.4.3. Reasons for codeswitching

Codeswitching is not merely a linguistic phenomenon but has mainly a social and psychological background and its analysis allows for detecting often complex mechanisms and relations between the participants of a given conversation, or even members of a particular community. Codeswitching is not a chaotic mixing of languages but a systematic tool used by speakers of two (or more) languages in particular situations for concrete communicative purposes. It is usually possible to determine the purpose of codeswitching. Myers-Scotton (2002) argues that codeswitching is used to achieve two major goals. She claims that it can either "call for a change in the dynamics of a conversation or an overall pattern of switching codes can index the speaker's desire to project themselves as persons with the identities associated with more than one language; that is, they project dual identities". The reasons for the latter behaviour may be various, depending on the extralinguistic circumstances. If the codeswitching is done by a speaker of a less prestigious language functioning as the matrix, it may signify his willingness to enter the dominant language community. Alternatively, if the same speaker uses the dominant language as a matrix frequently switching to his mother tongue it may mean that his goal is to stress his identity connected with the ancestral language and unwillingness to fully assimilate into the dominant language community. If this codeswitching is done by a second-generation immigrant child in a home language context, it may also signify the psychological need for independence.

Myers-Scotton and Bolonyai (2001) give an example of an eight-year-old Hungarian-English bilingual who tries to assert independence by codeswitching in a conversation with his mother in Hungarian as the matrix language:

Mother: Kértek salátát, úgy-e?
Would you like some salad, wouldn't you?
Kristóf: **I'll make my own salad**
Mother: Mi?
What?
Kristóf: **I'll make my own salad**. Ilyen kicsi tányérokban csinálják a restaurant-okban
They make it in such small plates at the restaurants
Kristóf: **I need some salad please**
Mother: Odaadtam az egészet.Tegyél hozzá mást is.
I've given you all. Add something else to it too

(in Myers-Scotton, 2002: 47)

Myers-Scotton (2002: 48) claims that the child chooses to use English as a manifestation of his independence, as this is the language he uses when outside parental control, at school and in interactions with peers. I would also argue that there might be another motivation for the switch in this particular instance, namely that of assimilation into the dominant language culture. Perhaps the child uses English to emphasise that the salad he is making is an element of the culture belonging to the dominant language (the one served in local restaurants) and is different from the one prepared by his mother and associated with Hungarian tradition.

The most basic reason for codeswitching, especially in its intrasentential form, is incomplete competence of one language in a given domain. It is most frequent where the home language differs from the official language or the interlocutors use different languages in social situations and at school/work. In such cases different domains are assigned separate languages and competence developed in each sphere of life is not repeated in the other language. Thus, when it comes to lexical competence, one may say that the interlocutors have a monolingual competence in certain domains and when talking in one context about a different domain they will use language items characteristic for both situations. When, for instance, a casual conversation is about work or school, the bilingual will switch codes introducing vocabulary items referring to the other domain to complete the message.

Codeswitching also occurs when there is no word in the matrix language that would allow the speaker to express exactly what he has on mind (or the word is not available to the speaker in the given moment) or the lexical item in the other language expresses his intended meaning better than its counterpart in the matrix language. In the example below an English-French bilingual child talks about his (French) school in a home setting (English).

FINN: We've got a new maths teacher, but he isn't *titulaire*... our real math's teacher is on a *stage*. (Approximate translations: titulaire – a teacher who has an established post, stage – an in-service training course) (Harding-Esch, 2003: 64).

There are two possible reasons for this switch: Finn may not know the language items in English which would convey the message equally well (or there simply are no ideal counterparts as a result of differences in education systems) or English, being the medium of home communication does not refer to school-related topics which evoke codeswitch.

This basic situation where change of linguistic code is motivated by gaps of knowledge, referred to by Zantella (1997) as *crutching*, although possible, is not as common as one would imagine. Myers-Scotton states that "switching mainly to fill gaps is neither typically true nor the major reason that speakers switch codes" (2002: 44). Her argument is that speakers who engage in codeswitching are usually highly proficient in both languages and they switch codes for stylistic effect rather than out of real need. Gumperz (1982) talks about frequent codeswitching in the case when the message includes quotations (in Shin, 2005). The quotation is rendered in original, while the matrix language may be different. It is especially justified when the quoted person is culturally different from the interlocutors. Romaine offers an example of a Papua New Guinean girl who retells a story previously watched on video. Although the matrix languge is Tok Pisin, the exact words of one of the characters are quoted in English:

Lapun man ia kam na tok, 'OH YU POOR PUSIKET', na em go insait (The old man came and said, 'Oh you poor pussycat', and then he went inside).

The author notes that the switch is appropriate as the character is white and the action takes place outside Papua New Guinea so it would be highly unlikely for the character to use Tok Pisin (1995: 162).

Codeswitching is also used for reiteration whose aim is typically emphasising the message. Shin gives an example of Korean-English bilinguals' interaction in a school setting (2005: 19):

YOONI: **Can I use your eraser?**
GRACE: [silence]
YOONI: Na **ERASER** sse-to-toy?
Is it ok. if I use your eraser?
GRACE: Ne iss-cyanha keki ey
you have it over there

The author claims that the switch of codes serves as a communication strategy. The lack of response may have been interpreted by Yooni as a misunderstanding or rejection of the request. Either way, it led to communication breakdown, which was repaired by Yooni by means of a repetition of the initial request in another language that the girls shared. Shin claims that the ability to change linguistic codes is an additional communicative strategy in the bilinguals' repertoire. If this tool was not available to the interlocutors, Yooni would probably choose a different strategy typical of monolingual speech like repetition, paraphrase, voice modification, body language, etc. This example shows a situation in which reiteration aids communication in that it gives additional explanation in case there should be a lack of understanding of the first message. It is worth noting that the repetition, even though it is rendered in Korean, still includes the referent in English suggesting that the word itself belongs to the classroom language and as such is expressed in English only (it seems possible that the girls do not know the word in Korean at all). Therefore, even if we assume that Grace did not understand the request, the first time due to imperfect language competence, she must have understood what object Yooni is referring to, as in the reiteration it is not rendered in Korean and still Grace gets the message. If we assume that Grace understood the word for the referent the first time she heard Yooni's request, it is rather unlikely that she could not make out the whole message from the context.

Thus, Yooni might have used reiteration to reinforce her initial request. Baker quotes Roberts' (1994) study which showed that nurses at a Mid-Wales hospital use reiteration with codeswitching to assert authority, as in the case of telling off a patient:

Peidiwch a chanu'r gloch Mrs Jones - **do not ring the bell if you do not need anything**! (2001: 114)

The repetition in the majority language stresses the nurse's position. A similar example is reported by Baker who quotes a teacher emphasizing his authority by codeswitching between French and English especially in short commands like:

Taisez-vous les enfants! **Be quiet, children**!' (2001: 115).

It seems that the strengthening of a request may also be achieved through codeswitching without reiteration. An example noted by Leopold (1954), based on a case study of his daughter, quoted in Harding-Esch and Riley (2003) shows a manipulative power of codeswitching consciously used by children to achieve their extra-linguistic goals. The example features Leopold's German-English bilingual daughter who tries to convince her father to stay with her until she falls asleep. To make her request more effective, the girl constructs a bilingual message:

Papa wenn du das Lich ausmachst, **then I will feel so lonely**
Daddy if you put out the light (65)

It is possible to suspect that the girl knew how interesting for her father her bilingual skills are and so she used her ability to make a greater impression on her father and thus increase her chances of achieving her aim.

Codeswitching may also serve as a tool for clearly indicating the intended recipient of the message. Romaine quotes McConvell's (1988) example of a switch between Kriol and Gurindji

Where, 'nother knife? Walima pocket knife karrwa-rnana?
Where is the other knife? Does anyone have a pocket knife? (1995: 163)

The message is directed at those who can comprehend it, in this case a group of butchers working together. Anyone who could not understand the message was excluded from this exchange for the simple reason that he was not its addressee. However, through codeswitching interlocutors may exclude other participants of the discourse if they want to keep the message from them. The additional language serves as a secret code in which bilinguals communicate in the presence of monolinguals if they do not want them to participate in the conversation. Such behaviour is typically perceived as hostile towards the participants of the conversation who have no command of the language shared by the rest. However, there are also instances which show that such exclusion does not necessarily entail negative feelings towards the excluded person but, on the contrary, is done for their own good. The example offered by Harding-Esch (2003: 65) presents a situation where a seventeen-year-old Emily engages in codeswitching from French, which is common language for all interlocutors, to Swedish which she shares with her mother in order to help her German friend, Anne, at a dinner.

MOTHER: [to Anne]: Tu reprendras un peu de ça?
would you like some more?
EMILY: [to her mother in Swedish]: Jag tror inte att hon tycker om det.
I do not think she likes it

Although Emily excluded her friend from the conversation by codeswitching into a language the girl did not know, her intentions were rather friendly. By not stating her thought openly, she saved Anne the embarrassment it would have caused otherwise.

On the other hand, codeswitching may play an opposite role, that is include a person into a conversation in a situation where the main conversation is held in a language that one participant does not speak. In this case codeswitching to include this person into the conversation is an act of showing friendship. Conversely, a person who only has a basic command of a language in which a conversation is held may try to use what little language he has to indicate his desire to belong to the group. As Baker puts it, "Someone with a rudimentary knowledge of a language may inject words of that new language into sentences to indicate a desire to identify and affiliate" (2001: 103). It is worth stressing that this language does not necessarily have to be the majority or dominant or prestigious language. Although it is probably most common for the speakers of a less respected language to try and assimilate with those of mainstream language, it is not inconceivable to imagine a situation in which the users of the dominant language have a desire to join a group of minority language speakers.

However, the latter situation, probably much less common, might ironically be more difficult. In the case of minority language speakers wishing to enter the dominant language community (as it typically is in the case of immigrants) resistance might be little as there is common understanding that sooner or later those people will become members of the community they aspire to, and it will be beneficial for both sides (e.g. in workplace communication). In the opposite case, however, the motivation might be unclear and, as such, arouse suspicion on the part of minority language users. In fact, the situation in which a dominant language user wants to enter the minority language community is, in a sense, unnatural since it offers little practical advantages (hence, speakers of English rarely speak other languages). Why would any dominant language speaker want to learn the minority language? It seems possible to imagine a few reasons. First, minority language speakers (like first generation immigrants or indigenous people of an invaded area) are typically manual workers who will strive to learn the majority language to improve their lot. They will usually work under a dominant language speaking supervisor who might want to learn some of their language to exert better control. Also, civil servants in countries with high immigration rates may decide to have a limited command of immigrants' languages for more effective communication. Secondly, business is usually conducted in the more prestigious language but traders might want to learn some of the other language to have a more direct contact with the speakers of the less prestigious language and to seemingly lower the distance between their cultures in order to be perceived as more friendly and, thus, conduct business more efficiently. Yet another case of such a direction of acquisition is linguists who are genuinely interested in the language and eager to become members of a minority speech community in order to explore and analyse the language. The last situation that comes to my mind (but this is surely not an exhaustive list) is that of personal, emotional engagement with a member of a minority language culture who is not willing to assimilate into the mainstream.

In this case the motivation might be strong enough to acquire the less prestigious language together with its social and cultural heritage, which could possibly lead to giving up the majority language identity and becoming a full member of the new community. With a possible exception of the last case (if treated in its extreme form), all reasons for acquiring the language of a lower status reflect a patronizing attitude at best and a total lack of respect at worst. Therefore, any dominant language speaking newcomer showing intentions to enter the less prestigious language community by codeswitching into this language, has to tread softly and be prepared not to be welcome with open arms immediately just because he is showing interest in the language.

In monolingual environments the same phenomenon occurs within linguistic subsystems in dialects, slang or jargon. To emphasize one's willingness to belong to a given subculture, social or professional group, people use linguistic elements characteristic for these environments. Such behaviour is justified when all discourse participants belong to the group and understand the language which becomes a form of a secret code incomprehensible to unauthorized public. In a bilingual situation such peppering of the matrix language with alien elements when not all participants have a sufficient command of the other code may be perceived as rude or arrogant. It is not uncommon to hear students of English, who otherwise share a common native language, engaging in conversations full of English words or even elements of grammar. While within this particular community codeswitching, whose aim is typically a presentation of wittiness, humour or play on words, is understandable through the context of environment, the same activity outside the community (especially in circles where this added value of codeswitching might not be understood) is rather frowned upon and socially unacceptable. By using English as an element of their language the students stress their belonging to the same group.

In a similar fashion codeswitching from a dominant into a minority language may be used to emphasize the connection between people forming a community within a more prestigious language society. Baker quotes Di Pietro (1977) giving an example of immigrants telling jokes in English but with the punch line in Italian where codeswitching serves to underline their cultural belonging to a non-mainstream community (2001: 102). At the same time it excludes monolingual participants of the discourse showing the desire to emphasize their bonds with other immigrants and unwillingness to fully assimilate into the English speaking community.

An opposite situation is possible when codeswitching between members of the same community is used to show distance between them in terms of social status or position. Quoting Myers-Scotton and Ury (1977), Baker describes a conversation between a Kenyan shop owner and his sister. The siblings greet each other in the local Luyia dialect but then the brother switches to Swahili, '*Dada, sasa leo unahitaji nini?*' (Sister, what do you need today?) while his sister goes on speaking in the dialect (2001: 103). This switch might have been used to indicate the difference of their status in this particular situation. However, another explanation is possible. Swahili is a Kenyan language of trade and as such is ascribed to this domain. The man naturally switched from the local dialect (low variety) used in the domain connected with home and family life to Swahili (high variety) used in official, professional situations. Similarly, regular codeswitching occurs when the topic of conversation changes indicating that a part of the discourse belongs to a different domain than the other as in the example given by Valdés-Fallis (1976; quoted in Baker, 2001) of Spanish–English bilinguals in the South West United States who use English to talk about money "*La consulta era* ***twenty dollars***" (the visit costs) (104). Baker concludes that "this reflects that English is the language of commerce, and often the dominant language of the mathematics curriculum" (2001: 104). It may suggest that the social binding of language to a given domain is stronger than the psychological drive to ascribe one's dominant language to certain inner functions as listed by Mackey (1968: 565), that include counting, reckoning, praying, cursing, dreaming, diary writing, note taking, speaking to oneself or thinking aloud (in Romaine, 1995: 31).

The multitude and diversity of roles that codeswitching plays may suggest that the above list is far from exhaustive. Additionally, each communicative situation may be interpreted in various ways and it is not always possible to determine one clear reason for codeswitching beyond reasonable doubt. In fact, as Peter Martin puts it, "it is not possible or indeed useful to attempt to assign a 'cause' for every instance of codeswitching in a given set of data" (2003: 72). Because there may be so many explanations for the reason codeswitching occurs, its analysis resembles interpretation of poetry. Unless the author of a given utterance states his intentions clearly (although he himself may also have problems identifying the underlying reasons), we may only determine a set of possible explanations rather than interpret a given communicative behaviour in one definite (often biased) way.

2.5. MULTIPLE ADVANTAGES OF BILINGUALISM

Rarely does it happen that a bilingual in his linguistic repertoire has languages that are equally prestigious and generally respected in all contexts and situations. It seems that the most common situation is when a speaker has a command of the superstrate language that is perceived objectively as more powerful or respected and gives this person a badge of being educated, modern or having a high social status. The other language (often concealed) is the ancestral language which in the dominant code environment may be perceived as a sign of being backward, unintelligent, poor and not ambitious.

However, in the substrate language environment, command a of the heritage language may be perceived as showing respect for the elder, tradition and history of the country of origin, while monolingualism in the dominant language may be seen as betrayal, disrespect and arrogance. Thus, it is usually the substrate language environment that promotes bilingualism by stressing the need to keep it and add the new one instead of merely replacing the old language. In general experience, more is usually better than less. Ownership of two cars is better than one, so is having two incomes, two university degrees, or even two wives. Why, then, isn't a command of two languages so obviously more beneficial than being monolingual? Acquiring an additional language has its consequences. Li Wei presents a list of possible outcomes of becoming bilingual. If a child is raised in a family where the parents speak different languages, he or she may interact with each parent in their preferred language, which may lead to forming "a subtler, finer texture of relationship with the parent" (2005:

19). In relation to family, bilingualism helps the speaker to bridge gaps between generations, which allows for learning more directly about one's heritage and, thus, gives the sense of belonging and rootedness. Being bilingual also allows to form social bonds outside home. When the languages of home, social life and school or workplace vary, being able to communicate in many different domains offers the opportunity to meet more friends and thus become more open, tolerant, knowledgeable.

On a more global scale, bilinguals may serve as messengers of their families, communities or even societies who may help to communicate in order to create "friendly relationships of mutual respect" (Li Wei, 2005: 20). A personal advantage for the bilingual speakers, referred to by Li Wei as *linguistic sensitivity*, may help them better understand communicative needs of their interlocutors leading to more effective communication. The ability to switch codes in order to find the best way to express their intensions, makes bilinguals aware of the intricacies and complexity of languages, which may in itself bring satisfaction from more conscious, fuller use of language tools. Increased language sensitivity contributes to a better understanding of foreign cultures. Hamers and Blanc (2000) claim that "by encountering multiple cultural and ethnic groups and values, bilingual individuals can develop unique cultural and ethnolinguistic identities, separate from those of monolinguals" (in Butler and Hakuta, 2006: 132).

While monolingual travelers may explore foreign countries in a rather superficial way, bilinguals have the opportunity to fully appreciate their cultures largely encoded in the language. A full appreciation of literature is possible only through the media of the language it was created in, since any translation will corrupt the true spirit of the book. From a more practical, down-to-earth perspective, knowing more than one language opens the world of professional opportunities. In today's global world practically every job with any prestige requires from the candidates a command of at least one additional language. This condition seems obvious when taking into consideration the fact that international trade is conducted in the world's major languages and local business goes better when one can show respect and interest in the partner by addressing him in his first language. Li Wei also mentions cognitive advantages. Being more linguistically aware and having the opportunity to constantly compare languages, bilingual speakers are more elaborate thinkers, have a deeper understanding of the underlying meaning of words and culturally dependent values hidden in the language, and "are able to extend the range of meanings, associations and images, and to think more flexibly and creatively" (2005: 21).

2.6. MULTIPLE FEARS AND PRESSURES

If there are so many advantages, why is bilingualism not viewed with greater enthusiasm? Initially, bilingualism was approached with suspicion, to say the least. Well respected doctors, psychologists, teachers and others advised against bilingualism predicting a range of problems and perceiving bilingualism as "a burden on the brain, mental confusion, inhibition of the acquisition of the majority language, identity conflicts, split loyalties, even a schizophrenia" (Baker, 2001: 135).

Detrimental effects of bilingualism discussed by Cummins (1984) and summarized by Baetens Beardsmore include fears that "bilingualism will handicap a child's speech development, intellectual progress, educational chances, emotional stability; may cause character difficulties so that children become aggressive and anti-social; bring about schizophrenia; make children ambivalent; cause cultural disorientation or opposing pulls of loyalty; make children morally untrustworthy and engender linguistic sloppiness (2003: 18).

Obviously, most of these imaginary problems have long been rejected. Others have been proven to wrongly ascribe an issue to bilingualism when the real cause lay elsewhere (e.g. emotional tension of immigrant children was not language induced but rather caused by the inconvenience of general circumstances they found themselves in). However, there are still fears connected with bilingualism that hunt various environments engaged in the issue. Baetens Beardsmore identifies four groups of fears, namely, parental, cultural, educational and politico-ideological. The author claims that fears of the parents arise from two possible situations: the parents either come from monolingual environments and project their experience of learning the other language on their children, or even though they are themselves bilingual, they live in a monolingual society which "pressurizes them into worrying about bilingualism in their children" (2003: 11). It is generally assumed that learning through two languages is more difficult than through one language. A child exposed to two languages at the same time but to a greater or lesser extent and possibly in different domains, may initially show slower linguistic development (e.g. bilingual children tend to have a delayed onset of speech). However, as was shown by Swain (1981), although it may take longer for bilingual children to reach a competence of their monolingual peers, they will with time catch up or even surpass their proficiency in at least one of the languages (in Baetens Beardsmore, 2003: 13).

Another potential problem parents fear is that of emotional nature. They are afraid that their bilingual children will have problems with asserting their identity established in connection with the values and cultural heritage encoded in a language. Surveys conducted in a study of Housen and Baetens Beardsmore (1987) have shown that "the majority of subjects had no polarized stances towards the language groups they were involved with, lacked stereotyped attitudes towards members of other groups they were involved with and maintained dual or multiple loyalty patterns" (in Baetens Beardsmore, 2003: 13).

Far from being in danger of losing their cultural rootedness, bilingual speakers gain an added value of becoming members of two different cultural entities from which the can draw to create a complex mosaic of personality. First generation immigrants express fears connected with a possible loss of values encoded in the ancestral language by their children who often strive for assimilation into the mainstream culture. Although acquisition of the superstrate language may entail a partial (though perhaps temporary) withdrawal from the ancestral language culture, it may simply be a manifestation of independence and, as such, an element of growing up. After the initial rebellion, second generation immigrants may return to the values respected by their parents and incorporate them as elements of their identity.

Cultural fears are based on the relationship between languages and cultures in contact. To the four types of individuals described by Fitouri (1983), that is monocultural monolinguals, monocultural bilinguals, bicultural monolinguals and bicultural bilinguals, Baetens Beardsmore (2003) adds that of "bilinguals who undergo a form of disorientation or acculturation brought about by cultures in conflict. Ironically, the first situation is rather uncommon since most people in the world are more or less bilingual and live in constant contact with other cultures. Monocultural monolinguals are people who live in considerable isolation from other cultures and languages. Seemingly, in such a situation there are no worries connected with cultural identity of future generations.

However, in such isolated groups that have no opportunities for exchange of thought and experience, development might be slow or even non-existent, which may lead to demise. Additionally, individuals confined to such unified conditions might rebel against the stagnation and sacrifice the ancestral language and culture for the sake of personal development. Monocultural bilinguals are typically people who have acquired an additional language in a home country. The threat to the ancestral values is small in this case due to limited contact with the other language culture. However, if language is treated as a medium of culture, it is impossible to separate the knowledge of language from the understanding of values that it encodes. Surely, an individual may choose whether or not to identify with certain cultural elements of the additional language, but I would claim that the command of another language (even at a basic level) induces the acquisition of another way of perception through the specific cultural associations typical of the other language. Thus, it seems hardly possible to find a bilingual who has no understanding of either of the cultures represented by his languages or no elements of either culture incorporated into his construct of personal identity. Bicultural monolinguals are those who have undergone language shift losing the ancestral speech but retaining the traditions and values characteristic for the previous generations. Bicultural bilinguals have acquired the additional language and culture without losing their ancestral language and values. They constitute an interesting patchwork of linguistic and cultural elements of both languages.

The fifth, added category of bilinguals who go through a transitional period when they have problems with reconciling the two cultures reflected in the languages they know, presents a case where the anxiety is probably most justified. The situation is the more difficult, the more differences exist between the cultures in contact. As McLaughlin (1985: 39) puts it, "if the bilingual's two cultures are mutually exclusive it is impossible to harmonise them (in Baetens Beardsmore, 2003: 16). The example presented by the author is that of Arabic–French bilinguals in Tunisia where the attitude towards bilingualism depends on social status.

The more open-minded upper levels welcome bilingualism as stimulating and enriching, while the conservative lower levels, focused on tradition and indigenous values, view bilingualism as a violation of their culture and aggression. As a result, in elite bilingualism there are minor cultural tensions, while folk bilingualism is marked with apprehension and distrust. Fears of Arabic-French bilinguals (in Morocco) were also examined by Bentahila (1983), who found that the majority of Moroccan bilinguals perceive themselves as divided between two cultures neither of which they fully belong to. They also agreed that bilingualism in Morocco leads to cultural crisis and lack of identity. Despite such opinions, Bentahila reported that a vast majority of respondents viewed bilingualism as a positive phenomenon, acknowledging its practical value (in Baetens Beardsmore, 2003: 16).

Educational context arouses probably most fears as it is almost always viewed with a monolingual bias. Bilingual children's underachievement during their first years at school is typically attributed to a detrimental effect of the acquisition of two languages. However, the comparison of educational success is made between the results obtained by bilingual children and their monolingual peers. It seems unreasonable to expect those children to perform at an equal level during the first years of formal education and, as Baetens Beardsmore puts it, "a child who receives input divided across two languages often in unequal proportions, should not be compared with a child who receives input in one language, as it is often the case, or we could be expecting the bilingual to live twice" (2003: 13). In the

US bilingual children of immigrants are referred to in educational context as LEP (Limited English Proficiency), which has a rather negative meaning as it suggests that the students have a sort of deficiency rather than an advantage of having a command of two languages (one of which is as yet incomplete). They are offered remedial classes and are generally perceived as 'special needs' students along with those with behavioural, psychological or other problems, which may hamper the development of their true potential.

Baker claims that assigning bilingual children such a label "can accentuate children's perceived deficiency rather than their proficiencies, children's perceived 'deprivation' rather than their accomplishments, their lower, marginalized, minority status through majority eyes rather than their bilingual potentiality" (2001: 5). The hidden aim of remedial education of bilingual children is often transition, which is helping the children to move into unilingual education provided in the superstrate language disregarding their additional asset of having a command of another language but treating it as an embarrassing obstacle instead.

The last group of worries identified by Baetens Beardsmore is politico-ideological fears. The author quotes Nelde (1987) who claims that whenever languages come in contact there is tension between them resulting from a clash between "differing standards, values and attitude structures which strongly influence identity image, education and group consciousness" (2003: 21). This view implies that there is no possibility of friendly contact between communities speaking different languages. Sad as it may seem, at least at a more global level, it is a fact that whenever two languages representing different cultures, encoding uncommon beliefs and reflecting dissimilar ways of thinking meet, a friction (if not an open conflict) is inevitable. However, it is possible to imagine situations where individuals speaking different languages come in frequent contact without any hostile intensions and build a bond from which both sides benefit (e.g. borderline neighbours). On a more global scale, though, languages come in contact, in the first place, in circumstances that almost always entail unequal power relations. When one language community feels superior in relation to the other community (e.g. in cases of military invasions or immigration) the cultures, and consequently languages of these communities, will be in conflict. However, the tensions may not result from bilingualism itself. In fact, the ability to communicate in each other's languages could be a factor mitigating frictions by offering the members of both communities an insight into the culture of the other and fostering mutual understanding.

The conflict arises rather from the lack of bilingualism which makes effective communication impossible and the attempts to prevent the development of bilingualism by either isolation of the minority language or forcing the less dominant community to shift to the other language. Such frictions may be observed in Belgium, where the majority language, Dutch, was stigmatized as having low prestige and public recognition while the minority language, French, was recognized as having strong economic and political power and associated with intellectual prestige. Such perception of the imbalance between those languages has led to massive shift in people aspiring for higher social positions.

The ultimate fear of communities speaking a minority language is that the contact with a superstrate language will in various ways lead to the eradication of the indigenous language when its speakers choose, for various reasons, to give up their ancestral language for the sake of the new one. As Myers-Scotton puts it, "the future of a language depends on the number of people using it, the existence of a community of speakers and the domains in which a language is used" (2003: 48). When the new language is more attractive in that it offers better job opportunities, self-development and upward movement in the social structure, it may discourage children of the substrate language users from learning their ancestral language or even lead to language attrition in those who already know the language. In a situation of contact between languages the bilingual will be pressurized to use one language (typically, but not always the dominant one) rather than the other. Mackey provides a list of these pressures which include economic, administrative, cultural, political, military, historical, religious and demographic. In many cases the acquisition of the dominant language is an economic necessity. Parents will typically encourage their children to focus on the superstrate language in order not to be underprivileged when it comes to professional development. As a result, children develop the languages to different extent with the ancestral language having a lower priority and consequently achieving a lower level of proficiency.

Administration favours multilingualism since in many countries the command of minority languages by civil servants helps to ease social tensions by providing effective communication with all citizens. Cultural pressures, on the other hand, urge people who aspire to constitute an intellectual elite to acquire an international language (e.g. English or Arabic depending on the region) as a medium of communication in printed material. The most obvious pressures, though, are exerted by political tensions with the more powerful country forcing its language upon the weaker one as in the case of military invasion where "the foreign colonial language may become the dominant one, develop a regional standard, and be used as the official language of the country" (Mackey, 2005: 31).

The results of a political pressure, if effective, can thus be long lasting. However, as Baetens Beardsmore points out, "official attempts to destroy a language have often merely promoted tension without achieving language shift" (2003: 21).

Indeed, Welsh for example, is still a living language despite the Act of 1535 that banned it from official use. In fact, historical events may determine the pattern of bilingualism in a country. Joining the army during the time of war offers new opportunities for bilingual development. Soldiers may be required to learn the language of a country they are in conflict with or another army that has signed a military treaty with their home armed forces. The final outcomes of such conflicts often include changes in language policies. The language of the party who have gained dominance in a given area is typically superimposed on the indigenous language users. However, steps are typically taken to maintain the language of the defeated parties. As a result, the minority language users may have a legal right to educate their children in the substrate language in mainstream education.

Sometimes fluency in a substrate language may be motivated by religion. The ancestral language community may exert pressure on its members to maintain the indigenous language for religious reasons. The added value of this motivation is the fact that very often the language encodes the community's beliefs and religious rites which constitute an inherent element of culture reflected in the language. Thus, the community members make the connection with their ancestral language deeper through religious experiences.

Finally, demographic pressures determine a bilingual's pattern of language use. Language vitality in an individual depends heavily on the opportunities he has to use his languages. This, in turn is determined by the frequency of contact with people speaking those languages. If a bilingual starts his life in a village populated mainly by people using his ancestral language, his development in this language will be more rapid than in the dominant one which he may encounter outside the community. Once he leaves this village to become a member of mainstream society (for educational or professional reasons), his encounters with the ancestral language will become scarce and he runs the risk of attrition (Mackey, 2005: 32). Whatever the reasons for language conflict, the dominant more powerful communities try to impose their languages upon the substrate communities, which on the other hand, strive to maintain their own languages.

The motivation for the dominant language to aggressively eradicate the substrate varieties may be twofold, depending on the circumstances. If the dominant language is one of a country engaged in military invasion, imposing the language upon the defeated community may serve as a tool for destruction of indigenous culture that may potentially encourage upheaval. On the other hand, if the dominant language is spoken by the majority of society, the obligation to learn the dominant language may be thrust upon the immigrant minorities as a means of inclusion in the mainstream society in order to prevent separatist movements.

It seems that substrate languages are under considerable threat of extinction. Krauss (1995) warns that "50% of the world's languages are no longer being reproduced among children and an additional 40% are threatened or endangered" (4). In the light of these numbers and the understanding of the need to maintain linguistic diversity, steps should be taken to increase linguistic vitality. A language's vitality is defined as "the range and importance of the symbolic functions a variety serves, that is, the degree to which a variety is used" (Ryan and Giles, 1982: 4; in Myers-Scotton, 2001: 50).

Summarising Landry and Allard's study (1992), Myers-Scotton observes that majority and minority language speakers treat bilingualism differently, i.e. for the former sufficient contact with L2 will result in additive bilingualism, while for the latter acquiring the other language will ultimately mean language shift. Although language shift is generally perceived as a negative phenomenon that leads to the loss of language together with all the cultural heritage it represents, Edwards (1985) perceives it as alternation, which "accords with social dynamics and, in any event there is never a question of a loss, sure and simple, with nothing to replace the abandoned form. Another language comes to serve and, in the transitional period, bilingualism is the usual bridge" (in Myers-Scotton, 2001: 51).

If we look at languages as colours, knowing one is like having a monochromatic view of the world, perceiving reality in endless shades of, nonetheless, the same colour. A command of two languages allows for seeing two different colours in their diverse tints and blends. A bilingual is like a painter who has at his or her disposal two different colours of paint. He or she can use either of them in different shades but a skilled master will also learn how to blend them in various proportions to create a new reality. One in which they will not only coexist but also overlap and intertwine creating a picture full of contrasts and smooth transitions. A bilingual is able to see the world beyond the language that describes it. He or she has the privilege to observe reality in the state of constant recreation by the various connotations and complex meanings that two different languages attach to it. A command of two languages offers an insight not only into the mechanisms of language itself but also into the history and culture of the people who have created and recreated it over centuries. The more languages one speaks, the fuller and more colourful one's perception of life is. It may be claimed with reasonable certainty that no one knows all the estimated 6000 languages or even one percent thereof. However, even one additional language is a key to a whole new world, which is known but presented, in a different light.

3. THE PLACE OF LANGUAGE TEACHING IN FORMAL EDUCATION

Foreign language education is an integral part of curriculum at all levels of education. Foreign language is an obligatory subject in primary education in almost all European Union countries and the percentage of children not enrolled in this type of instruction dropped from 32.5% to 21.8% between 2004 and 2010 (2012). Early introduction of foreign language instruction seems beneficial for the learners. However, lower primary-level students teaching practice needs to be carefully planned and adjusted to children's developmental capacities. The challenge of creating an effective foreign language learning environment calls for a revision of the pedagogical approaches in use and a construction of a new young learner-friendly methodology.

3.1. PEDAGOGY

Pedagogy comes from a Greek word *paidagogos*, which means 'to lead a child'. Although it is typically used nowadays to refer to the science of teaching the original concept included more than a mere focus on knowledge transfer. The main focus of pedagogy in its initial sense was the child himself as an active participant of his own educational process understood as gaining experience from the surrounding environment and reflecting upon it. The child was guided by an adult in the explorations of the nature of the world and himself to construct meaning through interaction. To lead a child does not mean to transfer a given amount of subject knowledge to him but rather to help him understand the world mechanisms in a meaningful way. It means to embark on a fascinating journey which will not only develop the learner's experience but also enrich the teacher's knowledge of the nature of learning and allow him to gain a fresh perspective on many issues as seen through the eyes of an uncorrupted mind. Therefore it seems that pedagogy refers to a wider spectrum of educational processes focusing on allowing the students to find their own path to reach their full potential, as Taubman points out:

Pedagogy as the science of teaching is holistic, in the sense that it must address the whole subject and object of teaching, giving a coherent model of the component parts. Pedagogy is the DNA of teaching, the deep structure informing, guiding and constituting in all its parts the purposes and execution of teaching (1999: 61).

It follows that pedagogy is superior to teaching and formulates the major principles to be followed in the educational process. While teaching is typically understood as conveying subject knowledge to students, pedagogy provides a wider picture of their personal development in which teaching of a particular subject ads another piece of puzzle to the formation of an inner image of the outside world, the concept of self and their interrelations. Any teaching has to reflect a certain approach towards an understanding of pedagogy or as Alexander puts it:

[Pedagogy is] the act of teaching, together with its attendant discourse. It is what one needs to know, and the skills one needs to command, in order to make and justify the many different kinds of decisions, of which teaching is constituted (2004: 11).

Teaching is a complex social interactive process. The interaction is crucial, as the process does not limit itself to a mere presentation of content by the teacher to be internalized by the students. It this were the case, than any teaching could be done in a form of distant instruction. In reality it is however possible only on a limited scale. This is because teaching is a process of activating students' abilities to reason and to do it effectively they need to interact to check and modify their hypotheses and find answers to questions triggered by the content input in order to gradually get to a deeper understanding of a given problem. According to Schoenfeld "tutoring is a knowledge-intensive activity with the specific goal (problem) of getting someone else to understand a particular body of content. Thus tutoring can be seen as a complex form of problem solving" (2010: 245).

The report issued by the American National Association for the Education of Young Children states that,

Too many schools narrow the curriculum or adopt instructional approaches that are incompatible with current knowledge about how children learn and develop. Specifically, schools often emphasize rote learning of academic skills rather than active, experiential learning in a meaningful context. As a result, many children are being taught basic academic skills, but they are not learning to apply those skills to problems and real situations. They are not developing complex thinking skills, such as conceptualizing and problem solving. (Bredekamp & Copple, 1997; in Berk, 2001: 216)

It seems, thus, that a more holistic approach to teaching young children that would engage them in meaningful analysis of their surroundings would contribute to raising more independent and critical thinkers in the future. Early education in this form would create essential grounds for later development of academic skills.

3.2. THEORIES OF LEARNING INFLUENCING LANGUAGE TEACHING

The structure of teaching practice in any classroom depends heavily on the approach adopted by the teacher based on his understanding of how knowledge is internalized in the process of learning. Historically there have been a number of theories attempting to explain the mechanics of knowledge transfer. They have informed and influenced everyday classroom practice through shaping the patterns of interaction and curriculum structure. Some of the most widely utilized (consciously or not) theories in classrooms are *associationist learning theory*, *constructivism*, *learning as problem solving*, *connectionism* and *situated learning*. As all these theories still have a major impact on the character of formal education, it seems justified to see how they shape the concept of teaching.

3.2.1. Associationism

The *associationist theory* sees knowledge as a network of small, interconnected elements of experience. Learning, thus, is a process of creating new associations and sustaining them at ready disposal. The theory defines most favourable conditions for learning, which are formulated as laws of contiguity, practice, effect and identical elements (Desforges, 2004: 68). Law of contiguity states that elements of experience that occur close in time are more likely to be associated. In terms of early second language teaching this would imply that any content knowledge delivered through the medium of this language would foster a creation of a link between a language item and the referent it was used to describe. The law of practice claims that the establishment and retention of links is fostered by repetition. A given activity or extralinguistic entity referred to repeatedly during the process of language learning will strengthen the association between words and actions or referents. The law of effect indicates that positive effects of link establishment make the association stronger. Praising children for correct linguistic performance should then foster the associations. Finally, the law of identical elements states that associations made in one context are likely to be triggered in another context if it bears significant resemblance to the one in which they were initially established. A lasting effect of language-real life association would therefore be expected to occur if the educational situation of link formation aimed to reconstruct to some degree a real life context. It comes as little surprise to notice that all these principles of associationist theory are deeply influenced by behaviourism and the laws reflect the basic principles of conditioning resting on the belief that the reinforcer must immediately follow the response and must be contingent on the response. The emerging behaviour has to be repeatedly reinforced or else it will vanish (Woollard, 2010: 64).

3.2.2. Constructivism

In opposition to associationist theory, *constructivism* sees little use in learning through making links between experiences as learners are perceived as active inventors and constructors of general theories following their experience. Knowledge is hence the effect of intellectual process of experience analysis. During this process learners construct mental schemata, which can later be applied to any other situation to which they are applicable. Unlike associationist theory constructivism understands knowledge development not as adding further elements but a reconstruction (or replacement) of the existing schemata so that they become applicable to the new experience. It is of course possible that existing schemata based upon repeated prior experience are challenged by a new event that contradicts an established theory. They are not automatically reconstructed to account for a one-time event but ignored until they occur often enough to falsify the existing theory and lead to a new schemata creation. The new more complex schemata are transferable to other situational contexts than the one they were constructed in. In the example given by Desforges (2004: 67), children who develop a schema for conservation of substance should in the light of constructivist theory apply this knowledge to all substances under all types of transformation. The author points out, however, that evidence shows that students who are able to conserve substance in the case of plasticine being rolled and squashed they cannot apply the same schema to it being cut up or to a different substance like sand. In terms of language education learners would be expected to form schemata of linguistic structures and apply them in the formation of novel forms to try out the theories formed on the bases of previously analysed samples. Then, basing on feedback, they would make changes to the existing schemata or abandon them and create new ones.

The view of learning as a *problem-solving* activity rests upon the works of John Dewey and Gestalt psychology. In this approach learning is defined as a process of "analysing and defining the issue before them, in planning possible approaches, in making decisions about how to tackle the matter, and in monitoring, evaluating and reviewing the effects of any action taken" (Desforges, 2004: 73).

3.2.3. Connectionism

The main principle of *connectionism* is that thinking processes can be shaped by interconnected networks of simple units (Shultz, 2007). The aim of educational process is to provide a multitude of examples that will build and expand the networks influencing a child's perception of the world by incorporating new data that will confirm, falsify or enrich the existing state of knowledge. In connectionist view learning is a time consuming process if it is to result in reaching accurate conclusions and is heavily influenced by the context. To ensure the understanding of particular elements of the network teachers are advised to decontextualise their use by providing examples of the same units in a variety of contexts. The main task of the learner is to identify possible connections between a new item of knowledge and the familiar ones and place it in an appropriate spot of the network reshaping it to form a new view on a particular matter. As the author puts it:

> In connectionist learning, knowledge representations are constructed and abstracted by the learner, rather than merely memorized. Moreover, this learning is particularly effective when lessons are well structured, building more complex ideas on top of simpler earlier ideas, and well practiced, with detailed information about correct responses (2007:1501).

The connectionist theory of learning has influenced the practices of teaching reading and mathematics. Since the theory applies to general idea of networks it is not strictly aimed at human education but includes the learning processes of animals and artificial computer networks. For this reason there are some important limitations like focus on learning from examples rather than direct instruction, omission of the social aspect of learning and learning goals.

3.2.4. Situationism

Situated learning theory sees knowledge acquisition as an intellectual apprienticeship in which children are presented with practical situations of any particular skill application. The claim of this theory that knowledge does not transfer between contexts is backed by examples of people able to perform a complex cognitive function in one authentic context but unable to do the same in another. Desforges (2004: 76) gives an example of Brazilian street traders who easily perform mathematical calculations including pricing, inflation and discount but fail school based tests that require the use of the same skills. It seems thus that they do not possess the knowledge of mathematics but of trading. In terms of formal education this implies that,

> Pupils and students will not learn to use and apply their knowledge met in classrooms if it is experienced in the form of ordinary classroom work or college lectures structured by textbooks and standard assessment tasks. If pupils are to master a discipline or a domain, then they must learn through the authentic experiences of that domain (78).

Formal education seems to be suffering from a slightly schizophrenic condition with its declared mission to prepare students for real life challenges on the one hand but creating learning environments that have hardly anything to do with authentic settings. The abstract purpose and outcome of most in-class learning activities are also a far cry from the real life situations. Another example by Desforges is that of counting three-quarters of two-thirds. In a classroom setting children would learn how to multiply fractions and they would work out the result in a form of digits written in their copybooks but in all probability they would not internalize this knowledge for later use in the kitchen when preparing a pancake using two-thirds of a real cup of cottage cheese.

In the context of primary foreign language teaching this theory would explain why children who have learnt a considerably large number of lexical items are unable to use them in real life communication through the inability to transfer their knowledge form classroom setting to another situational context. In the situated learning perspective knowledge is not an abstract content stored in a mysterious part of the brain but a set of the working practices of particular subjects.

3.3. DEATH OF A METHOD

After decades of psychological, sociological, linguistic and philosophical developments that led to the emergence of multiple approaches towards learning and teaching reflected in numerous methods, it has been concluded that none of them is universally applicable to all learning contexts. Furthermore, although different methods may be based on different, sometimes opposite, principles they are not as dissimilar in their basic practices as their authors would wish. Since teaching methods are based on the existing body of knowledge they may be placed along the same continuum of particular principles underpinning their theoretical grounds. Thus, grammar-translation and communicative teaching may be perceived as extremes on the line of focus on form and meaning with a number of less radical approaches to this issue in between. A good number of more modern methods of teaching that claim to be original are, in fact, clusters of existing approaches or well-known methods presented under a new name with only few original elements (e.g. Berlitz method). As Kumaravadivelu (2006: 161) states, "In all probability, the invention of a truly novel method that is fundamentally different from the [existing] ones is very slim, at least in the foreseeable future".

Throughout decades teaching practice has seen a closed cycle of emergence, decline and return of a variety of approaches. The cycle begins when a seemingly original method is conceived and implemented into classroom practice only to prove imperfect and undergo harsh criticism of the teachers, students and researchers themselves. Then, it is typically replaced by another miraculous method of gaining linguistic competence which, with time, leads to disillusionment and another replacement. This cycle goes on until it returns to the original idea to rediscover its previously unseen potential and so on. Trapped within this vicious cycle teachers and other specialists fail to adjust the teaching process to the existing local conditions. It seems unreasonable to expect that any given method will be fully functional and beneficial to all students in all circumstances.

The new perspective on language teaching has evolved from the postmodern philosophy. Presented in Table 1 is a summary of features of the new movement as proposed by Pishghadam and Mirzaee (2008). Postmodernism sees the notions of truth and preference as social constructs to be eliminated. Just like proponents of relativism, postmodernists perceive knowledge as dynamic and theories as canceling and distorting reality that can only be approached pragmatically. They question the authority of experts as the only creators of knowledge and the universal nature of their findings. Instead, postmodernism values subjectivism and diversity.

Table1. Modernism and Postmodernism in a nutshell

Modernism	Postmodernism
objective	subjective
rational	irrational
scientific	anti-scientific
global claims	local claims
positivist	constructivist
utopian	populist
central	fragmented
the best	better
linear	non-linear
generalizing	non-generalizing
theoretical	practical
abstract	concrete
unification	diversity

Source: Adapted from: Pishghadam and Mirzaee (2008: 95).

By accepting the postmodern perspective, education has shifted from a more authoritarian and prescriptive, towards a more liberal and descriptive approach to language teaching. As a result the notion of method has been devaluated as a theoretical model based on abstract assumptions and disregarding the uniqueness of teaching environments.

Allwright comes up with six reasons why a method is an unhelpful concept to build a teaching practice upon. Firstly, its main focus is the differences between the proposed approach and all other methods while even the concepts that differ significantly in theory are not that dissimilar in a real classroom practice. Secondly, it has a tendency to over generalize and fail to cater for individual differences between the students and even between various teaching contexts. Thirdly, Allwright points out that learning how to implement a given method into classroom is time consuming and takes the teachers' attention away from the far more important planning of actual activities. What is more, as a result of extensive training teachers may develop blind loyalty towards a given method and focus on proving its superiority over others thus fostering unnecessary competition. Another risk involved in following a given method is the false impression that all issues considering the nature of learning have been resolved and the answer to them is the method in use.

Finally, it provides an externally created and imposed on the teachers impression of coherence. They are forced to believe in the effectiveness of the method, without a critical analysis of the applicability of its principles to the particular educational context they operate in. Instead of reaching the sense of coherence of educational practice from the actual application of a variety of approaches in a classroom, teachers are expected to apply a set of practices whether or not they perceive them as beneficial for the students and the learning process in their particular case (Allwright, 1991; in Kumaravadivelu, 2006: 170).

It appears that teaching practice has reached a moment of raised awareness of the situation in which the fact that continuous recycling of the existing methods does not lead to improved practice or enriched theoretical background of this field, should clearly be acknowledged. This conscious agreement to break the vicious cycle and readiness to venture beyond the limits of a single method is what Kumaravadivelu calls the *postmethod condition*. It rests upon the acknowledgement of method as an artificial construct limiting the opportunity for the teacher and for the students to reach their full potentials by enforcing a rigid set of practices within which they have to operate. Having reached this point, language pedagogy shifts from method to a broader understanding of learning and teaching procedures. This *postmethod pedagogy* is a three-dimensional system governed by three pedagogic parameters: particularity, practicality, and possibility (2006: 171).

Particularity is considered by Kumaravadivelu to be the central aspect of postmethod pedagogy. He claims that it 'must be sensitive to a particular group of teachers teaching a particular group of learners pursuing a particular set of goals within a particular institutional context embedded in a particular sociocultural milieu" (Kumaravadivelu, 2001: 538). Since there is an abundance of factors influencing any learning situation, it seems unreasonable to expect any single approach to be applicable to all teachers, learners, educational contexts, classroom environments, etc.

The second parameter of *practicality*, relates to the transferability of theory into practice. It empowers the teacher to take the responsibility for monitoring and constant assessment of his own teaching practice. Instead of implementing a ready-made theoretical approach into the classroom practice, the teacher creates optimal conditions for learning, through active research and experimentation, trying out different techniques and methods to establish a coherent pattern of operations that really work for this particular context. This bottom-up view of creating good practices by teachers in service allows them to adjust all available resources to best fit the context in which they work. On the other hand, it assumes that teachers are willing to actively shape their practice and take responsibility for any possible failure instead of blaming it on a method imposed on them. In line with this approach Edge (2001: 6) points out that 'the thinking teacher is no longer perceived as someone who applies theories, but someone who theorizes practice". By giving teachers the power of shaping educational process, the practicality parameter acknowledges the importance of their insights gained through teaching experience and intuition, the often unexplainable by any theory awareness of what works best in a particular teaching context.

The parameter of *possibility* reflects the understanding that any pedagogy is related to power and dominance. In the process of education, it is essential to emphasize teacher's and students' individual identities. In a traditional teacher-dominated classroom the unequal distribution of power is evident and may lead to tensions. The possibility parameter advocates the explicit acknowledgment and use of students' experiences and knowledge which they bring into the classroom. Thus, the teacher is not the only expert and new knowledge is constructed by means of interaction between all participants of the process and built upon the pre-existing experiences of the students.

Breen et al. have designed a model, presented in Figure 8, of the interrelationships between the teacher beliefs and principles and the actual classroom practice. Perhaps not surprisingly, teachers' beliefs strongly influence pedagogic principles that rest upon them. They are also largely context-independent. The principles, that are not imposed on a teacher by a particular theory, but rather result from his prior or ongoing teaching experiences, mediate between the more abstract beliefs and the actual teaching situation. If a teacher believes, for instance, that communication is crucial in language development, his pedagogic principle will be to find ways in which to engage students in communication. Implementing this principle into a particular class will entail designing tasks serving this purpose and at the

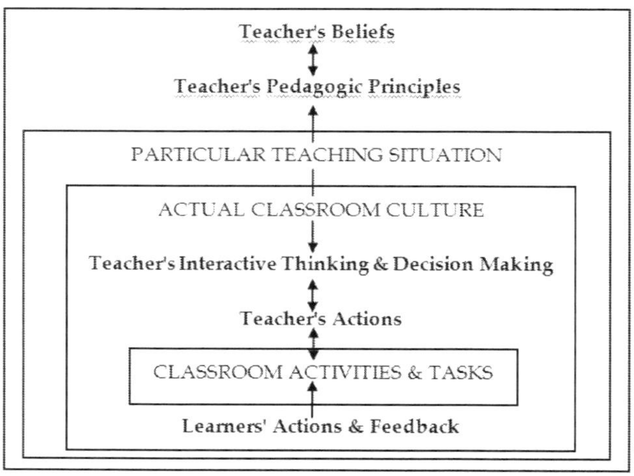

Figure 8. Teacher conceptualizations and classroom practices

Source: Adapted from: Breen's et al. (2001)

same time responding to students' immediate learning conditions. Working within a particular teaching situation imposes certain constraints on the teacher regarding the materials, the space, the available teaching aids and the broader context of the immediate environment outside the classroom. Therefore, a teacher's decisions as to particular actions and the resulting learning activities, result from striking the right balance between what the teacher believes is beneficial for students and what is feasible in a particular situation.

3.4. MODELS OF POSTMETHOD PEDAGOGY

Postmethod pedagogy operates beyond the constraints of any single method. Nonetheless, it does propose teaching solutions encompassing certain strategies and techniques to be implemented into a classroom by a reflexive teacher basing on his prior and ongoing experience of effective practices. Their common feature is a definite brake with any existing teaching methods and flexibility in approach that allows for its application in a multitude of pedagogic contexts. Kumaravadivelu (2006) considers three such models to be representative of the postmodern pedagogy concept. These are: Stern's (1992) *Three-Dimensional Framework*, Allwright's (2003) *Exploratory Practice Framework* and his own Macrostrategi. c Framework. Brown's (2008) *Principled Approach* seems to fall into the same category and thus deserves to be mentioned as well.

3.4.1. Three-Dimensional Framework

Stern's concept is a collection of strategies and techniques. Strategies, are understood here as any instances of intentional actions and techniques as occurrences of particular practical activities (Stern, 1992: 277). Therefore strategies may be perceived as elements of broader teaching policy whereas techniques are tools for their practical implementation in actual teaching practice.

Stern's idea of learning and teaching procedures rests upon three dimensions. These areas of teaching practice interest have been identified by the author on the basis of his earlier considerations of the major language learning problems (1992: 401). The first issue is that of inevitable inequality of competence between the first language and other languages present in a speaker's mind. Stern labelled this issue the L1-L2 connection and then translated it into the teaching perspective as the *intralingual-crosslingual* dimension (1992: 278). The second problem faced by additional language learner is the manner in which the language in absorbed, be it by conscious, deliberate action or in a more intuitive, automatic way. This dilemma is what Stern refers to as the *explicit-implicit* option. The third difficulty is posed by the inability to focus on the form of the new code and use it for effective communication at the same time. This problem was described by the author as the code-communication dilemma, which in the teaching perspective became an *analytical-experiential* dimension. To deal with these problems language teachers employ a number of strategies that draw from both ends of each continuum to some extent adjusting each dimension to the current needs of a particular pedagogic context. Each of the dimensions is characterized by means of juxtaposed features that constitute extremes of continua.

The intralingual-crosslingual dimension

The intralingual-crosslingual dimension in the teaching practice context refers to all actions taken in the classroom that make use of the first and the target languages to build a structure of all pedagogic activities. On the one end of the continuum intralingual/intracultural techniques involve the target language and the target culture, while on the other crosslingual/crosscultural techniques draw on the features of native language and culture for comparison purposes. Practitioners adopting a strong intralingual approach would advocate immersion as a way of instruction in language teaching. They would also be against any forms of translation or cross-reference between the languages and would therefore apply the elements characteristic for direct and communicative teaching methods. The aim of their actions would be some form of co-ordinate bilingualism. At the opposite end of the continuum, teachers believing in the crosslingual approach would use students' L1 and its culture as a system of reference frequently comparing emerging elements of knowledge. Due to its trust in translation, the strongest form of the crosslingual attitude towards teaching would be the set of classroom practices that constitute the grammar-translation method.

Stern himself is a supporter of a balanced approach in which L1 does not disappear from the language classroom but rather assists the learner in grasp the full meaning of L2. Stern offers three main reasons why L1 use in L2 classroom is beneficial for the learning process. He states that studying another language implies a preexistence of a previously acquired mother tongue. Although this is true for numerous formal educational settings, this statement seems not fully justified in early bilingual contexts where the acquisition of two or more languages happens simultaneously. Although it could be argued that even in such circumstances parts of extralinguistic knowledge are gained in one language earlier than in another, it would be difficult to agree that each item of information undergoes a process of translation when it already exists in the mental lexicon.

The other reason offered by Stern is that "it is in the nature of linguistic and communicative competence that we behave as if the L1 (or a second language previously learnt) is the yardstick and guide to our new L2" (1992: 282–283). This would suggest that learners of L2 make constant references to their L1, which again is not a typical feature of balanced co-ordinate bilinguals. At least not at the conscious level. Stern's third argument relates to learners' personal identity, which is closely connected with the native language and culture. Since "learning a new language and culture demands a personal adjustment" (1992: 283), it is important to retain constant contact with L1 as a point of reference for the newly arising identity. During the process of additional language learning both intra- and crosslingual strategies are applicable in a classroom setting.

The Analytic-Experiential Dimension

The Analytic-Experiential continuum reflects the discussion about the importance of form and message encoded in the target language. The core of the dispute seems to be the power relation between the focus on code and communication in language teaching. The analytic end of the continuum is explicitly directed at the formal aspects of language. The experiential strategy, on the other hand, suggests a focus on message and communication.

In an analytic teaching context, students' work on decontextualised language where emphasis is put on accuracy and the resulting interaction is linguistic in nature. Analytic teaching strategies are often employed in controlled practice phase of a lesson where the predictability of response is high but rarely reflects real life use. The experiential strategies value communication and interpersonal interaction. The focus is not on the form of the language used but on the effectiveness of reaching communicative purpose. It is characteristic for information gap, problem solving and discussion tasks where fluency gains superiority over accuracy and language is contextualized by the task. Again, the author suggests that effective teaching practice apply elements of both strategies.

The Explicit-Implicit Dimension

The third dimension of teaching strategies relates to the issue of conscious versus unconscious/subconscious L2 learning. Depending on the teacher's approach, each of the strategies described above i.e. intralingual, crosslingual, analytic and experiential can all be utilized in a form of explicit or implicit processes. The interrelations between all the dimensions are presented in Figure 9.

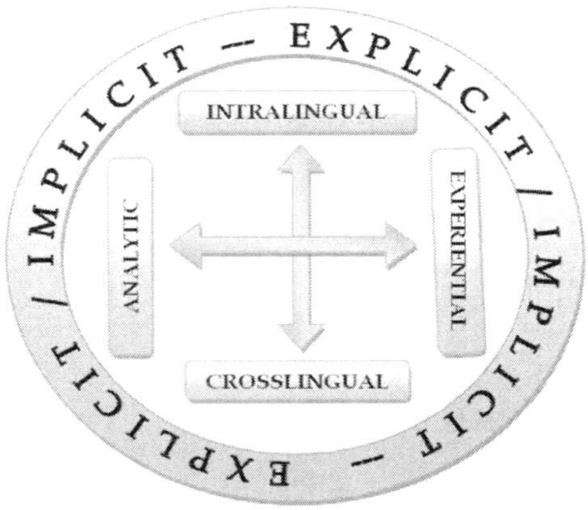

Figure 9. Stern's Three Dimensional Model

Source: Adapted from Stern (1992)

The explicit extreme of this dimension stands for conscious, deliberate learning resulting from a formal, intellectual approach to L2. It rests upon the cognitivist theory and makes use of systematic study of the target language. The Implicit end places language learning within the behaviourist and empiricist models and perceives language learning as an intuitive process of subconscious acquisition, that is incidental in nature and results from extensive exposure to language in use.

An explicit strategy allows learners to gain knowledge about the language itself so that they "know how the language functions, how it hangs together, what words mean, how meaning is conveyed, and so on" (Stern, 1992: 334). An implicit strategy acknowledges the fact that the formal complexity of any language is much too extensive to be described by rules which could all be remembered by the learner and applied effectively during spontaneous conversational exchanges. Individual preferences of the learners may also determine the extent to which the four strategies are put into action in an explicit and implicit form.

3.4.2. The Exploratory Practice Framework

Allwright's Exploratory Practice Framework is based on a strong belief in the value of experience gained from actual teaching practice. He believes in reflexive teaching that, not only implements the ideas emerging from scientific educational research, but also analyses critically the outcomes of these actions and improves the teaching procedures accordingly. Allwright describes his model in the following way:

> This is what we mean by 'exploratory teaching': teaching that not only tries out new ideas but that also tries to learn as much as possible from doing so. In fact, you do not even have to try out 'new' ideas to be an exploratory teacher. Any good experienced teacher will no doubt spend a lot of class time on ideas that are tried and trusted. Turning that 'good' teaching into 'exploratory teaching' is a matter of trying to find out what makes the tried and trusted ideas successful. Because in the long run it is not enough to know that ideas do work: we need also to know why and how they work. Until we can throw more light on those issues, successful teaching will remain a mystery (Allwright & Bailey, 1991: 197).

Exploratory Practice is based on three concepts: the supremacy of life quality in the language classroom over instructional efficiency; teacher's understanding of this life quality, that is superior to developing new teaching techniques; and their acknowledgement of the social nature of such life quality and its benefits to the all practitioners. In other words Exploratory Practice involves ' 1. practitioners (e.g.: preferably teachers *and* learners together) working to understand: (a) what *they* want to understand, following their own agendas; b) not necessarily *in order to* bring about change; (c) not primarily *by* changing; (d) but by *using* normal pedagogic practices as investigative tools, so that working for understanding is *part of* the teaching and learning, not extra to it; (e) in a way that does not lead to "burn-out," but that is *indefinitely sustainable*; 2. in order to contribute to: (f) *teaching and learning themselves*; (g) *professional development, both individual and collective*.' (Allwright, 2003: 127–128, italics in original). Such an understanding of the framework led Allwright to formulate seven principles of teaching practice:

Principle 1: 'quality of life' is of central concern to teachers and learners.
Principle 2: Work to understand language classroom life rather than improve it.
Principle 3: Involve everybody.
Principle 4: Work to bring people together.
Principle 5: Work for mutual development.
Principle 6: Work for understanding continuously.

Principle 7: Integrate your work for understanding into the existing curricular practice (Allwright and Hanks, 2009: 149-154).

Beside the core issue of classroom ecology, the second pillar supporting Allwright's model is cooperation. The framework is based largely on interactions between the parties involved in the educational process and mutual understanding. There is a sense of collaboration aimed at achieving goals that are negotiated and agreed upon by teachers and learners alike. This concept of collegiality is multidimensional and concerns a number of personal and institutional identities. Allwright distinguishes between six aspects of collegiality. At the most basic and direct level the concept involves teachers and learners who form a partnership where the balance of power is more equal than in traditional models. Another layer of collegiality is that among teachers in the same institution. This calls for close and frequent exchanges of ideas and implemented procedures that lead to constructing a coherent educational environment providing conditions for holistic approach to teaching. The flow of information among staff members involved in teaching procedures contributes to the development of their own teaching practice and a clear, unified vision of education in the institution itself.

The third level concerns the relationship and hierarchy within an employing institution. The cooperation at this level is that between staff and headmasters, managers, administrative authorities and any other bodies that govern the institution. To ensure proper functioning of a school all these parties need to share a common understanding of pursued goals and an agreed upon set of institutional means through which to achieve them. In a well-functioning educational setting, teachers are aware of the need for constant training. The next level of collegiality involves cooperation between the practitioners and teacher trainers. Reflexive practitioners are aware of the need for constant training and exchange of ideas. New developments in the field of education should be transferred directly to those who are in power to put them into practice. Thus, educational institutions should be open and willing to cooperate with scientists, offering the settings for their research whose results and recommendations should, in turn, be made available to the practitioners. The last level of collegiality is the professional relationship between teachers across educational settings. Teacher associations offer support for practitioners in areas of professional development and administrative challenges encountered in the profession. Associations also have political power of representing the educational body on the national policy arena and, being representative of a particular sector of economy, are potentially capable of introducing major and far reaching changes into the system.

The Exploratory Practice is an action research model whose stages can be clearly identified and described in a series of steps. The first step involves identifying a puzzle. The whole process starts with a practitioner finding something puzzling in a teaching and learning situation. The teacher then reflects upon the puzzle in order to understand it. Understanding is prior to taking any direct action. Obvious as it may sound, it is not uncommon for an educational environment to introduce improvements to situations that are not well analysed and understood. Such immediate remedial actions often result in more confusion and damage than the original problem caused. Therefore, step 3 involves close monitoring of the puzzling phenomenon that allows the teacher to better understand its nature. In order to do this, the practitioner takes direct action to generate data. This is done by using standard classroom activities rather than academic data-collection techniques.

The next stage involves reflexive analysis of the outcomes and taking decisions as to future actions. The teacher needs to decide whether further investigation is justified or more data is necessary to formulate any conclusions. Having reached adequate understanding, the practitioner decides on what type of steps to undertake choosing from such options as discussion with students, adjustment of expectations, expressing dissatisfaction with the state of affairs, taking personal action to improve the situation, or taking formal steps toward transforming the educational system. The final stage of Exploratory Practice is going public. Provided that a full understanding of the puzzle has been reached, appropriate actions have been taken and they have led to an improved "quality of classroom life", the practitioner has a professional obligation to share this benefit with others and to receive feedback from them. This stage involves the teacher to give workshops, conference presentations, or publish papers in professional magazines (Allwright, 2003: 135).

3.4.3. The Macrostrategic Framework

Kumaravadivelu's model is based on the understanding of the inability to predict all possible teaching contexts in order to prepare practitioners to cope with all situations they may potentially generate. The author believes that the only reasonable solution is to help teachers develop a capacity to come up with "varied and situation-specific ideas within a general framework that makes sense in terms of current pedagogical and theoretical knowledge" (Kumaravadivelu, 1992: 41).

In the author's view, teacher education should, therefore, focus on equipping the future practitioners with a set of general skills that could be easily modified and adjusted to any pedagogic situation they may encounter in their profession. Kumaravadivelu saw these abilities and *macrostrategies*.

Macrostrategies are general plans derived from currently available theoretical, empirical, and pedagogical knowledge related to L2 learning and teaching. A macrostrategy is a broad guideline based on which teachers can generate their own location-specific, need-based microstrategies or classroom procedures. In other words, macrostrategies are made operational in the classroom through microstrategies (2006: 201).

These strategies are not based on any particular theory of teaching, nor are they conditioned by any of the existing methods. They are a set of principles reflecting the postmethod pedagogy that goes beyond any prescriptive rules and focuses on a holistic approach to teaching. Kumaravadivelu designed a model that comprises 10 macrostrategies that are presented in a form of recommendations for the teacher. These ten points of focus can be analysed as pertaining to different areas of teacher activity in the classroom. It could be argued that the first two refer to the teacher's skill of organizing classroom interaction. These are (1) *maximize learning opportunities* and (2) *facilitate negotiated interaction*; The first one implies a willingness of teachers to constantly adjust their lesson plans to the ever changing dynamic situation in the classroom. Since the classroom interaction is cooperative in nature, teachers must acknowledge all contributions from partners engaged in the process. They also need to notice and utilize all potential learning opportunities spontaneously emerging during classroom practice.

The second macrostrategy concerns a meaningful classroom interaction between learners and between learners and the teacher in which the students are free to initiate and manage the exchange rather than simply react and respond to cues. Negotiated interaction requires the learner to be actively involved in the process of learning. The following two macrostrategies could be perceived as calling upon teacher's skills of working on the cognitive level of students' development. They include rule (3) *minimize perceptual mismatches*; and (4) *activate intuitive heuristics*. The third principle is based on a view of communication "as a gradual reduction of uncertainty" (2006: 204). As a result, in every L2 lesson some kind of disagreement between teacher intention and learner interpretation is imminent. The sources of this mismatch can be cognitive, as the students' mental processes governing the way in which they gain conceptual understanding of the reality may differ from those of the teacher. They can also result from unequal distribution of linguistic tools and communication strategies between the practitioner and the learners. When the students and the teacher do not share the understanding of short- and long-term objectives, the disagreement has pedagogical sources. Similarly, when the practitioner expects the learners to use certain learning strategies to gain, store, and use information that they are reluctant to implement, the mismatch has a strategic source. The misunderstandings can also arrive from differences in the attitude towards L2 and the nature of its instruction as well as from different understanding of target culture norms.

The last group of possible sources of mismatch relate to the procedures used in the classroom and include controversies around evaluation models, procedures used to resolve immediate problems and instructional directions given by the teacher of course book. The awareness of all these possible sources of perceptual mismatches may help teachers to understand the nature of a problem in the classroom and allow him to modify his actions so as to adjust to the current interpretative abilities of the students and achieve his intended goal. The fourth principle encourages teachers to activate students' intuitive understanding of language system by providing enough textual data for them to infer the rules of form and function from contextualized examples.

The next three principles refer to the language instruction in the L2 classroom and they recommend the teacher to (5) *foster language awareness*; (6) *contextualize linguistic input*, (7) *integrate language skills*. By raising language awareness Kumaravadivelu means the actions undertaken by the teacher to draw learners' attention to the form of the L2 in order to reach a higher level of explicitness using strategies that foster understanding. In its natural form language occurs in context. Introducing learners to isolated items of the system deprives them of the necessary cues, and thus, makes the process of decoding the meaning harder. The author believes that contextualizing linguistic input is primarily the teacher's responsibility. Regardless of the course book used, it is the teacher who can create comprehensible context for the students using the knowledge that is specific for this one and only teaching environment shared by the learners and their practitioner. The last principle in this group concerns integration on the level of language skills. The natural process of communication involves a number of skills and language components used simultaneously. Focusing on separate skills creates an artificial condition in which the natural language behaviour is hampered and overall development made more difficult. As Kumaravadivelu emphasises, "as we learn from the whole-language movement, language knowledge and language ability are best developed when language is learned and used holistically" (2006: 206).

The final three macrostrategies in this framework deal with the socio-cultural aspect of L2 learning. They suggest the teacher should (8) *promote learner autonomy*; (9) *ensure social relevance*; and (10) *raise cultural consciousness*. Underlying the eighth principle is the belief that language learning is a primarily autonomous activity and thus learners should be equipped with metacognitive, cognitive, social and affective strategies to take control over and responsibility for their own process of learning. Since a language learning environment is not limited to the classroom but is situated in a much broader educational, social, cultural, political context, it is crucial for the teacher to be aware of all variables shaping the pedagogic situation. Understanding this broad context and its influence on the students, teachers should work to ensure that the extralinguistic knowledge that students bring to the classroom is used and shared in order to present a variety of personal perspectives.

Macrostrategies are designed as guiding principles based on current theoretical, empirical and experiential knowledge of L2 learning and teaching practice.

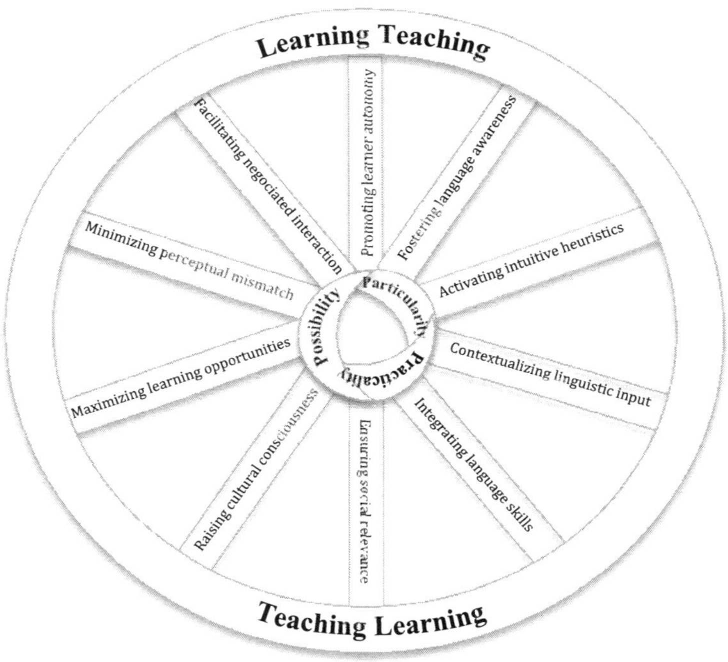

Figure 10. The pedagogic wheel

Source: Kumaravadivelu (2003: 41)

3.4.4. Principled Approach

According to Brown (2008) modern classroom practice is based on a number of general principles rather than any teaching method. He lists twelve such principles that are not much different (though at times they present opposite views) from the microstrategies proposed by Kumaravadivelu (2006). His approach differs, however, in the extent of practical applicability of the principles. While macrostrategies are defined in a more abstract scientific and sometimes overly complex manner, Brown's principles are recipes for teachers that suggest actual teaching practices that correspond to the general principles.

The principle of *automaticity* seems to go against the macrostrategy of raising language awareness. Brown believes that extensive language analysis does not contribute to a higher awareness of the system, but rather impedes acquisition of the skill to use a language item automatically. The principle of *meaningful learning* is similar to contextualized input strategy where content-centred approaches are advised. The behaviourist-inspired *anticipation of reward* principle does not seem to have a counterpart in Kumaravadivelu's model. It rests upon the belief that teachers should create multiple opportunities for reward winning, thus increasing students' motivation. This particular point appears controversial especially in the light of the following principle that is *intrinsic motivation*. If students' involvement is driven by constant anticipation of reward, there is hardly any room for developing a truly intrinsic desire to reach a learning goal where the only reward is the satisfaction and sense of achievement. What Kumaravadivelu called promoting learner autonomy, Brown presents as *strategic investment*. This principle is perceived as learner's own personal input of time, effort and attention to the second language learning. The *language ego* principle bears a resemblance to Stern's (1992) intralinguistic dimension of his model. Brown claims that learning a new language entails forming a new type of personal identity, which may cause inhibitions and defensiveness.

While it might be true for some learners, it is not impossible to imagine an opposite effect in which the rising proficiency in the new language empowers the learner and increases his self-esteem (e.g. in the case of minority language speakers learning the dominant language). This is closely linked to the next principle of *self-confidence*. Brown attributes better attainment to students' certainty they are able to complete a given task. Having achieved the sense of confidence in the additional language, learners want to venture beyond the limits of their actual current abilities using *risk taking* strategies. The *language-culture connection principle* pertains to the cultural consciousness raising macrostrategy focusing, however, on the target language cultural values rather than mother tongue connected identity. This places the strategy within Stern's intracultural dimension. As all the previously discussed models, Brown's principled approach also acknowledges the influence of L1 in the process of learning additional language which he calls *native language effect*. However, his interest in this area is more in the aspect of interference rather than explicitly made comparisons for linguistic enrichment. A natural consequence of this argumentation is the recognition of *interlanguage* as a stage of additional language development between initial incompetence and final attainment. Finally, Brown lists *communictaive competence* as a generally accepted principle of L2 teaching/learning. Thus, he recommends preference of language use over usage, fluency over accuracy and authentic language contexts over artificial classroom environment. Brown translates his model into a set of practical recommendations to the teachers:

1. *Lower inhibitions* by playing guessing and communication games, doing role-plays and skits, singing songs, using group work, laughing, having students share their fears in small groups;
2. *Encourage risk taking* by praising students for making sincere efforts to try out new language, using fluency exercises where errors are not corrected at that time, giving outside-of-class assignments to speak or write or otherwise try out the language;
3. *Build students' self-confidence* by telling them explicitly that you indeed believe in them, having them make lists of their strengths;
4. *Help students develop intrinsic motivation* by reminding them explicitly about rewards for learning English, describing jobs that require English, playing down the final examination in favour of helping student to see rewards for themselves beyond the final exam;
5. *Promote cooperative learning* by directing students to share their knowledge, playing down competition among students, getting your class to think of themselves as team, doing a considerable amount of group work;
6. *Encourage students to use right-brain processing* by using movies and tapes in class, having students read passages rapidly, doing skimming exercises, doing rapid 'free writes', doing oral fluency exercises where the object is to get students to talk without being corrected;
7. *Promote ambiguity tolerance* by encouraging students to ask questions when they do not understand something, keeping your theoretical explanations very simple and brief, dealing with just a few rules at a time and occasionally resorting to translation to clarify a word or meaning;
8. *Help students use their intuition* by praising them for good guesses, not always giving explanations of errors, correcting only selected errors;
9. *Get students to make their mistakes work for them* by recording their oral production and getting them to identify errors; not always giving them the correct

form, encouraging studnets to make lists of their common errors and to work on them on their own;

10. *Get students to see their own goals* by explicitly encouraging them to go beyond the classroom goals, having them make lists of what they will accomplish on their own in a particular week and getting them to make specific time committments at home to study the language. (Brown, 2008: 16–17)

In his analysis of post-method pedagogy Kumaravadivelu included only the propositions that truly and consistently break with the much-criticized concept of a method. Brown's Principled Approach would not be a part of his considerations. Although the author of this model treats it as a framework for educational practice in the post-method era, it is not difficult to classify the above-described proposition as communicative language learning method. Perhaps in response to criticism of the post-method pedagogy (cf. Akbari, 2008), in his model Brown attempts to provide detailed guidance for teachers even suggesting actual techniques and activities that he believes adhere to his framework. Ironically, however, post method pedagogy makes sense only when it is delivered as a very general framework of principles that apply to a variety of educational contexts but with major adjustments to be made by the teachers who are actually working in these settings. By giving practitioners such a detailed description of good practice, Brown drastically limits their freedom to interpret the general guidelines in a way that is best suitable to their own teaching context. The author's recommendations reflect his own personal perspective of what is effective and beneficial in a classroom. However, this perspective takes as a point of reference a concrete particular learning/teaching context and cannot therefore be transferred to other educational settings as universal. What may work well in an American school, may not be at all appropriate in an Asian institution. The problem of the post-method approach is precisely that it does not offer teachers ready-made recipes for an effective lesson. It is highly unreasonable, however, to expect any pedagogical approach to be universally applicable. The challenge is to prepare teachers to take responsibility for the teaching process by constantly analysing the setting in which they work and creatively shape it within the general principles.

The criticism of the post method pedagogy centers around the issue of incompatibility of the idealistic approach with the reality of teaching practice. Ramin Akbari sees the weakness of this model in inadequate teacher preparation.

The assumption of postmethod proponents is that all teachers by default are qualified or willing to conduct a postmethod class with all its social, cognitive, political, and cultural requirements. That assumption, however, is questionable because many teachers lack the required knowledge or skill to teach in the postmethod fashion. (2008: 648).

This argument is not to be underestimated. It is clear that the teacher post-method pedagogy has in mind is a highly qualified specialist, aware of current developments in the field and willing to constantly improve his skills and contribute to the general improvement of teaching practice. To reasonably request such practitioners, the post-method pedagogy should first educate them. Therefore, the change in the way of perceiving teaching beyond method should start with teacher training at the university level. Instead of teaching students the core ideas of historic methods, educators should perhaps develop in them the willingness for creative development of strategies to be applied in different circumstances, foster the understanding of flexibility in planning and teaching the sensitivity and responsiveness to learner's needs. Although it seems rather challenging, it is by no means unfeasible. Therefore the following critical argument of Akbari is less justifiable.

> We should also remember that for many teachers, teaching is a job not a career (Johnston, 1997), and they are often not willing to participate in any professional development that would task them with extra responsibilities (2008: 648).

While this might regrettably be so, it does not mean that attempts to improve the situation should not be made. Perhaps, a better teacher training would inspire the students and result in a higher level of involvement of the teachers in service. The post-method pedagogy seems perfect to improve the situation as it offers the teachers an opportunity to take control over their own practice. It should not be viewed as a threat foretelling more demanding and time consuming preparation for every class but as an opportunity to create a *unique* learning/teaching environment where the teacher and students form a supporting team that works together towards not only linguistic but overall development.

3.5. EARLY FORMAL EDUCATION

Children are learning new things from the very beginning of their lives, even before they are born. A four-month-old foetus has already a functioning sense of hearing and touch (Salkind, 2002: 349). The first moments of life abound in stimuli that have to limited by the parents in order not to put too much stress on the new nerve system. In the first years of life children explore the world and absorb enormous quantities of information from the environment through experimentation and interaction. Although this process of learning about the world does not finish until the last moments of human life, at one point it becomes less chaotic and intuitive. This is when children enter formal education. The Eurydice report (2009a) states that in a vast majority of European countries compulsory formal education lasts nine to ten years starting as early as 4 or 5 and finishing at the age of 14 or 15 although a rising number of students choose to continue their education in higher secondary schools and universities (17.4% of all EU higher secondary school graduates became students in 2006). During these years children's natural curiosity and internal drive to explore the world is squeezed into formal constraints of educational system. They are now expected to learn academic skills and acquire knowledge about the world in a far less natural manner. Formal education follows a plan that is prepared for all children at a given age regardless of their former experience and acquired knowledge. By being unable to address all students' needs individually and required to teach a predefined amount of knowledge and skills, formal education hardly resembles the natural process of learning. The aims of formal education include a multitude of areas from social integration and development of positive habits and attitudes, through gaining independence in expressing opinions and using reasoning to simple memorization of facts and data. To achieve these goals formal education needs to follow a detailed plan in a form of curriculum.

Strauss (2004: 10) defines curriculum as "the external manifestation of an underlying conceptual system about: (a) the nature and structure of subject matter that is being taught, (b) children's conceptions (sometimes preconceptions or misconceptions) of that subject matter, and (c) mechanisms of cognitive change, i.e. learning and development". The amount of information to internalize is so big that sometimes the delicate balance between learning facts and understanding their relationships is shattered and students are forced to focus more on memorizing chunks of data than on their critical analysis and creative deconstruction. The final outcome of such attitude may be a production of specialists who are unable to apply their knowledge in unpredictable circumstances or modify it creatively to adjust to existing situations. The natural power of child's imagination and internal motivation seem to be hampered by the constraints of formal education.

3.5.1. Formal additional language education

Farrell and Jacobs (2010: 23) present a list of eight essentials for successful EFL language teaching which include *Learner Autonomy*, *Social Nature of Learning*, *Integrated Curriculum*, *Focus on Meaning*, *Diversity*, *Thinking Skills*, *Alternative Assessment*, *and Teachers as Co-learners* and is based on a post-positivist approach to education, whose principles are listed below.

- Emphasis on whole rather than separate parts
- Contextualization as opposed to the positivist decontextualisation
- Emphasis on integration rather than separation
- Emphasis on the specific rather than general
- Consideration also of subjective and the non-quantifiable as opposed to objective and quantifiable
- Consideration also of the "average" participant and insider knowledge-researcher as internal rather than expert and external
- Focus on understanding rather than control
- Bottom-up processes as opposed to the positivist top-down attitude
- Appreciation of diversity rather than an attempt to standardize
- Focus on both process and product rather than merely on the latter

The more humanistic approach to modern formal education results in a change to the structure of teaching processes focusing on elements that were given little thought in the past.

A shift towards *Learner Autonomy* means that learners are given greater control over their own foreign language learning in terms of content as well as the methods used to achieve this goal. One of the tools characteristic for this approach is self-assessment, which empowers students to evaluate their own learning progress and teaches them to critically evaluate their accomplishments. *The Social Nature of Learning* denotes the idea that learning a foreign language is not an individual task but rather a social activity that involves and relies on successful interaction with others. Cooperation is valued above competition in active search for and exploration of knowledge. *Integrated curriculum* maintains that different areas of the curriculum need to be connected to help students build a bigger picture of the world using the subject specific pieces so that English as a foreign language is not the odd one out but a legitimate element of the puzzle. Text-based learning reflects this principle, as its aim is to develop fluency in texts which are used across the curriculum.

Another example is project work which employs language in activities done outside the classroom context. *Focus on Meaning* is viewed as crucial for real learning. This idea is realized in field of foreign language learning in the form of content-based teaching where the emphasis shifts from the language itself to the topic which is being covered in this language and belongs to a different subject area. Modern attitude to teaching acknowledges *Diversity* as a positive element in a learning context. It is understood as a multitude of learning styles, experiences, interests and needs that make the process more valuable as students may share their ideas and learn to respect other people's opinions on the one hand and maintain theirs on the other thus leading to non-conformist attitudes. One of the top essentials for successful EFL teaching is the focus on *Thinking Skills*, which should help to develop critical and creative thinking. Students do not learn the language for its own sake but to develop more complex thinking abilities that will be useful and applicable to real life situations outside the classroom.

Since academic achievement loses its priority in the sense that it does not prepare students for life, *Alternative Assessment* needs to complement the traditional testing to reflect learners' achievements in all the soft skills that are less measurable than memorization of subject knowledge. As process becomes as important as the product, the assessment should take into consideration all the steps students went through, the progress they have made and the knowledge and skills they have gained on their way to the final outcome. The modern approach to teaching sees *Teachers as Co-learners* in the sense that their role is not limited to transmitting subject knowledge but involves active participation in the quest for meaning and trying out alternative approaches to facilitate their students as best they can. The students-teacher relationship is not as unequal as it used to be in the traditional approach. Since the language itself is no longer the only focus of EFL instruction and other subjects content gains importance, the students become empowered in the sense of potentially having more expert knowledge in particular fields than the teacher. In language teaching, this attitude has resulted in reflective practice, action research, and other forms of classroom investigation.

3.5.2. Integrating knowledge – the foundations of holism

John Dewey formed a theory referred to as *instrumentalism*, claiming that people gather meaning through interpersonal activities and social contacts. Basing on this theory, Dewey defined good education as focusing on acquisition of a collection of particular skills rather than subjects.

Learning science means mastering empirical investigative and experimental methods or procedures rather than memorizing tables of elements and geography education is not learning facts about particular places on the planet but acquiring map-reading skills. (Dewey, 1958; in Carr, 2003: 125)

If knowledge is a collection of skills, then there seems to be no reason why they should be applied to particular fields of experience only. If knowledge is understood as the ability to investigate and experiment it is potentially applicable to all school subjects. Mathematical skills for instance are used not only in scientific subjects but also in art and music. Such an understanding of certain universality of skills reflects a *holistic* concept of knowledge where "different techniques of human inquiry are brought together or integrated for the investigation of this or that aspect of experience precisely in the interests of more vital and meaningful learning" (Carr, 2003: 126). Promoting the integrated approach and practical problem solving, Dewey was not in favour of the traditional, largely subject-centred schooling.

The underlying principle of holistic learning is the constructivist theory. Supporters of this concept see learning as a discovery and construction of mental schema by learners interacting with their environment on multiple levels. Taylor and MacKenney explain that this approach sees all knowledge as a web of interrelated phenomena, and thus "if education is broken up into segments, which are then taught independently of one another, then concepts become disconnected and disjointed" (2008: 144). Meaningful learning results from getting the big picture rather than from decomposing reality into pieces of separate information.

Since holism is based on constructivism, it also rests upon the same principles identified by Brooks and Brooks (1993: ix):

– Teachers seek and value students' points of view. This allows them to design lessons that correspond with students' interest and individual needs.
– Teachers structure lessons to challenge students' suppositions. Even the youngest students come to the classroom with some prior experience and beliefs. In order to learn they need to identify them and confront with new knowledge.
– Teachers recognize that students must attach relevance to the curriculum. If the content is relevant to the students, their motivation to learn will be sustained
– Teachers structure lessons around big ideas, not small bits of information. As a result they can see the point in learning the particular elements of the big picture
– Teachers assess student learning in the context of daily classroom investigations, not as separate events. Students' developing competence can be observed

along with the task they are striving to complete. Therefore, their performance should be assessed as a sum of efforts made during the whole process rather than on the basis of a singular test.

These principles sound particularly reasonable in the case of young learners who eagerly undertake challenges to gain new skills or knowledge if their interest is properly evoked. The structure of early primary education allows for creating conditions in which the classes are spun around big ideas to which all subjects can relate. Also the form of summative assessment seems fair for children who may fail at one time performance, but that would not necessarily reflect the actual learning progress which may take time to become internalised.

Holistic education does not only see the student as a whole person requiring instruction in all possible modes or the subjects content as interrelated and coherent elements of knowledge to be internalised through active interaction but also the classroom as an environment taking part in the process of learning. Thus, it is essential that every student is included in every activity and no one is ever left out. Since no classroom is a homogeneous environment, teachers must employ a variety of strategies to ensure that all children are involved. Miller (1998: 47) suggests four such strategies: *transmission*, *transaction*, *transformation* and *connection*. Transmission is a one- directional mode of instruction in which the interaction is between the teacher or the course material and the student. The aim of this mode is to gather factual information relevant for the current topic. The interaction between the teacher and the students is increased in the transaction mode when problem solving and tasks developing cognitive skills are used. During transformational learning all aspects of child development are considered including intellectual, emotional, moral, spiritual and aesthetic areas. The activities characteristic for this mode are storytelling and the arts. Connection occurs when the student engages into contact with his environment making the learning integrated. This integration may be achieved by designing lessons that centre around a core theme. This mode also promotes collaboration as students interact with others to cooperate in tasks involving exchange of thoughts and experiences.

3.5.3. Cross-curricular approach

Adopting a holistic concept in teaching requires designing a method of formal instruction that refers to all subject areas and aims at supporting the child in his social, psychological, physical and cognitive development. To address all these diverse needs *cross-curricular* approach to teaching has been proposed. It is characterized by sensitivity to, and a synthesis of, knowledge, skills and ideas from various subject areas. This attitude towards content of education enriches pedagogical activity and promotes exploration of wider sensitivity through a diversity of methods. Jonathan Savage (2011) lists the purposes of cross-curricular teaching and learning which are to:

– motivate and encourage pupils' learning in a sympathetic way in conjunction with their wider life experiences;
– draw on similarities in and between individual subjects (in terms of subject content, pedagogical devices and learning processes) and make these links explicit in various ways;
– provide active and experiential learning for pupils;
– develop meaningful co-operation and collaboration between staff leading to the dual benefits of curriculum and professional development;
– contribute towards a broad range of teaching and learning opportunities located within individual subject teaching, across subjects and in relation to specific external curriculum themes or dimensions;
– promote pupils' cognitive, personal and social development in an integrated way;
– allow teachers the opportunity to evaluate and reflect on their teaching and to be imaginative and innovative in their curriculum planning;
– facilitate a shared vision amongst teachers and managers through meaningful collaborations at all levels of curriculum design (42).

In terms of teaching an additional language the purposes above determine the structure of subject curriculum in a number of ways. Firstly students, no matter how small, are not empty vessels, which are waiting to be filled with knowledge. They come to the classroom with prior experience in many spheres of life which they are eager to share with others. In terms of early formal language education this approach would advocate using the students' emotions, experiences and ideas to teach the language on content that is truly interesting for them and thus motivating enough to enhance learning. Secondly, since life is not a sequence of separate events that happen one after another but rather a complex mix of stimuli from all fields of knowledge bombarding a child all the time, it is justified to use this accidentally acquired knowledge of the world in formal education. This approach shifts the focus from teaching facts specific for a given subject to a deeper understanding of the phenomena and experiences that are shared between different fields of knowledge. Furthermore, it stresses the need to make these links explicit and thus make children aware of the multitude of interdependencies between subject areas. Language becomes, thus, a vehicle for delivering content knowledge from a variety of subjects and learning the principles of its structure and use becomes incidental.

Cross-curricular approach also puts emphasis on active acquisition of knowledge through experimenting, forming hypotheses, checking them out and drawing conclusions rather than getting ready-made solutions. Therefore inductive teaching of additional language is preferred over deductive and implicit techniques over explicit ones. One of the most important principles of this approach is collaboration between specialist teachers of various subjects. Since knowledge is a shared commodity and largely does not belong specifically to one subject area, teachers representing different academic disciplines need to cooperate to help their students understand the links between subjects and their interdependencies to see the coherent nature of knowledge. As Brinton, Snow and Wesche (1989) have noticed,

> When various subject areas are taught jointly, learners have more opportunities to see the links between subject areas. By appreciating these links, students develop a stronger grasp of subject matter, a deeper purpose for learning and a greater ability to analyse situations in a holistic manner. (in Farrell and Jacobs, 2010: 45)

Teresa Kennedy raises a neurological argument for integrating content claiming that the growing understanding of the brain's ability to create neuronal networks through simultaneous mental operations on different cognitive areas and "the tendency for the brain to consider the entire experience and to search for meaningful patterns calls for thematic, content-based interdisciplinary language instruction at all levels" (2006: 480).

Since young children in many educational systems in Europe follow an integrated teaching curriculum in the first years of formal instruction where learning is organized in topical units with elements of various subjects intertwining, there seems to be no reason why foreign language teaching should be excluded from this format. Language is the natural medium of expression in teaching all other subjects. If students use their mother tongue in the classroom they could also be encouraged to use elements of an additional language to perform the same tasks involving non-linguistic subject knowledge. Cross-curricular approach also assumes that individual subject knowledge will benefit from the contact with other fields through becoming enriched by elements traditionally belonging to a different school subject. Children, if encouraged and trained, will naturally transfer their knowledge gained from one experience to another one crossing the borders of subject classification. Additional language may enrich students' understanding of physical phenomena by reflecting elements of subject knowledge in a different way than the mother tongue, hence adding additional information. For example the name of astronomical phenomenon *northern lights* includes information about the place where it may be seen. This approach, promoting active quest for knowledge and integrated subjects instruction, will naturally involve extensive cooperation between students working on various projects through which whey not only gain experience and understanding of the world but also develop critical thinking and reasoning skills. Additionally, they learn how to cooperate with each other and because no activity is focused on one particular subject, all students participating feel competent and expert in at least one part of the task. Cross-curricular teaching obviously requires a lot of planning and involvement of all subject teachers. Although it is a rather demanding and challenging endeavour for the school staff, it also allows them to avoid professional burn out through constant learning of facts which, being elements of different subject areas than their own, may be totally new to them and through widening the scope help them create more innovative and creative tasks and thus lead to both personal and professional development.

The above described purposes of cross-curricular teaching in terms of foreign language instruction seem to rest upon the Communicative Language Teaching, whose principles, as summarised by Richards (2006: 22), include the believes that "second language learning is facilitated when learners are engaged in interaction and meaningful communication". To fulfil this condition teachers need to arrange learning situations in which the use of a foreign language seems natural and serves a purpose different than simply memorising the abstract in its nature word or phrase. Effective classroom learning tasks and exercises "provide opportunities for students to negotiate meaning, expand their language resources, notice how language is used, and take part in meaningful interpersonal exchange" (ibid.) Again, a meaningful interaction between students or students and the teacher depends on the real need to communicate. A mere repetition of a word or phrase does not fulfil this condition by not being intentional on the part of the student who has no extralinguistic interest in repeating a string of words. Meaningful communication is a result of "students processing content that is relevant, purposeful, interesting, and engaging" (Richards, 2006: 23). In the context of lower primary classroom EFL instruction will meet this criterion if it is used in relation to an activity conducted as an element of another subject area. Communication is "a holistic process that often calls upon the use of several language skills or modalities" (ibid.) Students at the first stage of primary education will rely above all on oral communication due to the lack of literacy skills. They will, however, use all available means to convey the message. If the teacher introduces elements of a foreign language in a meaningful and comprehensible way, the students will readily incorporate them into their oral repertoire and try them out immediately in a conversation.

Language learning "is facilitated both by activities that involve inductive or discovery learning of underlying rules of language use and organization, as well as by those involving language analysis and reflection" (Richards, 2006: 23). Some elements of the foreign language will be acquired incidentally and become a part of the students' lexicons. Since the native language for early primary students in Poland is Polish, the newly acquired elements of a foreign language will be embedded in the matrix and given features of the mother tongue counterpart. The positioning and inflection of a foreign word in a mother tongue sentence will show whether or not its grammar has been analysed properly. Teachers may draw students' attention to the form, especially when it comes to words which sound similar as is done within the native language education at this stage. Language learning is a gradual process "that involves creative use of language, and trial and error" (ibid.). When learning their first language children often make mistakes that result from their creative search for accurate forms. The same process could be encouraged in case of a foreign language so that students can experiment with the new language items by putting them in different contexts and forms and adjusting their understanding to the corrective feedback. Learners "develop their own routes to language learning, progress at different rates, and have different needs and motivations for language learning" (ibid.). This is an argument for promoting diversity. Students have the right to differ from one another and to be offered education in a form that would suit their individual profiles. Successful language learning "involves the use of effective learning and communication strategies". At the lower primary stage children are still learning the rules of social behaviour and interaction. If encouraged, they will be willing to use all available resources and creativity to convey their message successfully. The role of the teacher in the language classroom "is that of a facilitator, who creates a classroom climate conducive to language learning and provides opportunities for students to use and practice the language and to reflect on language use and language learning" (Richards, 2006: 23). The teacher arranges situations in which the use of a foreign language is most natural and is there to help students if they experience communication breakdown. In the first grade of primary school students are not expected to show a wide range of linguistic abilities in the foreign language but the aim of the teacher should be to make sure they use the little language they have in a way that reflects their full understanding of its function and meaning. For example, in simple social interactions, when they are given something they are able to react naturally by saying "thank you". The final assumption is that "the classroom is a community where learners learn through collaboration and sharing" (ibid.). Learning a foreign language is not a solitary activity and one needs to have an interlocutor against whom he could test his linguistic hypothesis and from whom he could learn through active interaction. All these assumptions that form the basis of communicative approach are applicable to the form of foreign language instruction as an element of integrated curriculum.

3.5.4. Integrating language with other subjects

The understanding of the fact that language is an essential element in all subject teaching led to creating the concept of *language across curriculum*. There is obviously a strong interdependency between language competence and success in learning other subjects. Reading comprehension skills, for example, are a prerequisite in understanding scientific texts and good speaking abilities are essential in performing tasks that require oral presentations. Therefore, development of higher linguistic abilities helps students achieve school success in other areas. Subject knowledge, on the other hand, constitutes the material for language practice. Curricular integration in the case of foreign language instruction may also be introduced by means of content based instruction where language becomes a vehicle for subject content delivery. The main emphasis is on delivering subject knowledge and language development is a side effect. Curricular integration is also promoted by the use of projects that are multidisciplinary by nature. In an example given by Farrell and Jacobs a project on water pollution may involve science in analysing water samples, mathematics in calculating data gather from the analysis, social studies in the role of government, public and private sectors responsible for pollution and language in writing letters to these bodies and giving presentations summarising the project (2010: 45). Such a project, apart from having an educational value, also raises students' awareness of real life problems. Making links between knowledge and life outside the classroom in the process of formal education is often called critical pedagogy and defined by the authors as a concept that "encourages a view of learning as a process in which students actively take part in transforming themselves and their world, rather than learning being a process in which students passively take part in the transmission of information from their teachers and textbooks to themselves" (Farrell and Jacobs, 2010: 46).

Laura Berk (2001) describes a classroom of first graders she observes, where learning is organised in centres including the reading centre, the writing centre, the math centre, the life science centre, the physical science centre, the art centre, and the imaginative play/extended project centre. Every day children decide in the morning which centre they want to start with and the teacher sets the topic for the day. In the learning sequence described by the author the main theme of the lesson is amphibians and it can be inferred from the nature of students' work that the topic of a week/month is sea life. In the project centre students are labelling shells for a sea life exhibition that they are planning to open for parents and other students. In the reading area they are looking for information about frogs so that they may play the roles of experts for the visitors of their museum.

The teacher uses every opportunity to introduce an element of learning within one of her focus areas. When it is time for a drink she asks the students to count how many cups she needs if there are 22 students, one teacher and one guest in the classroom. Before going on a trip to a museum she asks the children to calculate how much money she needs to take if one ticket costs two dollars. These instances of application of the skills and knowledge gained at school constitute a direct link between formal education and real life, increasing their interest in participating in evidently useful classroom activities. Berk concludes that "students want to master reading, writing, and math skills not because an adult tells them to but because those skills are essential to pursuing real-world practical goals and compelling topics in literature, social studies, and science" (2001: 183).

One more path for subject integration focusing on language is the idea of teaching *Language for Specific Purposes*. This form is particularly popular with groups of professionals preparing to work in a foreign language environment. The main idea behind this concept is to teach only the elements of language that are going to be useful for this group in educational contexts resembling real life situations. The content of the course will then include subject matter often familiar to the learners only delivered in a different language.

In a primary classroom subject integration is usually implemented in three ways: through *parallel topics*, *interdisciplinary instruction* and *immersion experiences*. Farrell and Jacobs describe these methods in the following way:

– *Parallel topics* – instruction in several subjects is organized around a common topic such as Mexico. Students may study the history of Mexico in Social Studies, read literature from Mexico in language arts, and create Mexican folk arts in art class. Although the topic is parallel in each of the subjects, instruction does not emphasize making connections between disciplines.

– *Interdisciplinary Instruction* – instruction is organized to help students more readily find the connections between disciplines. Students might study the concept of proportion in math and art and the concept of fractions in math and music. The emphasis is on understanding a concept from the perspective of more than one discipline.
– *Immersion experiences* – learning is organized to more closely resemble life. Within this real-life context, students find meaning. Students might organize a service project to provide coats for children in need. Students learn skills and concepts from multiple disciplines within the context of real-life problems. (2010: 46).

The content integration level seems to rise from parallel topics where separate subjects are joined by a common theme but the activities students are engaged in are still subject specific, through interdisciplinary instruction in which the same problem is analysed from the perspectives of various fields of knowledge, to immersion where the links are made not only between the subjects but also with the world outside the classroom.
As Teresa Kennedy puts it:

> Combining language study with other subject areas not only increases academic performance, but it also allows students to see the connections between what they are studying and the world around them. In other words, content-based language learning provides students with a valid or meaningful reason for using the language they are learning (2006: 482).

Curricular integration, however, does not limit itself to the academic aspect of teaching. Especially at primary school learning does not constitute merely of gaining subject knowledge. Children at the age at which they start formal instruction are also entering the world of human interaction with its social, psychological and emotional aspects. Integrated instruction offers students ample opportunities for social interactions, development of critical thinking and reasoning skills, empathy and the ability to listen to each other and respect other people's opinions thus contributing to tolerance and open-mindedness in preparation for future education.

3.6. AIMS OF BILINGUAL EDUCATION

As it follows from the discussion in the preceding chapters, bilingualism can, by and large, be considered as a positive and beneficial if not uncommon feature. The ability to speak more than one language has potentially many advantages from a better understanding of other cultures, through language maintenance to better employment perspectives. In other words it is better to have a command of more languages than less regardless of whether one of them is perceived as less prestigious or hardly ever used. However, the way in which the additional language is acquired may be less straightforward.

The American National Association for Bilingual Education defines bilingual education as "any use of two languages in school – by teachers or students or both – for a variety of social and pedagogical purposes" (NABE, 2004; in Navés, 2009). The reasons why people enter formal bilingual education systems are in most contexts political in nature and the aims of the process are set by authorities who may attempt to manipulate power relations between different languages spoken in a given country at a given time.

Bilingual education programs are designed in accordance with a number of ideologies and perceptions of the assumed outcomes of the process. In the American context, as proposed by Wiley (2008: 71), the aim of bilingual education policies may be to promote English and one or more additional languages, help speakers of minority languages adapt to the English-only instruction, limit the use of a given language, lower the status of a given language or even eradicate it. All of the above goals of bilingual education seem to reflect an unequal power relation between the languages with English being the dominant agent threatening the minority languages. It is not impossible, however, to imagine bilingual education as a policy promoting linguistic diversity and striving to support the home languages and cultures of immigrants.

Unlike Wiley's view of imperialistic English thrown upon speakers of other languages, a more positive, though rather patronizing perspective of bilingual education in the same context is offered by González (2008: 885) who proposes a list of six different approaches to bilingual education: aesthetic (enrichment, pragmatic), civil rights (psychological, human development), cultural assertiveness, cultural pluralism, pragmatic (utilitarian, work-related).

The *aesthetic orientation* rests upon the belief that modern civilized societies acknowledge the beneficial influence of being exposed to a variety of languages and cultures as enriching elements of individual intellectual development. A well-educated person is seen as one who has the ability to understand other people and their cultures in a multicultural or non-English work environment. It is aimed at all children although in practice it tends to be elitist as not all parents are able to afford the program and the desired goals include the ability to communicate during foreign travels. *Civil rights orientation* stresses the legal and moral right of minority languages speakers to maintain their traditional values and cultures. The main aim is to assert the right to use the home language freely both at school and outside. A mother tongue is seen as a medium of cultural heritage of non-English speaking children and as such should not be threatened by the majority language and thus children have the right for bilingual education. English speaking children are welcome to join the system on voluntary basis although it is sometimes argued that all children living in an area with a substantial number of speakers of another language should be incorporated in bilingual education system (González, 2008: 888) to prevent conflicts resulting from the lack of understanding and appreciation of each other's cultures.

The core concept of *psychological orientation* is self-awareness and belonging. It is claimed that for proper cognitive development children need to have a clear idea of their personal national identity. The home language is seen as a tool for helping children gain educational success and adjust to the English speaking environment while maintaining respect for their uniqueness. The main goal of *cultural assertiveness orientation* is empower linguistic minorities to participate in the country's social, economic and political actions. The home languages are seen as assets in that they promote collective strength and solidarity of a given underprivileged group. *Cultural pluralism orientation* rejects the concept of society as a melting pot in which different cultures lose their unique features for the sake of uniformity. Language diversity is perceived as beneficial in that it helps language minorities adapt into the society. The ultimate objective of this orientation is to minimize the hegemony of English. Finally, *pragmatic orientation* sees multilingual Americans as more valuable and marketable employees and thus it seeks to prepare students to work in multilingual environment in the USA and abroad. In this orientation the emphasis on learning another language is not limited to language minority students but is equally enforced upon native English speakers.

3.6.1. Types of bilingual programs

Bilingual education may be defined in relation to educational goals and institutional means in which a school attempts to reach them. The goal of creating a bilingual policy of educational provision may be twofold – the process may be aimed at fostering the overall development of children including their cultural heritage and home language or it may aim to lead to a language shift through eradicating home languages for the sake of dominant language formal instruction.

Colin Baker proposes a more detailed classification of existing models of bilingual education which divides them into two broad categories of weak forms including submersion, segregationist, transitional, mainstream with FL and separatist and strong forms with immersion, maintenance, dual and mainstream bilingual. The weak forms of bilingual education do not support the very idea of providing students with the ability of speaking two languages but typically have other (usually political or socio-economical) goals. If they result in bilinguality it is in a form of a limited command of the additional language rather than a roughly balanced ability to communicate in two languages. The strong forms, on the other hand, are seen as genuinely promoting the ideals of bilingualism and biliteracy for promoting linguistic and cultural diversity.

Submersion programs are a type of educational provision where minority language students are incorporated into mainstream majority language instruction. The minority language children are expected to learn in a dominant language classroom alongside majority language students and teacher with no additional support in terms of language or academic content. A similar program called *structured immersion* functions in the USA where separate minority language students classrooms are formed and taught by a dominant language teacher who may modify her language input to suit the students' level but no home language support is offered. In both these forms there will be additional dominant language classes aimed at developing students' vocabulary, grammar and communication skills). The major problem of such programs is the limitation it puts on minority language speakers in terms of academic and general cognitive development. Valdés (1998) found that the skills of critical thinking, cooperating and questioning are not developed due to insufficient communicative ability in the majority language. She states that although the students had the cognitive capacity they could not move to higher order thinking level because they did not have enough linguistic devices in the dominant language.

Another variation indicated by Baker is submersion with *Sheltered Content Instruction* in this model minority language students are separated from the mainstream classroom and are provided with academic content in dominant language but modified to match their level of linguistic competence. This allows for eliminating the overwhelming feeling of constant incompetence, embarrassment and inferiority experienced by minority language students when confronted with subject content in a language they have not yet mastered. However, though attempting to help the minority students master the academic content, the program assumes a patronizing attitude and isolates them from the rest of the school, which may create an image of those students as being less apt or bright. The educational and societal aim of submersion programs is assimilation and a typical outcome – monolingualism in the target language and so they seem to support subtractive bilingualism. Additionally, as Romaine points out, there have been studies concluding that "the development of the children in both languages is fragmentary and incomplete" (1995: 246). The process, thus, leaves the children semilingual with not only the additional language deformed but also with the home language partly lost.

In countries where the power relation between two languages is profoundly unequal the elite may decide that speakers of a minority language are not allowed to enter mainstream education to maintain their subordinate role in the society. The disempowered minority speakers with seriously limited access to the majority language will not have the chance to learn it well enough to pose a threat to the ruling elite. For this reason *segregationist programs* are developed for schools where minority language students learn solely through their home language instruction. The aim of such a policy is apartheid and the outcome – monolingualism in the subordinate language.

The decision to educate children in the minority language only may also be an autonomous decision of a roughly uniform ethnic group living in a dominant language country without any direct pressures from the outside. In such a situation a minority group decides to create a rather closed community that emphasizes its difference from the rest of the society in terms of culture, religion and language. To ensure that the minority language is not threatened by the dominant one a *separatist program* may be implemented. The only language of instruction is the home language and children have limited opportunities to get the dominant language input from the outside, as the community is closed and largely monolingual. The societal aim of this program is detachement and autonomy and the educational outcome – monolingualism in the heritage language.

In the case of *transitional programs*, as Sarah Shin puts it, "bilingual education simply refers to the use of two (or more) languages of instruction to varying degrees in various instructional contexts and proficiency in two languages is not necessarily a desired outcome. (2005: 31). This attitude towards bilingual education promotes a shift from minority language to the one of formal instruction. Whether it is done in the form of early exit (L1 instruction is offered approximately for the first two years) or late exit (a part of academic content is delivered in L1 until sixth grade), the ultimate aim of this process is a shift resulting in monolingualism in the dominant language and suppression of the students' home languages through their eradication from formal schooling context. In the light of this philosophy underlying educational process it seems hardly justified to call it bilingual as the home language is used instrumentally only to foster the acquisition of the target language and little or no care is taken for its development.

Bilingual education policy is typical of countries with post-colonial past, strong immigration history or heterogeneous ethnical structure. However, in a vast majority of formal schooling systems students are expected to learn additional languages. In the European Union roughly 58 percent of lower secondary school students study at least two foreign languages and about 9 to 20 percent of all teaching time is devoted to these subjects (Eurydice, 2008: 101). Baker relates to this form of introducing additional language as mainstream education with foreign language teaching realized on the basis of *core* or *drip-feed language programs* (2001: 200). In such programs language is treated as any other school subject and despite a long-term investment it very rarely produces functional bilinguals. Although in the European Union countries average exposure to additional language in this form lasts between eight and fifteen years (Eurydice, 2008: 28), the outcome in most cases is a very limited communicative competence in the foreign language.

In all the above-described weak programs the term *bilingual* is used not to emphasize the desired outcome of the educational process but rather to characterize the students taking part in it. At the end their education they are either left monolingual in their home or target language or, at best, they end up with limited non-functional command of the other language. The strong educational programs, on the other hand, use the term *bilingual* to describe the ultimate goal of the process of preparing students to function in two languages.

Immersion programs aim to raise functionally bilingual and bicultural individuals. The second language is added without threatening the first. Unlike mainstream programs with foreign language instruction, the additional language is introduced as a medium of subject content teaching. As summarized by Swain and Johnson (1997), immersion programs use the same curriculum as the local first language, the school supports L1 development, L2 exposure occurs only in the classroom, students start with no or very little knowledge of the L2, all the teachers are bilingual, the classroom culture is that of L1 community. Immersion programs are introduced at different ages (early, delayed or late) and with varying intensity (total, partial). The idea originated in Canada where a group of Anglophone parents decided to set up a nursery school group of 26 children to be taught in French. The outcomes showed that the children acquired linguistic abilities in English identical with their peers in traditional education and additionally a competence in French that children in the traditional program could not meet (Baker, 2001: 205). The success of the experiment may be partly explained by the socio-political context. The languages involved in the Canadian study were of approximately equal status, which does not typically happen in other bilingual contexts where one of the languages is clearly dominant. In this sense the St. Lambert experiment was an example of elite education leading to additive bilingualism. The programs are implemented successfully in many other countries including Spain (Gardner, 2000 in Baker, 2001), Japan (Maher, 1997), South Africa (Martin, 1997). The societal aim of immersion programs is pluralism and enrichment and the educational outcomes are bilingualism and biliteracy.

Where minority languages have a lower status and run a risk of being eradicated by the dominant language *maintenance programs* are implemented which offer L1 only education at the early stages of formal schooling and support of home language development throughout primary education. Maintenance programs are introduced in contexts where home language may be threatened by the expansion of dominant language as it is in the case of post-colonial countries like Mozambique where there are over 20 local languages but the education until recently was conducted only in Portuguese (Rzewuski, 2010). In immigrant contexts the policy is often termed *enrichment programs*, which foster the development of additive bilingualism in children who acquire the dominant language without losing their L1 or even, in dual (two-way) modes, the dominant L1 speakers acquire the minority language. This program also aims to achieve pluralism and enrichment saving at the same time the heritage language from extinction. The students leaving school should be bilingual and bilateral.

When there are approximately equal numbers of students speaking a minority and majority language in the same classroom and they are willing to learn each other's language, *dual (two-way) language education program* may be implemented. Both languages are used for instruction and learning and thus the desired outcome are a roughly balanced bilingualism and biliteracy. As a rule the minority language is used at least 50 percent of all teaching time up to six years of schooling (in the American context). The level of language is adjusted to the current level of the students but made challenging and both languages are taught mainly through content. The languages are separated and typically one is used on alternate days, weeks or months as the only medium of communication on a given day or divided by subjects which have a prescribed language in which they are taught on a given day. Dolson and Meyer (1992: 115) propose seven aims to achieve in dual language programs: (1) development of proficiency in their L1; (2) achievement of proficiency in their L2; (3) ultimate achievement of academic performance at or above the level set for traditional educational models in both languages; (4) positive cross-cultural attitudes and behaviours; (5) high levels of personal and social competence; (6) academic excellence; (7) more positive attitude towards people of different cultural backgrounds, standard language competence in both languages and tolerance towards other nations.

The most important feature of a classroom pursuing dual language program is balance. The maintenance of equal usage of both languages is the essential condition for bilingual communication and integration. If one language group dominates the other may become excluded or forced to switch the language permanently. Another problem is that, although the advantages of the program for minority language students seen obvious in that they have a chance to learn partly in their L1 and acquire a functional competence of the majority language, the benefits for the majority language students are not so obvious. Baker notices that in American English-Spanish contexts "attracting language majority students to a dual language bilingual school is difficult. Where the monolingual mainstream school is as (or more) attractive to prospective parents, recruitment to dual language bilingual schools may initially be a challenge" (2001: 213 emphasis original). While it may be perceived as prestigious for a minority language speaker to learn alongside a native-English peer, a dominant language student may be resistant to learn the language of the subordinate culture and find it less than attractive.

A study by Thomas and Collier (2002) shows that language minority students achieve top results in academic achievement tests in all subject areas as well as in their home and majority languages. This form of education requires both language minority and dominant language students to learn each other's languages, the perceived status of which is equal. It also assumes high academic success expectations and parent involvement for closer home-school cooperation and emphasizes natural language acquisition through all content areas, tasks requiring cooperation between students, high level of interaction and discovery learning at all levels of proficiency (in Shin, 2005: 33).

Mainstream bilingual programs where the educational process is conducted in two majority languages is typical of communities were two or more languages of equal prestige are used (e.g. French and German or Dutch in Belgium – Eurydice, 2008). It is also employed where many mutually unintelligible regional languages are spoken and none of them is perceived as dominant. For practical reasons it is decided to introduce one additional language (typically English) to serve as a lingua franca within the country (e.g. Bahasa Malay and English in Brunei – Baetens Beardsmore, 1999). Although the majority of largely monolingual countries follow drip-feed language programs with the additional language taught as a separate subject with limited success there is a growing trend for using the L2 to deliver a part of the curriculum (Navés, 2009). International schools typically adopt these programs where the curriculum (UK, USA or local) is delivered through the medium of two majority languages, one of which is ordinarily English and the other one the national language of the country. The students attending these schools are children of diplomats, businessmen in multinational companies and organizations who can afford to pay the fee. European schools attended by children of the European Community workers adopt a similar solution. The medium of instruction is the first language of the children during the first years of education but L2 (English, French or German) is also introduced to later become the dominant medium of curriculum delivery.

3.6.2. Bilingual education research

In the modern world of abundant international communication foreign language education has gained a priority. In the majority of European Union countries foreign language is introduced at the onset of primary education. The average age of children entering formal education in EU countries is eight with some countries like Malta and several Spanish autonomies starting as early as three (Eurydice, 2008). In Poland children start learning the first foreign language at the age of six or seven when they enter primary school. By and large the chosen foreign language is English for a number of reasons including its popularity around the world and availability of teachers. The Eurydice report states that in around ninety percent of all EU countries the first foreign language taught is English (2008: 45) and the time devoted to its delivery constitutes ten percent of all teaching hours in the primary school.

In the European context, content based instruction emerged as CLIL (Content and Language Integrated Learning) in response to European Council's recommendations of 2005 concerning foreign language teaching policy (Tedick & Cammarata, 2012: 29). Depending on the country it was used in, it was given a variety of acronym like AICLE (aprendizaje integrado de contenidos y lengua extranjera), EMILE (Enseignement d'une Matière par l'Intégration d'une Langue Étrangère), BILI (Bilinguales Lernen) to name just a few. Grin (2005; in Coyle, 2007) recognizes 216 forms of CLIL programs differing in compulsory status, intensity, stage of education, initial linguistic competence, and duration. Most of the programs, however, can be placed on a grid in relation to two dimensions: intensity and focus. In terms of the former, a program can range from high time-intensive to low time intensive. As for the latter, the instruction may be content- or language-driven. As a result there are four general groups of CLIL programs: (1) high time-intensive content-driven, (2) high time-intensive language driven, (3) low time-intensive content-driven and (3) low time-intensive language driven (Tedick & Cammarata, 2012: 31) A graphic representation of these possibilities is presented in figure 11.

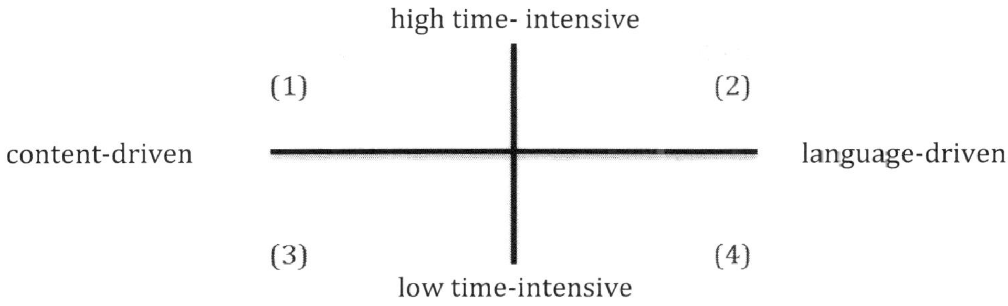

Figure 11. Dimensions of content and language integrating program

Source: Adapted from Tedick and Cammarata (2012)

In both content- and language-driven program the subject content is delivered through the medium of an additional language. The difference, however, is which of these elements is given priority. In content-driven approach the emphasis is put on the subject matter and language learning is treated as secondary and often even incidental. Teachers base their work on the subject matter curriculum and need to adjust language objectives and plan activities that correspond to the content (Met, 1999). This approach typically assumes that the subject teacher, with some linguistic competence in the second language, delivers his expert knowledge enriching it with elements of the additional language. The challenge here is to ensure that the students acquire the content knowledge and the linguistic goals are achieved. It seems inevitable that the subject teacher will lean heavily towards content attainment leaving the student's linguistic development behind. The other extreme is a language-driven program in which content is secondary to L2 learning. The curriculum is defined by language objectives and content attainment is incidental. This is the common approach of foreign language classes where the emphasis is often explicitly placed on the acquisition of linguistic forms and structures, while the textual and contextual means to this aim are largely disregarded. It seems highly implausible to conduct language classes without using any subject content to illustrate language use and structure. While students can be taught content matter without any use of L2, they cannot possibly learn an additional language without referring to other fields of knowledge. In the light of this argument, language teaching has always been content based in the form of language-driven model. However, since students' attention is rarely directed towards the content and the elements of subject knowledge in language teaching materials are chosen rather unsystematically and present the content superficially, the acquisition of facts is typically merely incidental.

Each of the CLIL program groups presented in Figure 11 seems to have its drawbacks due to favouring one of the extremes. It seems possible to predict that the high time-intensive content-driven model will result in attaining a high level of competence in the content matter and minimal progress in language. The high time-intensive language driven program, on the other hand, will lead to good results in reaching linguistic objectives but failure in acquiring adequate subject knowledge. Both focuses paired with low time-intensive dimension will lead to similar but less visible outcomes. The more a given program is situated to the centre of the grid, the more balanced approach it represents. If a given model can be defined as representing an approach placed halfway between content- and language-driven extremes, and is additionally time intensive, it is not unjustified to expect relatively high levels of attainment in both areas.

As early as 1987 a large-scale study of Genesee proved that French immersion (high time-intensive CBI) students showed similar content and L1 attainment as their monolingual peers, while additionally acquiring L2. More recently a cross-sectional study of Turnbull et al. showed that "in grade 6, immersion students' literacy scores were notably better than their peers' in English programs" (2001: 23) despite a slight lag in literacy skill in grade 3. A study in Switzerland showed that students in L2 CBI ultimately outperformed their peers instructed in L1. Not only did their mother tongue not suffer from the early immersion in L2 but it also developed as a result of the contact (Serra, 2007). However, a study of late English immersion students in Hong Kong described by Hoare and Kong (2008), reveals a more basic problem that CBI teachers may experience worldwide. The study results show that L1 instruction students did better in standardized competence tests than the immersion students but this might not have been caused by the inherent features of the program itself but the attitude of the teachers and quality of schooling. Hoare and Kong conclude that the results suggest "many Hong Kong immersion teachers do not have the pedagogical skills, nor the understanding of and commitment to immersion education, to integrate the teaching of language and content in the classroom in ways that can bring about the learning of both" (2008: 254).

A study of thinking and content learning processes (termed c*ognitional development*) conducted by Jäppinen (2005) in Finland produced interesting results in terms of age factor. Cognitional development of 335 CLIL students aged 7-15 instructed in English, French or Swedish was compared with that of an equal control group taught through their L1. The ability to form individual concepts and conceptual structures in maths and science were tested. The result showed that whereas the differences between the experimental and control group of children aged 13-15 were largely insignificant, younger CLIL students outperformed their L1 instructed peers. Jäppinen explains that "the amount of teaching through a foreign language was smaller in the third age group than in the first or the second [...] due to the level of difficulty of the subjects which restricts the amount of CLIL or, to the fact that eligibility for further studies that are, in general, in Finnish must be guaranteed" (2005: 162). A study of Hungarian high school students comparing conversational and academic level of competence in English between CLIL and non-CLIL students (Várkuti, 2010) revealed that although both groups are better at conversational English, the L2 instructed learners perform on average 24% better than the non-CBI students. The researcher concludes that "the findings of this research suggest that in largely monolingual societies the CLIL approach is a more effective means of language learning than intensive language programmes" (76).

Studies have also been conducted on the teacher's behaviours in CLIL and non-CLIL contexts. A study by Kong (2009) focused on the relations between the teacher's educational background (content or language) and the structure of pedagogical context in Hong Kong and Xi'an. He found that in order to be effective "new content has to be explored in depth and from different perspectives to enable complex knowledge relationships to be co-constructed by the teacher and students through the use of correspondingly complex language" (2009: 254). A similar study was conducted in the USA by Pessoa et al. (2007) in two content-based instruction classrooms taught by teachers coming from different educational backgrounds. It was observed that the teacher who was certified in both Spanish and elementary education used different discourse practices than the teacher who was a language specialist. The former constructed classroom talk focused on topic development involving diverse language functions. She asked open-ended questions and used varied lexemes to enrich vocabulary. The latter treated the content as material for lexical and structural analysis, using the sentences as examples of a specific grammar point to be worked on. Students in this classroom produced mainly single-word responses. The results of the study showed that the learners from the first classroom significantly outperformed their peers from the second group in function, text, impact, vocabulary, comprehension, and language control. The researchers concluded that "simply infusing academic con-tent into language lessons does not create a classroom discursive environment that promotes the students' ability to engage in target language interaction, academic or otherwise" (Pessoa et al. 2007: 111).

In a Dutch educational setting de Graaff et al. (2007) conducted an ethnographical study in various subject CLIL classrooms. They found that effective CBI included: scaffolding on the learners' level of language and content knowledge through adapted authentic materials, facilitation of meaning-focused processing by encouraging learners to request new vocabulary items, the use of implicit form-focused instruction, construction and application of communicatively feasible tasks and encouragement to use compensation strategies to overcome comprehension and production problems.

The studies mentioned above are only some examples of research activities undertaken in recent years in the field of CLIL. The abundance of data collection enterprises may suggest a rising interest of scholars in this mode of language teaching and reflect the current state of practice and demand in the educational sector. Thus, it seems justified to examine the issue in the sector of primary school since the general interest mainly focuses on secondary and tertiary level of education.

3.7. LANGUAGE EDUCATION IN POLAND

The implementation of bilingual education in Poland is a result of adopting the European Union education policy favouring multilingualism and formal education supporting various forms of CLIL. Profile Report on Bilingual Education in Poland (2008) is an outcome of a research conducted in Polish secondary schools offering some sort of CLIL programs offering and overview of this type of instruction in formal education in Poland. Nineteen schools participated in the project and the analysis of received data allowed the authors to distinguish four different curricular models: (a) Extensive English Language Medium Instruction, (b) Partial English Language Medium Instruction, (c) Limited English Language Medium Instruction, (d) Specific English Language Medium Instruction. A summary of these models is presented in Table 2:

The subjects taught through bilingual education were: biology, geography, mathematics, physics, chemistry and history. In all the observed models the preferred model of instruction was teacher-based with limited use of pair- or group work both in the case of content teaching and language instruction. Since collaboration is one of the main features of content-based language teaching offering students opportunities for genuine communication, such a mode of instruction is against the principle of CLIL. The authors of the report also enumerate the occasions when teachers use Polish. These instances include:

1. For translation of brief sections of teacher monologue (lecture)
2. For introducing a new topic: *Napiszcie sobie nowy temat – transport komórkowy* (*Write down a new topic – cell transportation* - biology)

Table 2. Features of bilingual models in Poland

Mode	A		B		C		D		
Use of English	Nearly 100%		50%		10-50%		Very limited		
Type	a	b	a	b	a	b	a	b	c
Focus	Content	Content and form	Content	Content and form	Content	Content and form	Content (lesson in English summarising a sequence of lessons in Polish)	Content (lesson in Polish based on materials in English)	Content and form (project in English based on knowledge delivered in Polish)
Goal	Expected content outcomes High language proficiency		Expected content outcomes High language proficiency		Expected content outcomes Limited language competence Cross linguistic development		Opportunities for specific use of English Complement a course in Polish		

Source: Based on Marsh et al. (2008: 26–27).

3. When introducing new terms: ***Land form*** *to formy terenu* (geography)
4. When asked for an explanation: ***Histology*** *to nauka zajmująca się budową komórki* (*Histology is the science which concerns cell structure*)
5. For giving clues following the use of prompt questions given in English, *Could you come to the blackboard and draw the set and explain the term mutually exclusive?* <upon receiving no answer from the learner> *OK, zapomnij o angielskim, wszyscy mają to zrozumieć, wytłumacz po polsku* (*OK, forget about English, everybody needs to understand it, explain it in Polish* – mathematics)
6. For classroom management purposes *Przeczytajcie tekst ze strony 23, Bądźcie cicho* (*Read the text from page 23, Be quiet – history*) (Marsh et al., 2008: 29)

Although the switch to Polish seems justified in the case of scientific term explanation to ensure understanding of content and acquisition of the word in both languages, some instances of first language use appear unnecessary. When the focus on content wins over linguistic objectives (like in example 6) the acquisition of the concept taught can be expected in the mother tongue only. It is important to remember that these classes are in fact content lessons with separate curricula and teaching aims to be achieved. English is an additional element to be addressed only if the acquisition of content has been ensured. It is therefore, surprising that English is not used when the interaction is not related to the subject content but results from natural discourse, like in examples 2 or 6. The application of English as a language for classroom communication could make these interactions more natural and offer a realistic context for language use. The lack of utilising such opportunities, together with minimal application of collaborative tasks limits the use of target language to the role of translation of the content lecture. In the same report students are noted to comment that what they miss from the bilingual instruction is the opportunity to use the language in real communication.

Papaja (2007) reports on the results of her study of the use of Polish in two bilingual secondary schools. The author observed 28 lessons of geography, biology, maths and physics conducted within the content-based instruction model. Out of all students observed, 75% had already passed Cambridge Certificate of Advanced English representing C1 level and 60% were preparing towards Proficiency exam. Despite this evident linguistic potential, the lessons are reported to have been conducted in 80% in Polish. If English occurred, it was nearly always a specific subject term (e.g. *frequency*, *soil*, *urine*, etc.) or, as in the physics lesson, a very simple topic connected sentence (e.g. *biomechanics is the science*). Teachers are also reported to give short lectures in English to then immediately translate them into Polish. Such practice seems counterproductive since it gives students no opportunity to process the information given in the target language and eliminates motivation to even listen to the first delivery and, instead, wait for the easier, Polish version.

Another problem of bilingual education expressed by students and teachers of content subjects is the disadvantage of curricular adaptation of the subject to the requirements of bilingual delivery. Tatoj (2008) reports on the state of bilingual Spanish-Polish instruction in secondary schools. Although the author acknowledges higher levels of linguistic attainment in bilingual programs, she stresses the frequent concerns of the participants regarding the level of content knowledge delivered in content-based instruction. All students in the study complained that the bilingual program did not prepare them for the advanced level of school leaving exam in any subject except Spanish. The main aim of content-based instruction is to deliver the same subject content using a target language. Thus the result should include a level of attainment in the subject content at least equal to the one of non-CLIL students and an additional benefit of (nearly) natural foreign language acquisition. Since students report that their knowledge of the subject is insufficient for the advanced exam, it seems that the goal has not been achieved. Perhaps the balance between the focus on language and on content was shattered making it impossible for the students to develop their full potential. It seems that in CLIL programs in Poland either the advanced language acquisition is at the cost of subject knowledge attainment or proper content learning happens at the expense of additional language development. Content teachers believe that the priority must be given to meeting the requirements of subject content while language teachers emphasize the necessity to work on linguistic form often forgetting that language serves only as a vehicle of content. Neither group, however, seems concerned with the need to introduce the additional language as an element of classroom communication not necessarily filled with content specific terms but used in real collaborative context.

As Pawlak (2010) points out, the evaluation reports on the current state of Polish bilingual education observe difficulties concerning the place of CLIL in educational system, qualifications of the teachers, forms of assessment, accessibility of materials or techniques of teaching. Thus, content based teaching of languages is still an egalitarian enterprise rather than an option available to all especially at lower stages of formal education.

Despite all these limitations, Pawlak concludes:

> Although one needs to be aware of such limitations, they should by no means justify the resignation from actions undertaken in order to develop CLIL in Poland. One solution could be tightening of cooperation between langue and selected content subject teachers so as to enable correlation between teaching some content, the more so because the national curriculum and existing course books include many elements that could constitute the basis for such integration (2010: 24).

In 2004 in Poland there were 40 schools with Polish-English bilingual program (Mobidic, 2004: 1). This number seems unimpressive when compared with the German educational system where in 2005 there were over 450 English bilingual schools (Vázquez, 2007). The distribution between different types of schools is summarized in Table 3. The difference is also visible in the distribution between the types of schools offering bilingual education. While in the Polish system this option is more popular at the secondary school level, in Germany the most numerous group of bilingual students study in middle schools. There may be a few reasons for this difference. Using an additional language in content learning must inevitably be more demanding for the students. The German education system appears to interpret this additional difficulty as less problematic at an earlier stage of education where students may still devote more time to learning and experience less stress caused by the major school leaving exam whose results will determine their future studies which is characteristic for secondary education. In Poland the decision to introduce bilingual instruction as late as the secondary level may rest upon the belief that students need to have a good command of the additional language on entering the program. Another reason may be teacher education. It seems that German subject teachers may be better prepared for delivering their content in English even working at schools of lower levels of education. Availability of comprehensible materials and the understanding of the value of bilingual education may also help to explain the difference.

Table 3. Distribution of schools with bilingual programs in 2005

Country	Primary schools	Middle schools	Secondary schools
Poland	2	9	29
Germany	5	349	104

In both countries, however, primary schools are largely underrepresented in the bilingual education system. The reasons for this might be similar to the ones described above including the shortage of adequately prepared teachers and materials.

Typically, bilingual programs in primary schools do not refer to early primary education and are more likely to exist in non-public institutions. As Iluk (2011) points out:

> In Andalucia 352 primary schools run bilingual programs. The intensive introduction of bilingual programs in primary schools in this country ensures dynamic development of this form of instruction at higher levels of education, which is proven by the fact that within the last five years the number of bilingual schools rose by nearly five hundred percent. Here [in Poland], we are observing an opposite tendency: secondary schools constitute the main body of bilingual institutions with no natural lower-level source of candidates (240).

It is to be regretted that the primary sector is practically excluded from this form bilingual education as the structure of curriculum often creates perfect conditions for a non-intrusive introduction of English as a vehicle for content teaching. The Polish National Curriculum for the first stage of primary school education (i.e. grades I–III) follows an integrated subjects approach (with elements of interdisciplinary instruction and immersion experiences) in which children learn about the world through activities belonging to a number of subject areas including: Polish language, music, visual arts, social education, science, mathematics, crafts and physical education. Additionally, children also learn ICT, religious education and a foreign language following separate curricula. In Poland the number of hours devoted to foreign language teaching at the early primary stage (grades I-III) is now 190[2]. In practice this means that students have two lessons of English a week that are typically taught by a specialist teacher.

The integrated subjects curriculum is organized around topical units where each day has a separate topic. The following tables present a short comparison of day 18 in week four between three different integrated subjects programs in grade I.

Topic

Teaching program	Topic of the week	Topic of the day
„Razem w szkole"	Welcoming Lady Autumn in orchards and gardens	Vegetables all year round
„Nowe już w szkole"	Autumn around us	Colours of autumn
„Wesoła szkoła i przyjaciele"	Forest in autumn clothes	Forest animals and their habits

Linguistic education (Polish)

Teaching program	Activities
„Razem w szkole".	Listening to a poem by W. Kostecka „Owocowa wyliczanka" (Fruit rhyme) . Listening to the text from the coursebook. Creating longer utterances inspired by illustrations. Names of fruit. Global reading of words. Dividing words into syllables
„Nowe już w szkole"	Utterances of children on the topic of upcoming changes in nature in autumn basing on the observations made during the trip, pictures, poems and feelings inspired by colourful leaves in autumn sun.
„Wesoła szkoła i przyjaciele"	Creating sentences to pictures and modeling them with white rectangles. Global reading of sentences. Phonetic analysis and synthesis of animal names. Drawing along traces in opposite directions - spirals.

[2] Framework for teaching foreign languages in public schools. Annexes to the Regulation of 7 February 2012 on the framework curricula in public schools (Ramowy plan nauczania języków obcych w szkołach publicznych. Załączniki do rozporządzenia z dnia 7 lutego 2012 r. w sprawie ramowych planów nauczania w szkołach publicznych)

Mathematical education

Teaching program	Activities
„Razem w szkole".	Revision: – creating sets and sub-sets, – comparing number in sets – recognising geometrical figures Terms: more, less, the same.
„Nowe już w szkole"	Selecting groups – gifts of autumn.
„Wesoła szkoła i przyjaciele"	Comparing number in sets *more*, *less*, *the same*.

Arts

Teaching program	Activities
„Razem w szkole".	Drawing creatures and dishes from potatoes.
„Nowe już w szkole"	A trip to a park or a forest – observing plants in autumn colours
„Wesoła szkoła i przyjaciele"	-

Science

Teaching program	Activities
„Razem w szkole".	Features of potato. What can you do with a potato?
„Nowe już w szkole"	-
„Wesoła szkoła i przyjaciele"	Recognising and naming forest animals. Lifestyle, feeding, habitats, Finding food.

Crafts

Teaching program	Activities
„Razem w szkole".	Design „Potato creatures".
„Nowe już w szkole"	Designing symbols of autumn.
„Wesoła szkoła i przyjaciele"	Making envelopes for pictures of forest animals.

Physical

Teaching program	Activities
„Razem w szkole".	General kinaesthetic exercises and games.
„Nowe już w szkole"	Kinesthetic games with music.
„Wesoła szkoła i przyjaciele"	Copying animal movements (crawling, jumping, running on fours etc. Kinaesthetic game „A walk in a forest".

Whatever the program on this given week students will be concentrating on the signs of autumn and on this particular day will be engaged in similar activities. The common theme for all these educational situations is exploring the outside world to recognise elements characteristic for this season and all subject areas use this concept in teaching content specific skills. Children listen to literature and music connected with autumn, draw, cut, glue and make out of plasticine elements associated with autumn and take part in dancing and physical activities connected with the same topic.

In the first three years of primary education students have obligatory six foreign language classes a week in the whole stage of early primary education. This is usually divided equally into the three years per 2 teaching hours weekly. If there was an English lesson on day 18 in week four of the school year in grade I, it would be lesson number seven. The following tables present a selection of lessons number seven in week four in different English programs.

Fairyland 1

Topic	Vocabulary	Grammar	Functions
Colour my world	words: *red, green, blue, yellow, sun, tree, cloud, sea, apple.*	Verb *to be (it is)* Questions *(is it + colour)* Shirt answers: *yes, it is* and *no, it isn't*	Describing a picture Asking and answering questions: *Is it red/green/blue/yellow?*

Bacpack Gold 1

Topic	Vocabulary	Grammar	Functions
Ready for School	Nouns: *backpack, book, chair, circle, crayon, desk, marker, paper, pen, pencil, pencil case, table* Adjectives: *blue, green, red*	Verb: *be (is)* Pronouns: *it, what*	Naming colours Using forms of the verb *to be* Questions: *What's this? What colour is this?* Answers

New Bingo 1

Topic	Vocabulary	Grammar	Functions
A big lion and a little mouse	big, little, head, nose, tail, eyes, ears, mouth, nose, arms, fingers, lion, mouse numbers: 1-10 funny monster many (toes)	Adjectives: *big, little,* Verb: to have got I have got… You can see! How many (eyes) have you got?	Describing appe-arance

Although English has been taught as an obligatory subject in the first stage of primary education in Poland since September 2008, there seems to be no correlation of content between foreign language program and the integrates subjects regardless of the course book. Moreover, different course books provide different topics at the same stages of school year. The material they contain seems to ignore the natural cycle of topics related to cultural and traditional events happening outside the classroom, which the integrated subjects curriculum incorporates into the teaching process. Some English course books offer holiday pages at the end of the book (e.g. *Bugs World 1*) but these only cover the major events of the year. It seems that the order of topics in English course books follows from the immediate, and hence more familiar surroundings to the more extended outside world but they are not at all adjusted to the order of thematic units children follow in their integrated subjects classes where it seems more natural and coherent. While all the above mentioned programs of early primary education show significant similarity, those used for teaching English vary widely in their choice of content.

The problem with this discrepancy between the integrated subjects curriculum and any of the EFL programs is that it introduces a clash between topics and often also activities the students are engaged in. Following the holistic approach to teaching, students should be allowed to create a coherent image of the world based on what they learn every day. Although, this seems perfectly feasible in terms of all subjects that are a part of the early primary education, English is the odd one out. In practice, on day 18 students would be cognitively engaged all day in different activities connected with oncoming autumn experimenting, exploring and coming in direct contact with nature, collecting data that would contribute to their understanding of the world. They would most probably be enthusiastically reacting to the new experiences and willing to share their knowledge about the topic. However, at the end of the day there would be a sudden change of two crucial elements of the learning context: the language and the topic. Students would be required to leave the safe area of integrated subjects education with its natural reference to the out of school reality and switch to thinking about pets, school or monsters depending on the course book chosen by the English teacher. Not only would they have to stop thinking about the subject matter they have been immersed in for the past few hours but they would also have to switch to this new information being delivered in a different code.

Since one of the principles of cross-curricular teaching is to draw upon similarities between subjects it seems unjustified that English is taught separately. If language is a medium of information transfer it could be a tool for delivering knowledge and not a subject itself. It is hardly possible to find a reading comprehension text in a course book devoted to word formation or a listening task dealing with the beauty of inflection. If English is not used to talk about itself there seems to be no reason why it should not be employed to deliver the same content as the mother tongue. All the materials in any language course book are devoted to some topics that are not linguistic in nature but rather apply to other fields of knowledge ranging from science to social matters. Every modern foreign language course book, like the integrated subjects materials, includes music, elements of arts and crafts and physical activities. The only difference is that the content is neither topically related with the latter nor with the real world outside the classroom at the time when they are planned to be introduced. It would therefore be beneficial for the students to integrate English with all the other subjects. This could be done at the level of materials if the course book was written in close relation with the integrated subjects curriculum. At the level of teaching the integration could be achieved in two ways: the English teacher could work in close relation with the integrated subjects teacher and plan his lessons according to the topic of a given day or week choosing appropriate elements of the existing course book or preparing his own materials; or the integrated subjects teacher could teach also English and incorporate it into the everyday life of the classroom. The observation described in this paper refers to the latter case where students have only one teacher for all subject areas including English and she tries to naturally introduce elements of this language in a variety of activities involving other subjects content and classroom language. As a result of such an implementation of foreign language education as a natural element of classroom interaction, parts of the national curriculum for the first grade of primary education are delivered in both languages. Therefore, the educational process in such a case resembles bilingual education.

4. INVESTIGATING LINGUISTIC BEHAVIOUR IN INTEGRATED EFL AND SUBJECTS EDUCATION IN A LOWER PRIMARY CLASSROOM. QUALITATIVE ANALYSIS

Language use in bilingual contexts, both formal and informal has been the subject of numerous studies described in the previous chapters. The context of the present observation differs, however, from those studies in terms of discourse organisation. The unique conditions for foreign language learning in lower primary context in Poland are created by the structure of general early formal education. Content integration, reflected in combined subjects teaching in the first three years of primary school, allows educators to introduce foreign language instruction as an integral element of the curriculum. Including elements of English in everyday instruction leads to distinctive communication patterns. It is, thus, interesting to observe linguistic behaviours of learners and the teacher, engaged in partly bilingual discourse in both educational and social situations in the classroom.

4.1. THE LANGUAGE CLASSROOM AS AN OBJECT OF RESEARCH INTEREST

Classrooms are fascinating places. Students spend most of their time inside a classroom where they interact with other students, teachers and the surrounding environment. Those are the places where they learn how to behave in social situations and discover their own identities through constant contact with other people in a myriad of contexts. They offer perfect conditions for research in the fields of psychology, sociology, linguistics, didactics and many others. It is in the context of a classroom that children grow up and become socialised, go through the long process of transformation from a child, unaware of their own endless potential, to a mature person with a well-defined personal identity and readiness to face the world outside the classroom. However, although these processes occupy a significant place in the so-called hidden curriculum, one of the main aims of a school is to provide students with subject knowledge and skills. In terms of a foreign language, students are expected to achieve a certain, precisely defined level of proficiency. But gaining competence in a language is different from learning any other subject in that it is a continuous process of constant enrichment and revision of what has already been learnt. Additionally, since the primary aim of language is communication, its development requires active participation in verbal interaction. Study in the field of discourse in formal education, thus, requires the researcher to record data *in* the classroom and over a period of time. This calls for extensive studies comprising ample data collection and detailed analysis of the language used, the communicative situations and participants involved, an approach referred to as *classroom ethnography*.

4.2. CLASSROOM ETHNOGRAPHY

Classroom ethnography is the application of ethnographic and sociolinguistic or discourse analytic research methods to the „study of behaviour, activities, interaction, and discourse in formal and semi-formal educational settings such as school classrooms" (Watson-Gegeo, 1997: 135). Unlike quantitative research, classroom ethnography focuses on sociocultural dimension of teaching and learning, includes participants' self-reflection on their behaviour, and promotes a holistic analysis of the entire context of classroom interactions. According to Toohey (2008), ethnography in language education aims to explore learners' and teachers' views on the ways in which languages and learned and taught in local and global social contexts. Ethnographic language studies rest upon the belief that learning is the outcome of active participation in culturally and socially organised practices.

Ethnographic studies of language teaching practices focusing on the opportunities they create for language learning to occur have recently gained popularity mainly in the naturalistic contexts in the USA and postcolonial environments (Grant and Wong, 2003; Goldstein, 2004; Hawkins, 2004; Gutiérrez, Baquedaño-López, and Asato, 2001).

Ethnographic research examining educational discourse has for several decades focused on how students are inducted or socialised into new subject matter at schools and other learning sites and how language and literacy practices mediate their learning and are themselves a goal and outcome of learning. There has thus been considerable emphasis on how students learn to engage in the sanctioned oral and written discourse practices of different disciplines and social groups, how they negotiate the routine questions, responses, and feedback behaviours of their teachers and peers, as well as other forms of accepted (or sometimes subversive) interaction, and how, in the process, they become more socio-linguistically competent participants in, or members of, these local cultures or learning communities (Duff, 2008: 107).

Data gathered as a result of ethnographic research may later be subject to analysis assuming different approaches depending on the main focus of the study. Hence, conversation analysts will give priority to the management of topic and discourse and turn taking mechanisms, while sociolinguistic approaches will focus on context affecting the degrees of formality and cultural factors influencing conversational style. Speech act theorists will look at the interactional factor in the discourse in terms of the speakers' intentions and functional aims of their utterances. Thornbury and Slade (2007: 281) identify also pragmatic and systemic-functional perspectives on ethnographic language data analysis. The former focusing on the co-operative function of linguistic exchange and politeness strategies while the later concerning the speakers' social identity at the levels of lexicon, grammar and discourse.

The present study, concerned with the way foreign language is used in an EFL classroom where it is incorporated into the content teaching, looks at the ethnographic data gathered mainly from the perspective of (1) discourse analysis and (2) language socialization.

4.2.1. Defining discourse

The term *discourse*, as broadly defined by Flowerdew (2013: 1), refers to language at its suprasentential level used in context. Classroom discourse, on the other hand, refers to „contextualized or situated language use in classrooms, as specific interactional contexts, that reflects cultural and social practices" (Luk, 2008: 121). Since spoken language is typically used in a communicative situation where at least one speaker and one listener take part, the interlocutors need to be aware of certain rules governing such a communicative exchange. In other words they need to be competent not only in terms of language but also other aspects of communication that accompany a given speech event. Communicative competence is, thus, a complex ability whose interrelated elements are presented in Celce-Murcia's model in Figure 12.

In her revised model, Celce-Murcia (2007: 46) distinguishes six major areas of competence crucial for effective communication. *Socio-cultural competence* concerns the speaker's pragmatic knowledge of the extralinguistic context of in-

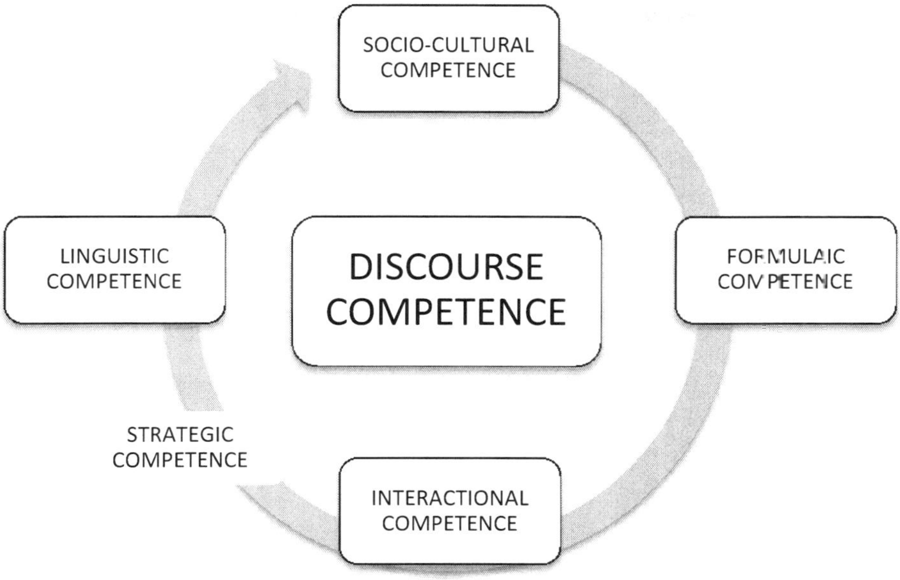

Figure 12. Celce-Murcia's model of communicative competence

Source: Adapted from Celce-Murcia (2007)

teraction. This dimension assumes the understanding of three main variables: *social contextual factors* like the participants' age, gender, status, social distance and their relations to each other; *stylistic appropriateness* based on the ability to use politeness strategies, the right genres and registers; *cultural factors* such as the background knowledge of the target language group. *Linguistic competence* consists of the speaker's knowledge of the target language phonology, morphology, lexis and syntax and his ability to use this knowledge in producing linguistically correct utterances. *Formulaic competence*, on the other hand, is the knowledge of fixed prefabricated chunks of language characteristic for everyday interactions like routines (*all of a sudden, How do you do?*), collocations (*spend money, statistically significant*), idioms (*to kick the bucket*) and lexical frames (*See you + later/tomorrow/next week/etc.*). In the case of foreign language learning in lower primary context, formulas seem to be a highly desirable language items since they offer children longer sequences of words that sound communicative and usually serve some pragmatic goal.

Another dimension of Celce-Murcia's model is *interactional competence* which comprises actional competence (the knowledge of how to perform common speech acts); conversational competence (the knowledge of how to conduct a communicative exchange, how to open, close and take turns); non-verbal/paralinguistic competence (body language, silences, pauses). *Strategic competence* helps the speaker to enhance his performance and overcome obstacles to avoid communication breakdown. The most important strategies for this model are: cognitive (which help use logic to organize thought), metacognitive (used for planning), memory-related (which allow the speaker to retrieve the right language items from memory), achievement (involving among others approximation and code switching), stalling (used for taking time), self-monitoring (which involves repair), interacting (appealing for clarification or confirmation), social (based on active search for opportunities to use the target language). The central role in Celce-Murcia's model is, however, played by discourse competence defined as „the selection, sequencing and arrangement of words, structures and utterances to achieve a unified spoken message" (2007: 46) especially in the area of cohesion, coherence, deixis and generic structure.

Discourse analysis

Discourse analysis may be defined as the study of language in context above the level of a sentence. Due to this wide scope of interest, more recently van Dijk (2001) proposed to refer to this notion more appropriately as discourse studies, treating discourse analysis merely as a tool for data description. Discourse analysis is based on those details of speech that are relevant in the context and in the light of the arguments the analysis is attempting to make. Gee (2011: 9) makes a rather convenient distinction between what he sees as two broad types of approaches to discourse analysis: descriptive and critical. The aim of descriptive discourse analysis is to explain the ways in which language interactions are structures in a given context. Critical discourse analysis, on the other hand, is also involved in the social and political dimension of any interaction. Since classroom discourse is clearly happening in a context where power is distributed unevenly among the participants of any interaction, it seems reasonable to observe the exchanges between the students and the teacher from the latter perspective.

Critical Discourse Analysis (CDA) is an interdisciplinary approach defined by Blommaert and Bulcaen (2000) and Collins (2004) as „the study of the relationships between texts (spoken, written, multimodal, and digital), discourse practices (communicative events), and social practices (society-wide processes)" (53). In terms of EFL classrooms, as Kleifgen (2008: 226) points out, discourse analysis is useful as a tool that is concerned not so much with the amount of time devoted to the foreign language in any given lesson as with the purposes for which it was used by the participants of the discourse. CDA has been conducted in a variety of contexts in terms of social environments (afterschool programs – Rogers, 2002; home schooling – Young, 2000) and school subjects (science lessons – Moje, 1997; literature lessons – Hinchman and Young, 2001). Although the scope and interest of CDA has been wide and comprehensive, Rogers points out that 85% of the studies concerned middle school, high school and higher education and only 15% elementary school students and children below the age of ten (2008: 57).

As a qualitative method, discourse analysis makes the findings of research more available to those readers who are less skilled in drawing conclusions from sophisticated statistical tables. As Anne Lazaraton puts it, „the results from discourse analysis are *observable*, in the form of transcribed data fragments, even when one does not agree with the conclusions at which an analyst may arrive" (2008: 202).

Language socialisation

Language socialisation, on the other hand, is a developmental process of acquiring knowledge and skills enabling a child (or anyone who is entering a new environment) to take part in the social life of a given community. The crucial ability central to language socialisation is the communicative competence understood as the ability to use a particular language and culture norms in socially accepted ways (Garrett and Bequedaño-López, 2002). Thus, language socialisation research is the study of social interactions conducted with the use of language including the study of how such interactions influence the development of individuals and larger systems of cultural meaning and practice and how they change over time. As a developmental process, language socialisation deals not so much with the learning or even production of well-structured and grammatically correct utterances but rather with the actual use of language in „socially and pragmatically appropriate, locally meaningful ways, and as a means of engaging with others in the course of – indeed, in the construction of – everyday interactions and activities" (Garrett, 2008: 189).

Young learners seem to be especially sensitive to noticing the relations between particular language structures that exert certain impact on interlocutors at the social level. Ochs' study (1996), for example, has shown how Samoan children acquired affectively loaded linguistic structures before neutral ones. They are reported to learn a special personal pronoun indexing a plea which is a preferred way of request in Samoan before they learn its neutral counterpart. Similarly, the research has shown that they learn the ‚e' particle implying anger or irritation of the speaker in such speech acts as threats and warnings very early in their language development. In a bilingual context this feature is reflected in the use of codeswitching quoted in Chapter One in which Leopold's (1954) daughter constructs a bilingual request (*Papa wenn du das Licht ausmachst, then I will feel so lonely* - in Harding-Esch, 2003: 65) to please her father and thus increase her chances of achieving her aim. These findings may suggest that foreign language learners could develop similar features if offered optimal conditions for the use of the target language in real social situations in the classroom.

Garrett (2008) proposes a list of key features of research allowing for language socialisation analysis that include: (1) longitudinal study design, (2) field-based collection and analysis of data, (3) holistic perspective and (4) attention to both micro and macro levels of analysis. In longitudinal study design researchers gather information on developmental changes in individuals or groups by periodically observing and recording their language behaviour across a selection of communicative experiences. The extensive period of time over which the studies are conducted allows them to collect a substantial amount of naturalistic data often in the form of audio or audio-video recordings. A holistic, ethnographic perspective is achieved by considerable amount of fieldwork based on ethnographic observation on the one hand, and familiarity with current theoretical bases for such methods on the other. The researcher is informed not only by the observation of individual events but also by the entire contexts in which they are observed. While analysing the gathered data, researchers are constantly looking for patterns and principles that may be applied to the whole context.

4.2.2. The uniqueness of classroom interactions

In the early days of classroom language analysis, discourse in instructional settings was perceived as significantly different from the speech events observable outside the school context. Especially in the 1980s classroom discourse was defined in stark juxtaposition to ‚natural' conversation. The main areas in which this crucial difference was perceived, as summarised by Dalton-Puffer (2007: 18), were: (1) the distribution of the talk among the participants; (2) the way questions are asked and answered; (3) the tripartite structure of most exchanges; (4) the way in which participants take turns in speaking. Studies focusing on classroom interactions showed that the discourse is largely monopolized by the teacher whose utterances take up to two thirds of the discourse (Mehan, 1985). However, not only the time of speaking but also the ways in which language was used were argued to be different from those in everyday conversations. This view was presented, among others, by Stubbs (1983) and Brock (1986) cited in Dalton-Puffer (2007: 18), but it still remains an important aspect of classroom discourse. Thornbury (2000) points out that:

> language classrooms are *language* classrooms, and for the teacher to monopolise control of the discourse - through, for example, asking only display questions - while possibly appropriate to the culture of geography or maths classes, would seem to deny language learners access to what they most need - opportunities for real language use. (28).

While it may be true that such teacher controlled discourse is more appropriate for content subjects than foreign language classes (at least in the modern school), Thornbury's argument seems to miss the point in the case of content and language integrated lessons or simply parts of regular EFL classes when the focus is shifted from the form of the language used to the content knowledge of the topic being covered. These days, it is not uncommon to discuss issues of science or social studies with the main focus on the subject matter rather than language structures practiced during the interaction. While it is possible that at times the teacher monopolised interaction concerns a specific language point, it seems to be more of a feature of a classroom discourse back in the eighties than the modern classroom. Specifically, for the present study, it is rarely observable in lower primary EFL setting today. Due to largely limited linguistic proficiency of young learners it seems unreasonable to expect that interaction will be spontaneously initiated by the students to the extent which will allow them sufficient practice in foreign language comprehension and use. Additionally, when EFL is not a separate subject but language events are incorporated into everyday classroom practice (which consists of tasks relating to all subject areas including the ones mentioned by Thornbury), English is not the main point of the majority of linguistic exchanges. It occurs occasionally in the form of code switches whose functions are discussed later in this chapter.

The third difference identified by Dalton-Puffer, the one concerning the triadic structure of linguistic exchange, is assigned by the author to the study of Burton (1981) who focused in his research on the repetitive pattern of tripartite interaction in the classroom. Finally, the way in which participants of a classroom discourse take turns in the interaction is claimed to be different from the real life linguistic exchanges. This last feature merits further explanation. Due to the roles of the participants involved in a typical classroom discourse, there are two main communication patterns available. The exchange is either between the teacher and the students or it happens between/among students themselves. Since the context of this study is that of a foreign language classroom (as opposed to second language environment), it is reasonable to expect that the ratio between these two patterns will be unequal. Since all learners share the same first language, the use of the foreign language in spontaneous interaction is not a communicative necessity. Therefore the teacher as the one who leads the learners to achieve certain learning objectives within a lesson initiates a vast majority of interactions. As a consequence of this discourse structure, teacher-students interactions take the form described by Sinclair and Coulthard (1975) as the *Initiation - Response - Feedback (IRF)* pattern. In terms of discourse analysis these steps can be perceived as opening a conversation, responding to the initial cue and providing feedback respectively forming a tripartite chain referred to as *exchange*. The authors, then, propose a classification of all such exchanges into two groups: *boundary exchange* and *teaching exchange* the latter further divided according to specific communicative aims as presented in Figure 13.

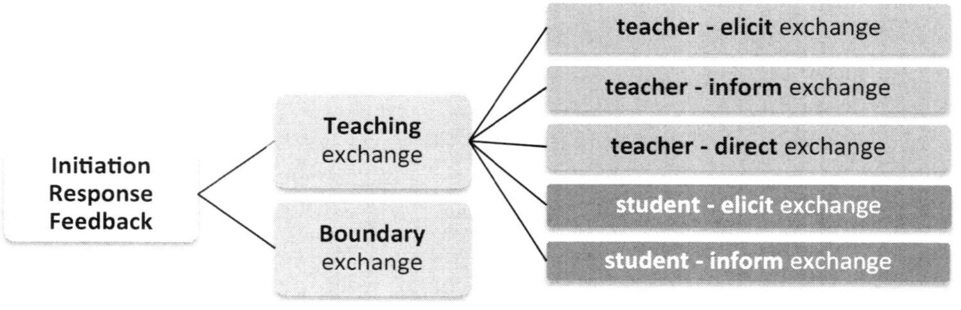

Figure 13. Sinclair and Coulthard's IRF model

Source: Based on Sinclair and Coulthard (1975)

Boundary exchanges announce the end or the beginning of a given stage of the lesson. They are typically announced by acts such as *right*, *good*, *okay*, and extra linguistically by an extended pause, and/or comments summarising the preceding or following discourse:

(1) **T:** right (.) now (.) last week we were looking at figurative language in poetry can anyone give me an example of what we mean by figurative language

(from Hardman et al., 2003: 211)

Teaching exchanges are further divided into five types: (I) *teacher-elicit*, whereby the teacher gets a student to provide a verbal response:

(2) **Teacher:** now when winter is over a new season will start do you know the name of the season?
Betty: January
Teacher: no, that's the name of the month what season will it be? after winter will be s---?
Betty: spring
Teacher: good girl springtime.
(from MacLure and French, 1980: 211)

(II) *teacher-inform* exchange in which the teacher provides an explanation that may or may not be followed by a student response:

(3) **T:** right so young people can be influenced by friends and we know that once you startsmoking it is very addictive as it is a drug and very hard to give up
(from MacLure and French, 1980: 210)

(III) *teacher-direct* exchange in which the teacher gets a student to perform an activity in response:

(4) **Sra. Soto:** [POINTING TO A BASKET ON THE FLOOR] ¿saben qué? este canasto, que está en el piso, por el espejo, ¿lo guardan también?
you know what? this basket, that is on the floor, in front of the mirror, will you put it away, too?
Sandra (English): [WALKS OVER TO THE BASKET AND PICKS IT UP]
Sra. Soto: Sandra, ponlos arriba del gabinete.
Sandra, put them on top of the cabinet
Sandra (English): [PLACES THE BASKET SHE JUST PICKED UP, ALONG WITH THE BASKET SHE ALREADY HAD IN HER HAND, ON TOP OF THE CABINET]
(from DePalma, 2010: 86)

(IV) *pupil-elicit* whereby a student asks a question usually targeted at the teacher and in which the teacher, if he is the addressee of the inquiry, always provides a response:

(5) **S:** can we have a seign of you?
T: seign=is it a signature
S: signature!

(from Dalton-Puffer, 2007: 195)

(V) *pupil-inform* exchange characterised by student offering an explanation which is typically commented on by the teacher:

(6) **T:** …What about this [GESTURES TO CLOTHING]
S: Clothes.
T: Clothes. Clothes.

(from Nunan, 1990; in Thornbury, 2007: 281)

The unequal power relations in this model are reflected in the lack of pupil-direct exchanges. Although both the student and the teacher are, according to the authors, allowed to produce elicit- and inform-type of exchanges, it is only the teacher who has the power to direct. In this model an exchange in which a student produces an utterance in consequence of which the teacher performs an activity is not present. However, such interactions are not uncommon. Direct exchanges initiated by pupils similar to example (7) may be observed in classroom situations.

(7) S: How do you spell it? Write this word on the board, please.
T: [WRITES THE WORD ON THE BOARD]

(own data from a traditional lower primary EFL lesson)

While it may be true that the IRF sequence as representative of classroom discourse may, as noted by Kasper and Rose (2001) limit learners' opportunities for interactional practice, the clear distinction between classroom interaction patterns and „natural conversation" is debatable. First of all, the perceived oddity of classroom discourse is based on its comparison with an abstract and rather elusive notion of everyday language. Such an approach, according to Dalton-Puffer, „firstly denies the very situatedness of language use itself and it also does not recognise pedagogic action as a legitimate kind of action that has its own specific determinants and requirements" (2007: 32). Secondly, such an approach assumes that there is only one model of real life communication that stands in striking contrast with the classroom interaction and vice versa, there is only one model of classroom discourse significantly differing from that of everyday speech. It seems more fair to acknowledge classroom discourse as one of many types of linguistic interactions happening in a social context. The situation in a typical foreign language classroom seems slightly different. Since both the students and the teacher share the same first language, there is no real communicative need to use foreign language to engage into conversations like (4) above. In this interaction, recorded in a two-way Spanish-English preschool context, the teacher instructs her student in Spanish to perform an activity (tidy up the classroom) although they can both speak English. This interaction, then, from the point of view of effectiveness of the task would probably benefit from being conducted in the student's L1 to avoid the risk of miscommunication. However, the main goal of this simple task is not to keep the classroom clean (although it adds reality to the exchange) but to practice comprehension of Spanish directives. This activity is done repeatedly in the course of the school year because of its pragmatic, extralinguistic dimension and children eagerly participate in it treating the task as a game. Although the use of L2 in a situation that is not a direct language instruction may seem unnatural, it is made real by having a pragmatic application.

In fact, teacher-students interactions often have pragmatic goals that is to say, language in an EFL classroom is not always used in order to introduce or practice lexical items or grammar structures. Teachers and students speak for a variety of reasons summarised by Walsh (2006: 67) in fourteen interactional features of classroom discourse presented in Table 4.

Table 4. Interactional features

Feature	Description
(A) Scaffolding	(1) Reformulation (rephrasing a learner's contribution) (2) Extension (extending a learner's contribution) (3) Modeling (correcting a learner's contribution)
(B) Direct repair	Correcting an error quickly and directly.
(C) Content feedback	Giving feedback to the message rather than the words used.
(D) Extended wait-time	Allowing sufficient time (several seconds) for students to respond or formulate a response.
(E) Referential questions	Genuine questions to which the teacher does not know the answer.
(F) Seeking clarification	(1) Teacher asks a student to clarify something the student has said (2) Students asks teacher to clarify something the teacher has said
(G) Confirmation checks	(1) Making sure that the teacher has correctly understood the learner's contribution (2) Making sure that the learner has correctly understood the teacher's instruction

Feature	Description
(H) Extended learner turn	Learner turn of more than one clause
(I) Teacher echo	(1) Teacher repeats a previous utterance (2) Teacher repeats a learner's contribution
(J) Teacher interruptions	Interrupting a learner's contribution.
(K) Extended teacher turn	Teacher turn of more than one clause
(L) Turn completion	Completing a learner's contribution for the learner
(M) Display questions	Asking questions to which the teacher knows the answer.
(N) Form-focused feedback	Giving feedback on the words used, not the message

Source: Adapted from Walsh (2006: 67).

4.2.3. Language behaviour in a language-rich lower primary classroom – an ethnographic approach

according to the core national curriculum, in Poland foreign language education is perceived as a continuous process of gradual building of competences throughout four stages of education. The context of the present study is an EFL classroom at the first stage of formal instruction (children aged 7-9) whose main goal is defined in the national curriculum as the development of spoken language understood as follows:

The main focus of foreign language education at this stage is listening comprehension and reacting to utterances as well as understanding of phrases, general sense of dialogues, stories and fairy tales. A student at the end of the first grade gradually develops his or her language awareness in the area of the foreign language as well as the mother tongue (National Curriculum, 2009: 68).

Apart from purely linguistic aims, foreign language education has to support general development of the learners by encouraging them to cooperate, creating friendly learning atmosphere and promoting physical development by introducing kinaesthetic activities.

The role of an EFL teacher, thus, goes far beyond a simple language instruction. The policy adopted by the core national curriculum is that in holistic education the teacher is more than an expert in his or her field, but rather an active participant in shaping the learners' overall competence in life skills. This seems especially important in the case of lower primary students who are just starting their adventure with education. All these specific goals need to be achieved in the process of language learning that takes place in the context of an EFL classroom.

Any language classroom is a speaking environment and, as such, merits analysis in the sphere of spoken interaction. The study of classroom discourse is concerned with the use of oral communication in educational processes. Since EFL classroom discourse is (or at least can be expected to be) characterized by the use of two different language codes, it is additionally interesting to see how they interact with each other and how they are used in response to particular communicative situations.

4.2.4. Research questions

A number of studies conducted in bilingual instruction have shown patterns of language use that differentiate those contexts from traditional EFL classrooms. Differences have been reported in the cases of bilingual English instruction in naturalistic settings (i.e. in contexts where English is one of the official languages used outside the classroom (cf. Toohey, 2000) as well as in formal educational settings where English is used (to varying degrees) as a medium of instruction in content and language integrated form. In the recent years there has been a considerable interest in the study of classroom discourse in the European contexts where additional language (typically English) is taught as a medium of instruction (e.g. Klieme, 2006; Falk, 2000; 2006; Nikula, 2007; Dalton-Puffer, 2008; Gassner and Maillat, 2006). However, a vast majority of research is conducted in lower and upper secondary level classrooms or even at the tertiary level of education. The few studies focusing on lower levels of formal education are conducted in specific context where education is structured in accordance with the British curriculum (García, 2008) or in naturalistic settings (DePalma, 2010).

In the Polish context research conducted in this field focuses mainly on the state of the art of bilingual education system (Marsh et al., 2008; Iluk, 2000) or has an evaluative character in terms of measureable test results (Kamińska, 2005) or students' and teachers' attitudes towards this approach (Roda-Sroka, 2010). As mentioned in Chapter One, the number of Polish schools where bilingual programs are implemented is rather unimpressive. Therefore, the studies conducted in this field are not only modest in number but also unequally distributed among all levels of education. In preschool education, some studies are conducted mainly due to a greater flexibility of curriculum (cf. Kamińska, 2005). Since bilingual education in Polish public schools is present almost exclusively at lower-, upper-secondary and tertiary level of education, there is little data from primary school and almost none from the lower primary sector.

Polish lower primary education, having an integrative structure, offers perfect conditions for implementing English into the existing system as one of the subject areas covered on everyday basis. If English is an element of classroom instruction and serves as a vehicle for subject content, it would be interesting to see how it is used in discourse. The present ethnographic study attempted to describe the elements of classroom discourse where English was used. The investigation addressed the following research questions.

(1) How is English used in relation to a whole day structure?
(2) What is the relationship between the context and language choice?
(3) What types of IRF exchanges predominate?
(4) What is the linguistic structure of these exchanges?
(5) What are the reasons for codeswitching?

Answers to these questions will attempt to provide a background for the interpretation of data and explanation of research findings in the next chapter dealing with quantitative analysis of results obtained in course of this study project.

4.2.5. Participants

The present study was conducted in a local public primary school in Łódź. The participants of the whole research consisted of (1) 23 students of a content and language integrated learning class (referred to as study group); (2) 23 students of a parallel class taught EFL as a separate subject (referred to as control group); (3) teachers of these students. Since the profiles of the participants differ significantly, they should be described separately in more detail.

(1) Study group

The study group consisted of 23 students coming mainly from the middle class backgrounds with no diagnosed educational problems who started their formal education on September 1, 2010. None of the students had any additional English classes and little or no contact with the language outside the school.

(2) Control group

The control group consisted of 23 students coming mainly from the middle class backgrounds with no diagnosed educational problems who started their formal education on September 1, 2010. Some of the students (8) were reported to have attended some sorts of English lessons (usually private tuition) for some time (at least one semester). Apart from that, they all had little or no contact with the target language outside the school.

(3) Teachers

The teacher of the study group holds two university degrees: a master's degree in education (five-year full time studies) and a bachelor's degree in English (three-year part time studies). At the time of the study, she has three-year experience in teaching in lower primary education and two-year experience in teaching English (as a separate subject) to young learners. She teaches her class in accordance with her own, officially approved, pedagogical innovation. She is the only teacher in her class (apart from religious education teacher). The teacher is responsible for delivering the lower primary education curriculum and the English curriculum binding for this stage of education. She uses *Nowe Już w Szkole*[3] as the leading course book (but very frequently supplemented by her own materials also prepared for the Interactive Whiteboard). She also uses *Bugs World*[4] for elements of English but only as a supplementary material and the content is not covered in the order it appears in the book but the topics are chosen by the teacher to suit the issues currently covered in the course of the lower primary curriculum.

The control group is taught by two separate teachers (and a religious education teacher). The English teacher holds a master's degree (five-year full time studies) in English and at the time of the study does not have much experience in teaching this age group (although she has taught English for many years both in Poland and abroad). She teaches English in all grades of lower primary education in this school and has two 45-minute lessons a week with the control group. She follows the official curriculum for EFL and uses *Bugs World* course book as the leading (and in fact the only) materials used in the lessons.

The other teacher is a very experienced graduate of five-year full time university studies holding a master's degree in education who has no competence in English. She follows the official early years curriculum and uses *Nowe Już w Szkole* as the leading course book (but very frequently supplemented by her own materials also prepared for the Interactive Whiteboard).

---

[3] Piotrowska et al. (1–2009, 2–2010, 3–2011) Nowa Era.

[4] Read, Soberón, *Bugs World* (1–2009, 2–2010, 3–2011) Macmillan.

In this part of the present research only the study group's discourse is observed and then analysed as an example of specific learning conditions.

4.2.6. Method and materials

This part of the present study was ethnographic in nature and consisted of a longitudinal non-participant observation of the study group from October 13, 2010 to January 13, 2013. The researcher observed the group once a week for four hours (60 minutes), which amounted to a total of 240 hours. The observations were video recorded and field notes were made. The recordings have been transcribed only in those fragments that contained data relevant for the present discussion. It is important to note that all day activities were observed and the scarce occurrences or English were marked. This is significantly different from observing specifically English lessons where English may be expected to be the predominant element of discourse as the focus is on its form and use. In the classes observed for this study there were long stretches of no English at all since they were not English lessons per se but general lower primary classes with occasional uses of the foreign language. Some of the samples retrieved from the recordings are representative of longer sequences of English use when the teacher planned for an activity to be conducted in English. Others are single utterances used for instruction or other communicative reason or represent spontaneous productions of the foreign language in otherwise Polish discourse. For the present discussion only the representative samples were selected when there were multiple examples of similar language use.

4.2.7. Data collection and qualitative analysis

The data collected in this study has been transcribed in fragments and given the following transcription conventions presented in Table 5.

Table 5. Transcription conventions

Symbol	Description
T	Teacher
S	Student

Symbol	Description
Sn	Marked as S1, S2, S3, etc. unique students in a given exchange and are not consistent across interactions
Ss	all or a group of learners in a choral response where it was impossible to identify the number of voices
[ ]	Additional information about the context
( )	non-verbal action described in the exchange
...	natural pause, anticipation of response, hesitation
(.)	unnatural pause, silence, waiting for response, searching for a word or plea for help
Bold	words appearing in English in the original context
Italics	translation of the of the parts of the discourse in Polish

Source: own elaboration.

Each excerpt is preceded by concise information about the condition in which it was recorded. The provided data include: grade (I, II or III in which a given behaviour was observed); subject area (the area of general curriculum covered within which a given behaviour was observed); topic (the topic of the day); context (the situation in which a given behaviour was observed).

The observed interactions were recorded and transcribed as speech events occurring within the matrix of an integrated subjects sequence of activities. It is important to remember that whenever English utterances appear in the exchange, they are not elements of an English lesson per se. Therefore, their structure is necessarily different from an EFL discourse where the focus is on the use of English and the attention is paid to the form and meaning in relation to students' L1. In other words, the following interactions were recorded in a general lower primary curriculum environment enriched by elements of English and <u>not</u> during EFL lessons. This distinction will be important from the perspective of the following discussion.

Lesson structure

One of the major features of the observed environment was the structure of a learning unit. In a traditional EFL teaching context, a learning unit is a 45-minute lesson conducted by an English teacher on a topic covered by following an EFL course book sequence. In the case of the observed class, a learning unit extended into the context of the whole day (or even a whole week) organised, in accordance with the lower primary curriculum, into topics involving activities from all areas of education. As a result, the teacher had to plan a coherent order of mathematical, social, science, reading and writing activities which were logically linked and included elements of arts and crafts, music and English. A typical structure of a day is presented in Figure 14 although alterations of the model caused by current requirements were not infrequent.

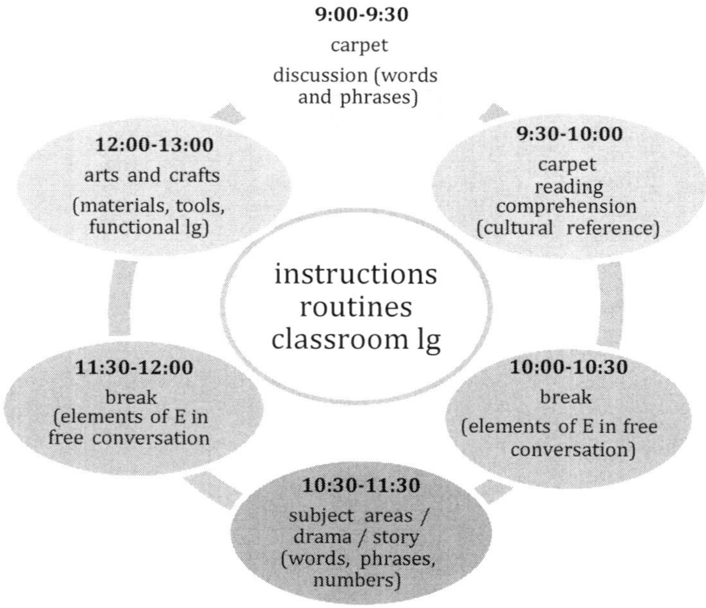

Figure 14. Typical lesson structure in the study group

Source: own elaboration

Elicit sequences

In a classroom context where teacher is in control of the communicative situation, his or her initial moves in the IRF model are necessarily more frequent than those made by the learners. Additionally, since the distribution of power and competence are unequal, the initial move in teacher-elicit exchange will most often be in the form of a question. Questions in the context of a (especially foreign language) classroom are, however, different from those asked in natural conversation. They may be classified in accordance with a number of dimensions, e.g.: range (display and referential) (Mehan 1979); goal (for facts, explanation, opinion, reasons and meta-cognitive) (Dalton-Puffer, 2007: 98); breadth (open, closed) (Barnes, 1969), function (procedural, convergent and divergent) (Brown, 1994).

Display questions are those to which the teacher already knows the answer, while referential questions encourage opinions or ideas that are not simple statements of facts and may not be easily anticipated by the teacher. Studies of EFL classroom interactions show, perhaps not surprisingly, that display questions largely predominate in the discourse. Shomoosi (2004) recorded 1335 display questions and merely 293 referential questions in his study of English teachers at a tertiary level of education in Teheran. These findings seem to support the earlier study by Brock (1986), in which the teachers observed asked 141 questions only 24 of which were referential. There is also a discussion over the definition of a closed versus open question. Dalton-Puffer (2007) maintains that closed questions are only the ones to which the answer is *yes* or *no* excluding form this category questions with limited choice of answers. The author states that "pre-defined sets of possible answers are hard to come by (…) apart from maybe a handful of meronyms such as the possible answers to the question *Which day of the week do you prefer?*" (97). In fact, however, in the lower primary EFL context a vast majority of questions have a limited choice of answers. The main reason for this is that young learners' lexicons contain only the items that have been presented to them in the classroom. The teacher can, therefore, easily predict the answers on the basis of the language previously taught.

(4.1)[5] [grade II; subject area: social education; topic: friendship; context: Ls talk about the characters in their set book – Winnie the Pooh]

1 T: to czego my się uczymy z tej historii?
what do we learn from this story?
2 S1: jak być przyjacielem
how to be a friend
3 T: właśnie jak być prawdziwym przyjacielem to teraz uwaga zaczniemy odDominisi what can you say about Winnie the Pooh (.) Winnie the Pooh is…?
exactly how to be a real friend so now we start from Dominisia
4 S2: silly

Although the question in move 3 could potentially be answered in many ways, S2 chooses the adjective that was ascribed to this character during text analysis (in L1) the previous day. A seemingly open question is, therefore, in fact very closed,

[5] If not indicated otherwise, all extracts come from own data gathered in course of the present study.

as there is only one answer possible (as expected by the teacher and as feasible in L2 on the part of the learner).

Another reason is that vocabulary is presented in pre-defined sets (domestic animals, fruit and vegetables, family members, etc.) each of which contains but a few lexical items. In a traditional lower primary EFL classroom students' responses will typically not go beyond these small sets. In content and language integrated contexts like the one observed in this study the range of items in the lexical sets may be larger and less predictable but still limited. It seems, therefore, that all questions assuming an answer that can be anticipated as coming from a limited set of possible responses should be considered closed. Open questions typically start with wh-question words and offer significant freedom of responses that are difficult or impossible to predict not in their content but in the choice of linguistic tools. Additionally, as observed by Cazden and Beck (2003: 177), teachers often expect a particular answer even if the question looks open.

Looking at classroom questions from the perspective of their function, at least at the lower primary level, their distribution seems unequal (Brown, 1994). *Procedural questions* (e.g. *Do you understand? Are you ready? Can you see the picture?*) dealing with class management and routines (and not with the content) are seen as helpful in managing the lesson rather than in supporting L2 development. *Convergent questions* elicit the material already taught and do not require higher levels of cognitive performance. They are used to promote simple interaction and involve students in the main theme of the lesson. They generate short responses and are used in the warm up sections of a lesson. *Divergent questions*, on the other hand, encourage learners to produce elaborate responses or at least longer utterances. They refer to learners' general knowledge and depend on cognitive abilities for drawing conclusions, evaluating and making analogies. These questions are used for developing more complex communication skills and allow students to add a personal element to the classroom discourse. In the context of lower primary EFL classroom convergent questions will most probably dominate teacher discourse. They are easier to manage and they generate little communicative risk. As they require no cognitive processing or personal input, the answers to convergent questions are more predictable.

The major disadvantages of classroom discourse dominated by convergent exchanges include little or no L2 processing, development of single word answers and low level of involvement. Procedural questions are frequently used in any low level EFL classroom and although Brown (1994) ascribes the merely managerial role, it seems that in the case of young learners they provide important (and repetitive) linguistic input. They offer ready-made utterances in the form of functional chunks that can be used by the learners imitating the teacher in suitable contexts. In other words it seems justified to treat procedural questions not only as a teacher's tool for class organization but also as a valuable source of linguistic input. Divergent questions are a rarity in lower primary education especially in contexts where the "L2 only" principle is applied. Young learners' linguistic abilities are insufficient to elaborate on issues requiring higher-level thinking. Due to this shortcoming young learners appear to be often perceived by their EFL teachers as incapable of conducting more complex cognitive processing. This belief that learners who cannot respond to questions calling for greater cognitive complexity in English are unable to do it altogether, seems to rule EFL teachers' perspective eliminating such opportunities for practice. As a result L1 discourse in lower primary classroom (where mainly divergent questions are asked with the aim of supporting general cognitive development) is significantly different from English lesson interactions. The following discussion of discourse examples recorded in the framework of the present study show the combined attitude of the lower primary and English teacher to the cognitive abilities of her students that is reflected in the way the interaction is structured.

Interaction patterns in the observed discourse bear close resemblance to any other classroom interaction in terms of the Initiation Response Feedback turn taking practice with extensive use of teacher elicit exchanges (excerpt 4.2). Most of the exchanges are initiated by the teacher who exerts control over the class. Due to the specific conditions in which EFL is taught in this class, however, the researcher has an opportunity to observe the learning process at a much wider scope than a single unit of a 45-minute English lesson. Since English is used in the classroom all day on daily basis, its occurrence is largely unpredictable even within activities belonging to the same subject area. While on one day multiple examples of English were recorded during reading activity, on another day the same type of activity involved few or no instances of its use. Similarly, it was not possible to determine which types of activities were more prone to attract English use (except stories and dramas which were meant to be staged in English on special occasions). Some instances of English occurrence were initiated by the students driven by the need to find out the name of a given object in the foreign language (excerpt 4.3).

(4.2) [grade I; subject area: drama; topic: fairy tales; context: L1 chooses a sticker from a set presented by T as a reward for participation]

1 T: wybierz sobie nalepeczkę (.) **what's this?**
choose a sticker

2 S1: **ladybird**
3 T: **ladybird**

(4.3) [grade I; subject area: science; topic: spring birds; context: T informs that Ls will hear sounds of birds and they need to recognize them]

1 T: posłuchamy teraz odgłosów ptaszków i będziemy zgadywać jakie to ptaszki wydają takie odgłosy. **ready**?
we'll now hear sounds of birds and we'll be guessing which birds make these sounds
2 Ss: **ready**!
3 CD: [SOUND OF STORK]
4 Ss: bocian!
stork
5 T: bardzo dobrze to jest klekot bociana.
well done this is a stork's clatter
6 S1: **and in English**?
7 T: **stork**
8 Ss: **stork**

The first part of interaction in excerpt (4.3) is an example of a teacher-direct exchange where the teacher is in control and dominates the discourse. The second part is similar to (4.2) but the roles of the learners and the teacher are opposite. While (4.2) is an example of teacher-elicit exchange, (4.3) in move 6 is a pupil-elicit exchange but both follow nearly identical IRF structure. In fact the learner initiating the exchange in moves 6-8 takes over control of the interaction by asking the exact same question as the teacher frequently uses in her teacher-elicit exchanges. This exchange is different also in the underlying reason for occurrence. It is typically the teacher who provides lexical elements when she decides they are useful. In this example the initiative is on the part of the learner who is curious to know the name of the bird that is being discussed in English. The word *stork* is not a typical element of the lower primary EFL curriculum and would not in all probability be explicitly taught by a teacher in the first grade were it not for the learner's interest. In the course of the observation many similar examples were recorded when some vocabulary was introduced not because it was planned in the English curriculum or presented in the English course book, but in response to immediate need and interest of the learners. Figure 15 shows yet another example of vocabulary enrichment motivated by students' genuine interest.

Figure 15. Students' initiated vocabulary enrichment

Source: own materials

Figure 15 illustrates a very characteristic feature of educational process in the observed classroom. The type of language introduced into the lesson is motivated by the topic of the day and students' interest rather than by the minimal requirements of EFL curriculum for this level. Names of flowers may not be included in a typical foreign language teaching program for grade I, but they appear in the general lower primary curriculum and there seems to be no reason why pupils should not be acquainted with them in L2.

While in excerpt (4.2) the reason for codeswitching is clear and is a part of classroom routine of asking pupils referential questions for them to provide lexical items in English, excerpt (4.3) is an example of role reversal when a student uses a form that is characteristic for the teacher for exactly the same purpose. Here the code switch may have been motivated by the rule of answering a question in the same code in which it was asked but it may just as well be a result of acquiring the question as a functional chunk through multiple exposition to the same structure used by the teacher in similar function.

Another interesting feature observed in the teacher-elicit exchanges is the length of pauses when T waits for response. She does not provide additional cues or translations but waits for the students to internalise her questions and respond accordingly (excerpt 4.4).

(4.4) [grade I; subject area: mathematics; topic: spring; context: Ls listen to a song on CD and answer questions by counting objects in the picture of a spring garden on theirworksheets]

1 CD: **how many flowers can you see? let's count together one, two, three** (.)
2 T: co teraz będziemy liczyć?
what are we going to count now?
3 Ss: **flowers**
4 T: **how many flowers can you see?**
5 Ss: (.) (.) (.) **six**
6 T: **how many?**
7 Ss: **six**
8 T: **let's check** [PLAYS THE CD]
9 CD: **six flowers**

The teacher waits for the students to make out the meaning from the context. She assumes that because the students know the content word and the rule of the task they should be able to comprehend her question. The extended pause could be expected to evoke pupils' requests for translation or indication of confusion, or urge the teacher to provide help (possibly in the form of translation). However, this excerpt was recorded in the second semester of the first grade and, thanks to the teacher's consistency, the students had not developed this habit. The code switch in this example is initiated by the learners who respond to the teacher's question in English taking the word from the recording directly preceding the question. The teacher continues the exchange in the language chosen by the students and does not return to L1 even in the face of possible communication breakdown.

Many teacher-elicit exchanges reveal the interest in the content of the utterance rather than its structure. While the sequence has a typical pattern, the learners' reactions concern the topic of the interaction rather than the linguistic form in which it was encoded (excerpts 4.5, 4.6).

(4.5) [grade I; subject area: mathematics; topic: spring; context: Ls listen to a song on CD and answer questions by counting objects in the picture of a spring garden on their worksheets]

1 CD: **how many suns can you see? let's count together one, two, three** (.)
2 S1: no **one sun**. wiadomo (.) przecież słońce jest jedno.
well, one sun that's clear (.) the sun is only one

(4.6) [grade I; subject area: social education; topic: days of the week; context: pupils revise names of the week in random order in Polish then the T decides to repeat the task in English]

1 T: **and what day is it today? do you remember?**
2 Ss: **Monday!**
3 T: **what's the next day after Monday?**
4 Ss: (.) **Tuesday**
5 T: **and after Thursday?**
6 Ss: **Friday!**
7 T: **and after Sunday?**
8 Ss:... **Monday!**
9 S1: a w niedzielę będzie **Sunday**
and on Sunday it will be

In these exchanges the teacher initiates an elicitation sequence, which is followed by the learners. However, the final comments in both examples suggest that the students' attention is drawn to the content of the utterances and not merely the fact that they are practicing English. The comment refers to the subject of the exchange rather than the lexical item. In excerpt (4.5) the context of S1's final comment is the solar system, content knowledge referring to science education covered a few weeks before. S1 is not only answering the listening comprehension question but displays a deeper analysis of the utterance expressing surprise that such an obvious question is asked. S1's reaction may imply that while listening to the recording the student is not so much focused on hearing the lexical items (*when I hear the name of an object, I have to find it on my worksheet and count*), but rather participates actively in the construction of meaning of the recorded task.

Teacher-elicit exchanges are also frequently used to raise pupils' awareness of language through analogies (excerpt 4.7) or to prompt learners to provide the required linguistic item not by translation but using riddles (excerpt 4.8) or body language (excerpt 4.9).

(4.7) [grade I; subject area: language; topic: winter; context: Ls read a story in their Polish course books about a bunny lost in the snow. One of the comprehension questions concerns the weather in the story]

1 T: króliczek się schował bo było mu…
the bunny hid because he was…
2 Ss: zimno
cold
3 T: no właśnie. Popatrzcie na ilustrację. **What's the weather like**?

Exactly. Look at the picture
4 Ss: **winter**
5 T: czy na pytanie **what's the weather like?** można odpowiedzieć 'zima'? jakie bym musiała zadać pytanie żebyście mogli powiedzieć że jest zima?
*can we answer the question **what's the weather like**, 'winter'? what question would I have to ask so that you could answer 'winter'?*
6 Ss: jaka jest pora roku
what's the season
7 T: a no właśnie a na obrazeczku jest właśnie… **in English** (.)?
exactly and in the picture it's…
8 S1: **snowing**
9 S2: **snowing** to jest że śnieg pada
means that it's snowing

(4.8) [grade I; subject area: science; topic: plants; context: Ls revise a topic ofgarden covered on the previous day, T elicits names of fruit and vegetables]
1 T: wczoraj rozmawialiśmy o ogrodach i na informatyce projektowaliście swój ogród dzieliliśmy też zbiory w **garden** na co?
yesterday we talked about gardens and on IT lesson you designed yourgardens we also divided the garden into what mathematical sets?
2 Ss: **fruit**, **vegetables** i **flowers** */and/*
3 T: rozmawialiśmy już dużo wcześniej o warzywach i wy różne warzywa jużznacie na przykład jakie warzywa znacie?
we talked much earlier about vegetables and you know various vegetables and fruit for example what vegetables do you know?
4 Ss: **lettuce**, **tomato** (.)
5 T: a takie długie z takimi wąsami?
and a long one with whiskers?
6 S1: **carrot**
7 T: **carrot** ale takie zielone długie
but a long green one
8 Ss: **leek**
9 T: a frytki się z tego robi?
and what are French fries made of?
10 Ss: **potato**
11 T: dobrze a jak się kroi to się płacze?
good, and when you peel it you cry?
12 Ss: **onion**
13 T: Weronika **what fruit do you like**?
14 S1: **I like strawberry**

(4.9) [grade I; subject area: language; topic: body parts; context: Students listen to a story on CD and look at story cards presented by the T, then T holds out story cards and tells the story herself]

1 T: **buzz, buzz, buzz. Is this a flower?** (.) [PUTS A PAPER BEE ON A NOSE IN THE STORY CARD]
2 Ss: **no!**
3 T: **no, it's my**... [POINTS AT HER NOSE]
4 Ss: **nose**
5 T: **it's my nose. buzz, buzz, buzz. Is this a flower**? (.) [PUTS A PAPER BEE ON AN EAR IN THE STORY CARD]
6 Ss: **no! ear!**
7 T: **it's**...
8 Ss: **it's my ear**
9 T: **it's my ear. buzz, buzz, buzz. Is this a flower?** (.) [PUTS A PAPER BEE ON AN EYE IN THE STORY CARD]
10 Ss: **no! eye!** (.) **It's my eye!**

Excerpt (4.7) is an example of teacher-elicit exchanges in which the teacher encourages learners to analyse the question-answer relation in a topic of weather and seasons. The focus of the interaction is on the use of language but the way of conducting this conversation is not typical of an EFL lesson where in all probability the teacher would present the difference in the questions by translating them into Polish. In this exchange students are asked to analyse the logical sequence of question and answer much like they would do in their first language interaction (as has been frequently observed in the study). Students are asked helpful questions which lead them gradually to analyse the issue in Polish but also in English. It seems that the interesting feature of this conversation is the fact that students analyse the logical relations between the questions and answers simultaneously in both languages.

Excerpt (4.8) starts with a boundary exchange where the teacher reminds her students about the previous topic which is followed by a revision of the already covered lexical areas. It seems that in this fragment of classroom discourse three unique elements are worth mentioning. First of all, the way the teacher offers cues is, again, characteristic for general lower primary education rather than EFL context. As a result the learners are practicing not only lexical retrieval of the L2 items (as they would if the task was based on the common EFL practice of translation) but also conduct a more complex cognitive operation of identifying a word on the basis of its description. Secondly, the words in the set are also not typical of a first grade English curriculum. Apart from the common ones like "potato" or "carrot", learners also have in their lexicon much less frequently taught at this level words like "lettuce" or "leek". The reason why these words occur in this exchange is that they were taught during an arts and crafts activity in which the pupils were creating figures made of different vegetables they had been asked to bring to school a few days before. Since learners' lexicons in this context are largely motivated by real need, the unusual choice of vegetable names in exchange (4.7) is a result of student initiated vocabulary enrichment in previous activities. Thirdly, the code switch in the final teacher-elicit sequence marking the end of the guessing game refers to a different set of vocabulary (fruit). Although it is a rather sudden change of both topic and function (from guessing to communicating), the learner indicated by the teacher has no problem with answering the question appropriately. Perhaps the learners already know that the teacher is not likely to translate her utterances in English and it is therefore important to focus more when she produces longer utterances. This fast and correct reaction may also be ascribed to well-developped automaticity of response in common recurring contexts. Whatever the reason, S1's response is an example of natural language use that is not so common in other classroom contexts.

Excerpt (4.9) is an example of involving children in a monolingual L2 discourse in the context of a story. Again, the way the activity is conducted by the teacher is characteristic of a corresponding task in L1 area of education. The children are encouraged to take part in the story telling by finishing lines provided by the teacher. In order to make this possible, the teacher offers them cues in the form of body language and gestures. The interesting element of this sequence is that the cues offered by the teacher are gradually reduced encouraging learners to produce ever longer utterances. The first time the structure occurs learners provide only one word which is repeated in the whole structure by the teacher. The second time the same phrase is needed, the teacher only starts the line for the pupils to complete. The third time she waits until the complete utterance is produced. By the third time the learners are familiar with the structure and correctly interpret teacher's silence as an invitation for a full response.

The basic goal of foreign language learning, according to the Polish national curriculum for lower primary education, is the ability to communicate effectively in the foreign language both orally and in writing. The emphasis is, therefore, on teaching "the skills of reaching a variety of communicative goals while linguistic accuracy, though they play an important role, is not the main teaching objective" (2009: 61). In order to achieve this aim all classroom practices should support very basic communication. In the observed context the learners are allowed to conduct a communicative activity in a way that does not perfectly reflect the model as long as they can understand each other. Although it is a common practice based on a communicative language teaching principle, it is rarely observed in lower primary classroom where communicative tasks (pair work, group work, interviews, surveys, etc.) are generally avoided as too noisy and difficult to manage. Excerpt 4.10 is an example of such an activity conducted in the first grade.

(4.10) [grade I; subject area: science; topic: fruit and vegetables; context: students are given worksheets with pictures of various fruit and vegetables and two columns "I" and "my friend".They are asked to complete the first column with happy or sad faces in reaction to the question "Do you like…?"]

1 T: **ok,** Wiktor **do you like grapes**?
2 S1: **yes**
3 T: **yes, I do**
4 S1: **yes I do**
5 T: Zuzia **do you like tomatoes**?
6 S2: **yes**, (.) **I do**
7 T: Patrycja **do you like leek**?
8 S3: (.) a jak **no** to co się mówi?
and if no then what do you say?
9 T: **no, I do not**
10 S3: n**o, I do not**
11 T: Michalina **do you like onions**?
12 S4: **no**, (.) **I do not**

(4.11) [subject area: science; topic: fruit and vegetables; context: students walk around the classroom and try to find other students who like and do not like each of the items on the list and complete the second column of the worksheet]

1 S1: **do you like strawberries**?
2 S2: **yes, I** (.) [L1 DRAWS A HAPPY FACE ON HIS SHEET] **Yes**.
3 S3: **do you like potatoes**?
4 S4: **no**.

In the first part of this activity the teacher makes sure that the learners know how to answer the question. In sequence (4.10) again the pauses are used with no additional cues for the learners to come up with a structure required by the teacher. In this case they are practicing short answers in present simple in the first person, a structure that can be expected in very basic communication at lower primary level. The teacher starts by asking a closed question, which is followed by a natural response. In move 3 the teacher repairs the learner's response and gives a model of a short answer, which is echoed by the learner. In other words in moves 1–4 she is teaching the structure of short answer to the question "Do you like x". In move 5 the teacher turns to the next student with the same question which is again answered in the natural way but a prolonged pause is used to give the learner time to self-repair, which she finally does in move 6. An interesting thing happens in move 8 where the learner appeals for help switching to L1. The code switch is motivated by the learner's desire to answer the question truthfully. This may suggest that for the learner this activity is not a grammar drill but she perceives the teacher as genuinely interested in the learners' preferences. Such interpretation may be supported by the use of "no" as an intrasentential code switch. The correct form is provided by the teacher and again echoed by the learner. The next student asked is expected to have paid attention and to be able to produce a grammatically correct response. The excerpt finishes with move 12 but the activity went on until all students gave their answers, all of which were grammatically correct.

This element of the lesson may be perceived as controlled practice where attention was paid to the form of the language used. It was immediately followed by sequence (4.11), which was planned as a communicative activity often referred to as *Find someone who...* which allows students to communicate in a context resembling real life. It is interesting to see that confronted with a communicative opportunity, students regress in terms of grammaticality of their answers. In move 2 the learner makes an attempt to recall the structure but fails and gives up. Other students rely on *yes/no* answers throughout the whole activity. A closer look at this interaction, however, reveals a mechanism that allows for perceiving it not as a failure but as strategy. Although S1 knew that she should say something more than just *yes*, this answer resulted in a correct reaction on the part of her interlocutor meaning that the communicative aim has been achieved. It also needs to be mentioned that the learners liked the activity very much and were on task at all times clearly enjoying the fact they could make themselves understood. If the simple answers worked, there was no need to elaborate on them. In all probability the answers in the form the learners provided would also have been understood in an L2 context. The teacher did not interrupt the activity, although she clearly wanted the learners to acquire the short answers in their correct form. The communicative value of this task was, however, more important to her than accuracy. Such an attitude seems to be more beneficial for the students that commonly observed teacher behaviour like in the excerpt (4.12) (data from Majer, 2003: 385).

(4.12) 1S: **my mum and my sister watching** "Klan" **all the time but it's too -** jak jest "nudny"?

how do you say boring?

2 T: **ask in English, please**.

3 S: **how to say** "nudny"?
boring

4 T: **no. say what is** "nudny" **in English, OK**?
boring

5 S: **what is** "nudny" **in English?**
boring

In this sequence the teacher reacts to an appeal for help with a request for an English form, an element of classroom language that can be also used as a strategy against communicative breakdown in a real life situation. By asking the learner to formulate his appeal in the target language the teacher might want to point out that a code switch to the student's L1 would not be helpful in a situation where the only common language among the interlocutors is English. However, the learner's reformulation in move 3 does not meet with acceptance on the part of the teacher, although it seems perfectly fine in the present context and not much different from what the teacher proposes in move 4. The artificial aspect of the teacher's repair seems to be the fact that in this particular context (or any other where at least one interlocutor was able to understand and translate the required word), the learner's initial question would be understood and would not lead to communicative breakdown. In a natural context, however, neither the learner's appeal in move 3, nor the teacher's repair would be effective.

Similarly, a tendency to use metalanguage in classroom communication is not effective in real life situations. Such a linguistic behaviour is characteristic of higher levels of education where students are expected to understand the underlying structure of the utterances. Authenticity of such exchanges as presented below is, however, questionable.

(4.13) T zaproponujcie komuś tą konstrukcją si plus imparfait zwiedzanie Paryża
use the si *plus* imparfait *construction to suggest sightseeing of Paris to somebody*

S **et si on visitait Paris?**
how about sightseeing Paris?

(data from Piotrowski, 2011: 224)

Although the elicited structure is a functional phrase, the teacher instruction evoking the response is neither likely in authentic communicative context nor possible at lower primary level where students' metalinguistic knowledge in their L1 is inadequate for such a task.

Excerpt (4.11) showed that a grammar structure was not immediately internalized by the learners to be transferred onto a communicative task. However, on many occasions it was observed that certain grammar features became acquired very quickly and efficiently. Excerpt (4.14) is an example of practicing the third person singular -s in the context of a follow-up activity of talking about food preferences of other students.

(4.14) [grade I; subject area: science; topic: fruit and vegetables; context: studentscome back to the carpet with completed worksheets and are asked to comment on their findings by answering teacher's questions]

1 T: mówiliśmy o sobie **I like apples**. Zuzia, **what fruit do you like**?
we've talked about ourselves

2 S1: **I like grapes**

3 T: świetnie, a teraz będziemy mówić o koleżance, koledze. **My friend likes apples**. Gabrysia zaczyna.
great, and now we'll talk about a friend Gabrysia starts

4 S1: **my friend likes strawberries**

5 S2: **my friend likes carrots**

In this sequence the teacher contrasts the verb in the first person singular with the third. This is typically done explicitly with the teacher drawing student's attention to the final -s in the verb. In this example in move 1 the teachers reminds the learners about the structure they have already practiced for some time but the focus is not on the form but on the content. She asks a referential question to confirm that students are able to answer it correctly and introduces a new structure that will be used to talk about the information they have just collected. Although the teacher provides the model in move 3, she makes no attempt to stress the grammatical feature of the utterance. Nevertheless, the student in move 4, and all the other students after her, produce perfectly correct sentences and none of them makes the common mistake of omitting third person -s. This observation is in line with the findings of Dalton-Puffer (2007) who noted that even the youngest learners in CLIL classrooms seemed to have no problems with the third person -s. The researcher is, hence, "inclined to speculate that in the case of the third person -s the increased exposure does indeed lead to the necessary degree of enrichment which brings about automatization of this notorious inflectional marker" (285). Although the extent of exposition and amount of input are not to be underestimated, since it is not only the quantity of language but also its quality that makes a difference, it would be justified to ascribe the better attainment of this grammatical feature to the shift of focus from form to meaning. Perhaps for the students it is much more meaningful to associate the whole verb *likes* with a friend and *like* with themselves than to internalize an abstract general grammatical rule of a foreign language they have just started to learn.

Inform sequences

Teacher-inform sequences typically take the form of mini lectures. In lower primary EFL context these longer passages of teacher talk cannot be conducted in L2 due to limited command of the foreign language and cognitive abilities of the children. If these monologues constitute a part of instruction, they are unproductive (cf. 4.21 below) and thus usually followed by immediate translation. In the context of lower primary EFL practice, longer passages of teacher talk are characteristic for storytelling, which, as discussed above, tends to contain language beyond the current level of the learners but is made clear enough by the context for the learners to follow the plot. Since the observed context is not an EFL lesson but a general lower primary class, the longer teacher-inform sequences are typically rendered in L1. If the topic of the utterance is connected with L2 in terms of vocabulary the teacher plans to introduce bilingually or revise a new functional structure to be practiced in L2, or is culturally relevant, the teacher inserts elements of L2 into L1 matrix as presented in excerpt (4.15).

(4.15) [grade I; subject area: arts and crafts; topic: Easter; context: students aregetting ready to make an Easter basket]

1 T: dostaniesz na ławeczkę szablony i można je wykorzystać żeby ozdobić nasz **basket** możesz wyciąć **Easter bunny** możesz zrobić z **Easter eggs** może być z **hen** może byćw ogóle sam wiosenny czyli z **butterfly.**
you'll get stencils and they may be used to garnish our… you may cut out… you may make… it may be with…it may as well be only spring [basket] so with …

Excerpt (4.15) is an example of teacher multiple intrasenetntial codeswitching sometimes referred to as code mixing defined as switched talk in the EFL classroom that is less predictable and unstructured (Majer, 2003: 405) and perceived as having a negative effect on language learning. While this may be the case in EFL classrooms where English is taught as a separate subject twice a week or in contexts where the learners are either older or at a higher level of L2 proficiency, it seems to be unfair in the case of partially bilingual learning environments as the one discussed in the present longitudinal study.

Majer (2003: 406) quotes a boundary exchange adapted from Brzostek (1994) as a negative example of classroom talk presented in (4.16).

(4.16) T: mówiliśmy o naszym **apartment**. powiemy sobie o innychpomieszczeniach, które mogą się w tym **apartment** znajdować. **for example it's a bedroom**. taki mały, ale **bedroom**. [...] **so what's it like**? nowoczesneczy nie?
we talked about our... let's talk about some other rooms that can be found in this... so tiny but a...modern or not

The above extract was recorded in a typical EFL classroom which, additionally, in all probability was not in lower primary context (since the data had been collected before obligatory EFL education was introduced in this sector). While there are obviously justified reasons to comply with the "L2 only" policy in language classes that are taught only a few times a week for forty five minutes to maximize students exposure to the foreign language, it is not applicable to the studied context where English is an element of everyday teaching practice. It seems that research is mainly conducted in the former contexts and thus the conclusions referring to the negative effects of language mixing are endemic to such context and not transferable to content and language integrated teaching at lower primary level of education. The most striking difference between those two contexts is that of matrix versus embedded language ratios. While traditional EFL lesson aims at providing as much L2 input and practice as possible and as a result creates an English matrix with only occasional relapses to L1, the context observed in this longitudinal study does the exact opposite, i.e. introduces situationally motivated elements of L2 into the otherwise Polish matrix. Additionally the major aims are different.

The classical EFL lesson focuses on teaching particular lexical element and structures that happen to be present in the leading course book, whereas in the studied context the elements of English teaching are motivated by the more general lower primary curriculum whose aims are superior to those in the EFL curriculum. In the case of mixed teacher talk in a typical EFL classroom, the instances of Polish are treated as unnecessary as they deprive the students of an opportunity for comprehension or exposure to new language. In terms of the studied discourse the embedded lexemes or phrases of English are valued as elements of vocabulary revision. In (4.15) above all the words used by the teacher in English are familiar to the learners at that level in this particular discourse. Should the teacher apply the “L2 only” practice, the learners would not be able to understand the instruction not only because the level of L2 would be far beyond their current command of English but also because of their insufficient cognitive development and familiarity with classroom practices at the outset of formal education.

Procedures like the one in (4.15), are also described in detail to the learners in activities that are not connected with L2 at all. It seems that the insertion of a few L2 items into the instruction is highly beneficial to the learners who relate the words heard with the actual objects and thus revise the vocabulary without resorting to translation. As a result of such practices, the observed pupils do not ever ask for immediate translation but rather conduct deeper analysis of the teacher’s utterances and take communicative risks to check their hypotheses much as second language learners do in naturalistic contexts.

Similar switched utterances can be found in the learners’ language as shown in excerpt (4.17).

(4.17) [grade I; subject area: ICT; topic: story; context: Ls draw in Paint a scene from a movie seen the other day]

1 T: **what is your picture**?

2 S1: to jest scena jak wodnik uwięził chłopca w jeziorze a w tym jeziorze pływają **fish**
*this is a scene in which the aquarius imprisons a boy in the lake and in this lake **fish** swim*

3 S2: na moim obrazku jest **sunny** i latają **birds**
*in my picture it is… and **birds** are flying*

4 T: **what can we see in your picture?**

5 S3: jak **fish swim** i jak chłopiec jest w morzu
when… and when the boy is in the sea

In this example S1 identifies the teacher’s question in L2 as an invitation to give an answer in the same language. In natural bilingual interaction move 1 would trigger a code-switch from Polish into English at least for one question-response dyad. The learners, however, are in grade I and their command of L2 is minimal after one month of language education. The pupils are not able to sustain the conversation in L2 but are eager to show that they have understood the questions (which is not at all obvious at this level of L2 education in a traditional model) and can use at least some elements of English that they remember from the previous classes. The switch from Polish into L2 in the case of the learners is motivated by their eagerness to practice and use in a meaningful context the language they have already acquired. This may suggest that the learners are aware of their learning process and make conscious decisions to take communicative risk in using words from newly emerging lexicons.

In order to facilitate the need for practicing language used in real life situations, the teacher provides her students with materials that support learning in context. This policy is also applied to assessment. Figure 16 presents a short test checking the understanding of rules for crossing the street safely.

Ponumeruj zdania zgodnie z czynnościami jakie musisz wykonać zanim przejdziesz przez jezdnię

_____ Look left!
_____ Stop!
_____ Look right!
_____ Go!
_____ Look left!

Figure 16. A short test checking the understanding of road safety rules in grade I

Source: own elaboration

In the test above the students are required to number the activities they do before crossing the street. It refers directly to the topic of the week "road safety" and constitutes an integral part of the integrated subjects curriculum.

An interesting feature of bilingual utterances is observed in learner-inform sequences where the interaction is not between the teacher and her pupils but among the students themselves. While the extract (4.14) above exemplifies the learners' acquisition of the third person singular -s form, (4.18) and (4.19) present sequences which reflect the correct use of plural -s in pupils' utterances where the plural forms are single embedded items.

(4.18) [grade I; subject area: language; topic: body parts; context: T gives out prompts]

1 T: kto miał te obrazki trzymać?
who was supposed to hold these pictures?

2 S1: ja miałam **girl**
I had a…

3 S2: właśnie tu widziałam jakieś **girls**
I just saw here some…

(4.19) [grade II; subject area: culture; topic: Easter egg hunt; context: students are looking for chocolate eggs in the school yard]

1 S1: znalazłam jajko
I found an egg

2 S2: znalazłam drugie już mam **three eggs**
I found another one, I've got..

3 S3: a ja mam **four**!
and I've got…

It is fairly easy to identify the reasons for codeswitching in each move of the above utterances. In excerpt (4.18) the occurrence of English lexeme in move 2 is motivated by its belonging to the L2 context as a prompt in an English performance to be staged. The use of the word "girl" at the end of S1's statement could trigger a switch in S2's contribution but her level of English does not allow for a full change of code. To follow the rule she goes on speaking L1 until she meets an element that she can utter in English and she does so at the same time correctly adjusting the number. This adjustment may suggest that S2 is not merely repeating S1's L2 contribution but analyses the matrix language syntax and changes the word accordingly. A similar mechanism is observed in (4.19) in move 2 where the adjustment may be supported by the earlier code switch. The noun is thus adjusted in number to the immediately preceding numeral also in L2. This code switch in turns triggers L2 utterance in move 3 again in the first possible position (when the English word is known and readily accessible at the moment of speaking).

Pupil-inform exchanges gain more elaborate forms with time. In the studied context the inserted utterances become longer when the learners gain competence. In accordance with the national core curriculum for languages in lower primary education, the observed teacher introduces songs and rhymes that children learn by heart just as they do in L1 in general primary education. This feature of classroom practice frequently present in this context is hardly ever observed in a traditional lower primary EFL classroom (typically due to the lack of time to cover all the material in a very limited period). The integrated curriculum in accordance to which the observed teacher is working stressed the need for cultural education. Since cultural diversity is promoted in the core curriculum it is introduced in the context of both Poland and English speaking countries and their traditions. The observed class is the only one of this kind in the school and treated as a linguistically but also culturally enriched environment. Hence, the learners were often encouraged to share their knowledge with the rest of the pupils during mini lectures or performances. Excerpt (4.20) comes from a recording made on the 31st of October 2012 and exemplifies a longer sequence of pupils production in L2.

(4.20) [grade III; subject area: social education; topic: Halloween; context: Ls give a performance for younger]

1 S1: **October thirty first is Halloween. on this day children in Britain and in the USA dress up as witches** /witʃez/ **and ghosts**

2 S2: **in the evening children go out in groups** /graʊps/ **and knock** /knɔk/ **to people's door. the children shout out 'trick or treat'**

3 Ss: **trick or treat, trick or treat give us something nice to eat**!

While it is obvious that the learners recited the above passages from memory, the length of the remembered passages is still worth acknowledging. The produced utterances are imperfect in terms of pronunciation but they are still impressive considering the fact that the learners have constructed the text together with only minimal teacher support. The fact that the learners could decide themselves on the content of their utterances based on a cultural mini-lecture delivered by the teacher and exchange of information among the pupils in L1 resulted in higher motivation and effective performance. If the words used in the text were less familiar for the students, it would be more difficult for them to retrieve them from memory and thus recite the text fluently. It seems justified to conclude that the performance was effective because the passages uttered were meaningful for the learners.

Direct sequences

Direct sequences initiated by the teacher's instructions for an activity are often followed by confirmation check. To avoid confusion and risk of misunderstanding teachers elicit feedback on the comprehension of the instruction. Such an interaction is natural in real-life communication when the speakers contributions are then reformulated by the interlocutors to confirm their meaning (*Do you mean to say that…*, *If I understand you correctly*, etc.). However, in a foreign language classroom this type of interaction is rather artificial and does not seem to fulfil its aim. The sequence (4.21) is an example of a very commonly used practice.

(4.21)

1 T: **and now have a look at these three questions, please. read the passage to yourselves and try to answer these questions. we've answered one and I would like you to answer what is the story about and when did it happen OK so what do you have to do** Maciek

2 S1: [SMILES]

3 T: **say something** cokolwiek co masz zrobić

anything what are you supposed to do

4 S1: [INAUDIBLE]

5 T: **you have to read the passage**

6 S1: to znaczy ja mam odpowiedzieć tak?
That means I'm supposed to answer right?

7 T: **mmhm read the passage first no read the passage**

8 S1: [INAUDIBLE]

9 T: [TO S2] **yes can you say it** Kasia

10 S2: mamy przeczytać tekst i odpowiedzieć na ten dialog
we are supposed to read the passage and answer [the questions on] that dialogue

11 T: **can you try and say it in English**

12 S2: **we have uh read this text and we have answer uh the questions**

13 T: **good perfect good so go on two minutes to read the passage and get the answers**

(data from Majer, 1998)

Obviously interaction (4.21) takes place at a higher level of education but it perfectly illustrates the problem with comprehension check in an EFL classroom. There seem to be a few reasons for this sequence to be of questionable communicative value. First of all, turn 1 which is a teacher-direct exchange, seems to be far too long and complex for at least some of the students to comprehend. The context of the utterance, on the other hand, is clear since it can be inferred that the students are all looking at a text (which they have probably read or listened to once) and they have already answered one of the comprehension questions. For a learner who is experienced in classroom practices the next task is obvious from the context. In fact, the pupil in turn 6 correctly identifies the task. Secondly, the teacher's comprehension check at the end of turn 1 has little chance of genuine success. What is it that the teacher expects the learner to say? Perhaps to satisfy the teacher the learner should repeat her instruction word for word. This however, would not check whether he understands the task. Additionally, such an answer would be rather unnatural in real-life communication. In EFL classroom this type of exchange appeals for translation, which in this example is rendered in turn 10. However, this does not satisfy the teacher, who requires L2 to translate the utterance back to English i.e. to repeat the initial instruction. Although it is obviously important for the teacher to make sure her instructions are understood and followed, it seems reasonable, sometimes at least, to trust learners' procedural experience, simplify the instructions or provide models, rather than resort to direct comprehension check questions.

A similar problem with overusing directness in comprehension check exchanges is often observed in the context of lower primary EFL classrooms. Extract (4.22) is an example of a frequent behaviour in teaching vocabulary to young learners.

(4.22)
1 T: [vocabulary revision; teacher shows a picture of a sheep] **what's this**?
2 Ss: **sheep**
3 T: **sheep** czyli co…?
which is…?
4 Ss: owieczka
s heep
5 T: [SHOWS A PICTURE OF A DUCK] **what's this**?
6 Ss: **duck**
7 T: czyli po polsku…?
so in Polish
8Ss: kaczka
duck

(own data from a traditional lower primary EFL lesson)

In this excerpt the teacher elicits translation, even though the learners correctly recognise the animals in the pictures. It seems obvious that in both turn 2 and 6 children's knowledge of the required vocabulary is checked and no additional moves are necessary. The appeal for translation would be justified if the children were acquiring the words in both languages simultaneously. However, in the case of seven-year olds it may well be assumed that they can recognize domestic animals and provide their names in L1. An additional potential disadvantage of such sequences seems to lie in the habit formation of obligatory translation. Initially, the learners provide L2 word in response to visual stimulus but constant encouragement for translation may develop a retrieval process necessarily involving the medium of L1. The policy of providing learners with pictures and translation at the same time can be often observed in students' notes. Figure 17 presents two different approaches to vocabulary development in the same lexical area. The first photo was taken in a traditional English lesson while the other was recorded in the observed context. Both sets of notes were made on the same topic of "nature" although the first lesson was conducted in October and the other one in March.

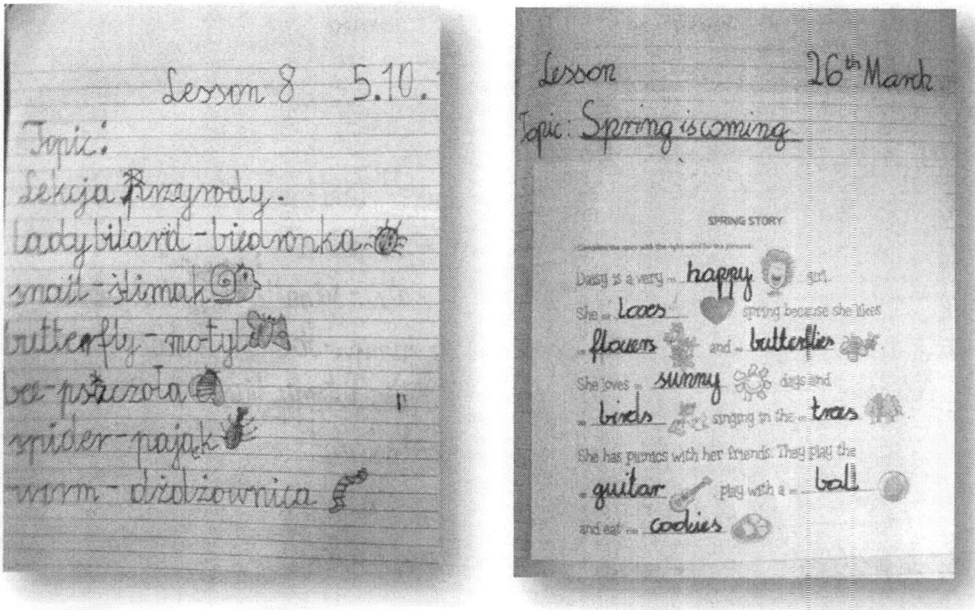

Figure 17. Vocabulary enrichment in traditional versus observed context

Source: own materials

While the notes made in the traditional context reflect the approach presented in excerpt (4.22) providing immediate translation for each word, the task completed in the observed classroom offers more varied vocabulary in a language rich context without any translations.

In the present study neither Polish-English picture dictionaries were made nor comprehension check sequences, like in excerpt (4.21) or (4.22) were observed. Instead, teacher direct exchanges were offered in the form of providing model reactions, which were often elicited from the learners (4.23).

(4.23) [grade I; subject area: social education; topic: Easter; context: students sit on the carpet in a circle, teacher holds a bowl of cross buns]

1 T: zrobiłam dla was takie specjalne tradycyjne angielskie bułeczki. one się nazywają **cross buns** bo mają tu taki **cross** [SHOWS THE SIGN ON THE ROLL] i w Anglii piecze się je specjalnie **for Easter**.
I've made for you special English rolls. They are called cross buns because they have a cross here and in England they are baked specially for Easter

2 S1: będziemy je jeść?
Are we going to eat them?

3 T: tak tylko musicie ładnie poprosić. Ja puszczę tę miseczkę w koło a wy będziecie prosić kolegę lub koleżankę… jak?
yes, only you have to ask for them nicely. I'll let this bowl go round and you'll ask your friend… how?

4 S2: **can I have a** (.)

5 T: **cross bun**

6 S2: **can I have a cross bun, please**?

7 T: super i potem będziemy koleżance lub koledze oferować **crossbun**… jak? *great, and then we'll offer our friend a crossbun… how?*

8 Ss: **here you are.**

9 T: no właśnie i jeszcze na koniec wypadałoby podziękować…
right, and finally it would be nice to thank…

10 Ss: **thank you**

11 T: **0k, so are you ready**?

12 Ss: **ready**!

13 T: no to zaczynamy od Juleczki
so we start from Julia

This excerpt starts with a teacher-inform exchange with a cultural content. The context makes it clear what the following task will involve, which S1 identifies correctly in move 2. The teacher encourages the learners to produce formulas they already know by associating them with particular elements of a typical sequence of moves in such a context. It is worth noticing that each time (moves 3, 7 and 9) the teacher refers to the function of the required phrase (*ask*, *offer* and *thank*), not the exact words to use. Once the procedure is agreed upon, everything is clear and the teacher only checks whether the students are ready. It is important to remember that all the interactions in the observed context are not fragments of EFL lessons where L1 is overused, but general lower primary education in which L2 is used very frequently. As a result there is no reason to pretend that L1 does not exist, as it is often the case in EFL classes following the "L2 only" principle. The instructions are, therefore, made clear by the use of L1 and L2 model ensuring a more relaxed atmosphere and higher motivation to participate in tasks whose rules are clear.

One of the most characteristic features of teacher-direct exchanges in the observed context is that teacher's instructions are not translated. Lack of translation in the case of these exchanges just like in teacher-elicit sequences provides the learners with meaningful input and supports cognitive processing skills. In typical EFL lower primary classrooms English directions are immediately followed by their translations (4.24).

(4.24)

T: **open you books on page seven**. otwórzcie książeczki na stronie siódmej.
open you books on page seven
look at exercise one. spójrzcie na ćwiczenie pierwsze.
look at exercise one.
listen and number. posłuchaj i ponumeruj.
listen and number
będziemy słuchać nagrania i wpisywać cyferki.
we are going to listen to the recording and write in numbers
are you ready? wszyscy gotowi?
is everybody ready?

(own data from a traditional lower primary EFL lesson)

Constant translation seems to be counterproductive in L2 development. Pupils quickly learn that there is no point in focusing on the teacher's instructions in English because they are always translated so the strategy is to wait for input that will require less effort to process. Even though such instructions belong to the procedural part of the lesson, it is a shame to waste an opportunity for real communication need. In the observed classroom the instructions, in a vast majority of cases are not translated and their effectiveness relies on the students' ability to interpret them in the light of the context and the little linguistic competence they already have. Such a policy is observed both in the case of procedural instructions (4.25) and inter activity directions (4.26).

(4.25) [grade II; subject area: science; topic: Space; context: students have revised the names of objects in space and are going to do a listening matching task in their English workbooks]

1 T: **open your workbooks on page thirty three**.
2 S1: [ASIDE] **workbooks** czyli ta [TAKES OUT HIS WORKBOOK]
so this one
3 T: [TO S2] dlaczego jeszcze nie masz książeczek na ławce?
why haven't you got your books on the table yet?
4 S3: która strona?
which page?
5 T: **thirty three**

(4.25) [grade I; subject area: mathematics; topic: birds; context: students are doing a task in their mathematical course books]

1 T: ile mamy ptaszków?
how many birds have we got?

2 Ls: siedem
seven
3 T: **seven**. to policzmy je
let's count them
4 Ls: **one, two, three, four, five, six, seven**
5 T: teraz mamy inne polecenie: pokoloruj ptaszki oznaczone numerami **three, five, seven.**
now we've got a different task: colour the birds numbered...
6 Ls: [ON TASK]
7 T: ptaszki z numerami **three, five, seven** [MONITORS]
birds numbered...

In excerpt (4.25) the teacher gives a typical instruction in L2, which in fact is a more or less consistent element in her discourse throughout the whole period of the observation. The instruction is correctly analysed by S1 in move 2. In move 3 the teacher switches back to L1 for disciplinary reasons but it does not distract her from repeating the instruction in L2 in response to S2's request.

While the L2 instruction in (4.25) is a part of a larger classroom discourse structure used in this context as an element of teacher talk, (4.26) is an example of L2 use in an activity that is not a part of classroom procedures, nor is it aimed at language development. The pupils are doing a mathematical task which is conducted in Polish until move 3 when the teacher's use of L2 indicates a code switch, which is then followed by the learners. Move 4 is used as a revision of numbers and exploited in the following instruction. It is interesting to see that in this excerpt (and all similar recordings of this sort) the learners do not appeal for translation, which nearly always happens in traditional lower primary EFL classes. The reason for this may be the learners' familiarity with the procedure and the fact that the teacher does not, as a rule, provide translation to her instructions so the habit is not formed. Additionally, the extract was recorded in the first grade indicating a very early onset of such practices.

The Sinclair-Coulthard (1975) IRF model described earlier ascribes the instructional element of classroom language exclusively to the teacher depriving students of the right to perform direct exchanges. It has however, been observed in the present study that, although teacher clearly dominates discourse in this respect, certain elements of direct exchanges can be attributed to learners' utterances as well. In excerpt (4.27) the students take control over the task to maximize their chances of success.

(4.27) [grade III; subject area: social education; topic: school; context: students watch a movie on IWB showing a classroom in which classroom objects appear. Their location is described orally]

1 T: za momencik obejrzymy filmik i waszym zadaniem będzie **to answer thequestions so the first question is Max read**
in a moment we are going to watch a film and your task will be…

2 S1: **where's the red pen**?

3 T: **Zuzia the second question**

4 S2: w**here's the green school bag**? [ETC.]

5 DVD: ***where's the red pen? It's under the blue chair. where's the green school bag? it's on the pink chair***. [ETC.]

6 T: **once again**?

7 Ss: **yes**

8 S3: a może pani zatrzymać po każdym jak powiedzą?
/but can you stop after each [object] they say?

9 S4: niech pani zatrzyma na obrazkach to my sobie sami napiszemy
*/stop [imperative]on the pictures then we'll write [the sentences] ourselves]*10T: ok

In this example recorded in the first semester of the third grade, there are significantly more elements of L2 than at the beginning of the study. The utterances are longer and the students have gained the skill of reading in English with few or no mistakes. Instructions are followed quickly and classroom language (move 6) is understood and responded to in L2. The above sequence starts with the initial teacher-direct exchange in move 1 but in the face of communication breakdown (no pauses between the dyads on DVD prevent them from writing the sentences down) students in moves 8 and 9 make a successful attempt to take control over the procedural part of the exercise. Move 9 is a request in imperative form directed at the teacher and thus it seems to be an example of student direct exchange that is missing from the Sinclair-Coulthard model.

Excerpt (4.27) also shows an interesting feature of learner language. The task requires the students to write down sentences describing the location of classroom objects in the film. These exact sentences are present as utterances in the video and require only transcribing. However, since the spaces between them are not long enough to write down the sentences, the learners suggest pausing the DVD. Interestingly, their request is not motivated by the desire to hear the required utterances better and remember them. They seem to have made a decision to ignore the dialogue as it is technically too difficult to follow and request for a chance to create the sentences themselves, rather than recreate them from the recording. The learners are, thus, willing to perform a more cognitively demanding task that requires the use of L2 without a model. This might suggest that they are confident enough to take a higher risk in L2 production.

Teacher direct exchanges are also used in procedural function to maintain discipline in the classroom. Extracts (4.28) and (4.29) are examples of two different ways of using discipline keeping strategies in L2.

(4.28) [grade III; subject area: procedural; topic: discipline keeping; context: students are talking among each other despite the teacher's requests for silence]

1 T: one, two, three…
2 Ss: quiet be
3 T: girls, boys…
4 Ss: stop that noise

(4.29)[grade I; subject area: procedural; topic: discipline keeping; context: students are notlistening to instructions concerning the next arts and crafts activity]

1 T: proszę wstaniemy w takim razie.
In that case please stand up
2 T: **touch your nose**
3 Ss: **touch your nose** [DO THE ACTIVITY]
4 T: **touch your tummy**
5 Ss: **touch your tummy** [DO THE ACTIVITY]
6 T: **jump**
7 Ss: **jump** [DO THE ACTIVITY]
8 T: **sit down**. czy jesteśmy teraz gotowi do pracy?
are we ready to work now?
9 Ss: **yes**

In both these examples the teacher resorts to L2 in order to discipline the students during an activity that is conducted in L1. This behaviour seems to be contrary to Baker's (2001: 115) findings quoted in Chapter One, where the researcher claims that in cases of indiscipline teachers switch to the L1 of the learners (e.g. *Taisez-vous les enfants!* ***Be quiet, children!***). In the studied group the opposite tendency was frequently observed. The recorded reactions of the pupils showed that the learners immediately shifted their attention towards the teacher at the moment of code switch. Perhaps due to the characteristics of the classroom discourse in this context the learners know that they need to pay closer attention the teacher talk whenever she switches to English. Extract (4.30) exemplifies a ritualised dyad of password-response sequence. The same technique is used by the teacher (and other general lower primary teachers) in L1 (cf. 4.2).

(4.3) [grade II; subject area: procedural; topic: discipline keeping; context: students are talking among each other while the teacher waits to start a reading aloud task]

1 T: chcę powiedzieć kilka słów…
I want to say a few words

2 Ss: my słuchamy a ty mów
we are listening and you speak

The characteristic feature of these short dyads is that they rhyme and form a kind of secret exchange that signifies an opening of a different activity. Lower primary EFL teachers in traditional classrooms rarely use such rhymes, which is a shame since learners are used to this formula in their integrated subjects lessons. Extract (4.29), on the other hand, uses the young learners need for physical activity relying on a TPR technique of bodily reactions to teacher's directions. The added value of this type of disciplining strategy is the opportunity to revise whatever language is being taught at the moment (in this example - body parts). Throughout the study period different lexical and structural elements involved in this king of activity were observed (classroom: *point to the door/window/blackboard*; verbs of movement: *fly/swim/turn around*; animals: *show me a rabbit/mouse/cat*; daily routine: *get up/get dressed/brush your teeth*, etc.).

Formulas

Classrooms are formal environments, which are governed by a fixed set of rules that also concern the use of language. Lower primary classrooms are especially prone to produce fixed behaviours to introduce order into the teaching and learning processes and develop appropriate habits. As a consequence, classroom language is rich in formulaic sequences that support communication and clarify the instructions. Wray (2001) defines a formulaic sequence as continuous or interrupted strings of "words or other elements, which is, or appears to be, prefabricated: that is, stored and retrieved whole from memory at the time of use, rather than being subject to generation or analysis by the language grammar" (9). Lower primary L2 education heavily relies on the use of such prefabricated chunks mainly due to inadequate analytical skills and low gramaticality of pupils' utterances. Lower primary foreign language education is a fairly recent phenomenon and teachers asigned to this sector are not always fully aware of the abilities and limitations of their pupils. The teachers tend to take one of two stands: they either treat young learners as fully aware users of L1 teaching them grammar explicitly or underestimate their abilities and focus on teaching vocabulary. Since the core national curriculum stresses the need to prepare students for communicative use of the foreign language, both these attitudes fail to comply with its requirements. If the main focus of young learners EFL classes is explicitly taught grammar or vocabulary, students may not be exposed to enough formulaic language to develop this particular competence to the right extent. As de Cock et al. (1998) put it:

> Because of their limited exposure to authentic input, and hence, fewer opportunities for acquiring output, classroom learners tend to underuse formulaic language, relying instead on their grammatical knowledge to generate well-formed but essentially unidiomatic language. (cited in Prodromou, 2007: 21).

In the light of the communicative principle governing early EFL in Poland, it seems reasonable to equip young learners with formulaic functional chunks with pragmatic application. Wray (1999) identifies four types of formulas used by children: (1) *underanalysed forms* like "wanna" that "display grammatical and/or lexical knowledge beyond the child's current generative capacities"; (2) *fixed formulas* like lines from songs or nursery rhymes as well as institutionalised ways of saying things like "May I leave the table?"; (3) *fused utterances*, i.e. original creations of the child's language which prove to be pragmatically useful and thus become fused into a fixed expression to be used frequently; and (4) *gestalt utterances* which are typically long appropriately used utterances picked up from peer or adult talk and which give the impression of precosity (220).

In comparison with a traditional lower primary EFL classroom, where pupils nearly exclusively use one-word utterances in response to teacher elicitations of task comprehension checks, formulaic sequences in the observed environment were plentiful. As a result of the assumed policy of functional language use in a variety of classroom contexts, the language presented and elicited from the students was very often structurally beyond their current level of linguistic competence. This was evident in the stories and fairy tales used in the classroom where the structurally and lexically complex content was clarified by the extralinguistic context. Another feature of the observed environment that promoted the use of underanalysed forms was the topical integration of content and language that often required the use of vocabulary and structures that were not within the typical lower primary EFL curriculum. One such example is presented in excerpt (4.31).

(4.31) [grade II; subject area: environmental education; topic: materials; context: students revise names of materials]

1 T: do wyrobu różnych przedmiotów używa się różnych materiałów i my te materiały wczoraj poznaliśmy.
to make different objects we use diffrent materials and we got to know them yesterday
to ja przyniosłam różne przedmioty i chciałabym żebyście mi powiedzieli z czego są zrobione **ready**?
so, I brought different objects and I would like you to tell me what they are made of
2 Ls: **ready**
3 T: [SHOWS A WOODEN BIRD] **it is made of**...
4 Ls: **wood**
5 T: [SHOWS A SPOON]
6 Ls: **it is made of metal**
7 T: [SHOWS A BAG]
8 Ls: **it is made of** (.)
9 T: **leather**
10 Ls: **leather**

In this example the whole phrase *It is made of* is used as an underanalysed form whose meaning is obvious but whose passive voice structure is beyond the learners' conscious analysis. Similarly, the vocabulary involved in the exchange seems to be rather sophisticated for lower primary classroom especially in the last moves. However, it is perfectly justified by the communicative need of being able to describe the objects in the learners' immediate surroundings. The day finishes with a project whose result is illustrated in figure 18 where learners work in groups to create posters.

Fixed formulas were present in rather complex sequences like the one in (4.23) above concerning the communication chain *can I have a... - here you are - thank you*, which was used throughout the whole period of the study in a variety of situations including weekly milk distribution (4.32); borrowing forgotten classroom objects from the teacher and distribution of materials for arts and crafts activities (4.33).

(4.32) [grade I; subject area: organisational; topic: classroom procedure; context: students get free milk once a week within a framework of a governmental program. Milk is available in 3 flavours, vanilla, chocolate and clear]
1 T: zapraszam pojedynczo do mnie.
come to me one by one
2 Ss: [LINE UP IN FRONT OF THE DESK]
3 T: **can I** (.)
4 S1: **can I have milk**

Figure 18. Project work

Source: own materials

5 T: **can I have milk…**
6 S1: **please** (.) **can I have milk, please**?
7 T: **what kind of milk**?
8 S1: (.)
9 T: **white or vanilla or chocolate**?
10 S1: **vanilla** (.) **can I have milk vanilla, please**?
11 T: **can I have… vani…**
12 S1: **can I have vanilla milk, please**?
13 T: **here you are** (.)
14 S1: **thank you**

(4.33) [grade II; subject area: science combined with a project of home economy "Od-grosika do złotówki"[6]; topic: Space; context: students are making a picture of space]

1 T: będziemy rysować **space**. **what can you see in the sky**?
we'll draw
2 Ss: **planets, astronauts, rockets, moon, stars**

---

[6] From a penny to a pound.

3 T: no właśnie. narysujemy galaktykę finanse. a ja tutaj mam, zobaczcie, **what's this**? [SHOWS SMALL CUT-OUT STARS]
right. we'll draw galaxy finances. and here I've got, look
4 Ss: **star**
5 T: możecie podchodzić i brać sobie te gwiazdki. tylko **in English**
you can come and take the stars. but...
6 S1: [APPROACHES THE DESK] **can I have stars please**?
7 T: **how many**?
8 S1: **five**
9 T: [gives L1 five stars] **here you are**
10 S1: **thank you**

Both (4.32) and (4.33) above show the use of the same sequence of fixed formulas used in the classroom for pragmatic reasons. It is also visible in these examples that formulas get internalised with time through frequent usage. The sequence recorded in grade I is clumsy and requires teacher cues (moves 3,5,9) and repairs (move 10). A similar communicative situation in grade II is handled by the pupils much more smoothly and effectively.

Fused utterances are not very common in the observed environment due to a rather controlled context of language practice. If a structurally erroneous utterance is used repeatedly in the discourse, it is corrected by the teacher and a new habit is formed. The few recorded samples of an imperfect phrase that nonetheless was pragmatically useful and thus repeated in other contexts include the example presented in exchange (4.34).

(4.34) [grade I; subject area: arts and crafts; topic: Easter; context: students are making a paper Easter basket]
1 T: **what colour do you want**
2 S1: **green** [TAKES A GREEN SHEET]
3 S2: **you have blue?**
4 T: **no**
5 S2: [TAKES A GREEN SHEET]

The above excerpt comes from a recording made in the first grade. The same procedure is used repeatedly throughout the study and the fused utterance in move 3 disappears later in the EFL education process. It is, however, not repaired in the above sequence as it does have pragmatic usefulness and, although grammatically incorrect, it constitutes evidence of early linguistic creativity. The teacher deliberately decides to assign this original L2 creation communicative value to encourage further risk-taking moves by the learners.

Gestalt utterances constitute a minor element of the observed discourse. Typically, the utterances are picked up from the teacher as the better-able user of the language like in excerpt (4.3) move 6 described above. They are also present in learners' own interactions imitating the teacher's utterances like the one in excerpt (4.35) recorded at a very early stage of grade I.

(4.35) [grade I; subject area: social education; topic: getting to know each other and the school; context: students are getting familiarized with the characters in their English course book]

1 T: [HOLDING IN ONE HAND A PUPPET OF A CATERPILLAR AND IN THE OTHER A LADYBIRD] **hello, I'm Colin. what's your name**? **hi, I'm Lucy. nice to meet you. nice to meet you too**! [turns to L1 holding the puppet of the caterpillar] **hello, I'm Colin. what's your name**?

2 S1: **hello**, (.)

3 T: **I'm**...

4 S1: **I'm Wojtek**

5 T: **nice to meet you**.

6 S1: **nice to meet you** (.)

7 T: ... **too**

8 S1: **nice to meet you too.**

9 T: [CONTINUES THE SAME ROUTINE WITH A FEW LS UNTIL THE BREAK]
[DURING THE BREAK LS SIT ON THE CARPET AND EAT SANDWICHES OR PLAY TOGETHER IN A TOY CORNER]

10 S2: [TAKES A PUPPET OF A DUCK AND PUTS IT IN A MAKESHIFT PUPPET THEATRE] **hi, my name is** kaczka. **what's your name**?
duck

11 S3: [TAKES A PUPPET OF A MOUSE AND PUTS IT IN A MAKESHIFT PUPPETTHEATRE] **hello, my name is** myszka. **nice to meet you**! [LAUGHS]
[diminutive] mouse

In this fragment of classroom discourse the learners adopt the teacher's model, although it is not immediately clear from the teacher (puppet)-learner dyads. While students struggle with the exchange in the first, practice part of the teaching sequence, they seem to have no problem with the structure in a free practice activity entirely initiated and run by the pupils themselves. This extract is different form (4.3) where the learner uses a teacher phrase that is not meant for learners. Here, the intention of the teacher is to transfer the fixed phrases to the student's communicating repertoire. The learners take the structure from the teacher and use it in a novel environment exhibiting features of linguistic creativity which is briefly discussed below.

Creative language use

Although much of the classroom interaction is based on predictable routines and formulas, the most interesting element in the ongoing discourse is creativity. Jeffrey and Woods (2003: 3) maintain that teaching is creative rather than formulaic and see its aim in providing conditions for "creative learning, with children coming to their own knowledge and skills being enthused and changed by the process, and having some control of the learning process, but under teacher guidance". However, allowing pupils to show creativity without equipping them with basic skills will not result in meaningful learning. Creative L2 behaviour was recorded frequently in the present study in contexts where learners were offered a frame that could potentially be filled with their own ideas as in the example of trying out the new language (4.35) described above or (4.36) below.

(4.36) [grade I; subject area: language; topic: body parts; context: Students rehearse a story in groups]

1 S1: **buzz buzz buzz is this a flower**?
2 S2: **no, it's my nose**!
3 S3: [FOOLING AROUND WITH L4 POINTING AT HIS LEG] **is this flower**?
4 S4: **no, leg**! [LAUGHS]
5 S3: [pointing at L4's arm] **is this flower**? [LAUGHS]
6 S4: **no, hand**! [LAUGHS]

This excerpt was recorded in the context of a rehearsal for a dramatized story already described in example (4.8) While that excerpt illustrated students' active linguistic participation in story telling that relied on a word perfect text reconstruction, (4.36) is an example of creative construction of novel utterances based on the rehearsed structural frame. The repetitive question-answer sequence in the original story referred to *nose*, *eyes*, *ears* and *mouth*. In the above extract, however, this limited repertoire is enriched with other body parts known from a different context. The boys involved in the creation of new sentences fused the lexical items learned on previous days with the new context proposed by the teacher. They were also clearly enjoying the process of playing with the language, which seems invaluable in the context of early EFL learning, even if the utterances were not perfect in terms of structure. Bowkett (2005: 3) argues that creativity is a set of mental processes that "incorporates playfulness, curiosity, sensitivity, self-awareness and independence". Therefore, linguistic creativity requires conditions that are rarely provided in traditional EFL lessons that are not integrated into the bigger picture of lower primary teaching practice.

It seems that the practice of frequent codeswitching (which does not occur as immediate translation) promotes the development of language awareness through making analogies and the general atmosphere of the classroom allows for creative use of the new language, which is illustrated in excerpts (4.37) and (4.38).

(4.37) [grade II; subject area: routine; topic: calendar; context: changing the date on 30.03]

1 T: **today is**…

2 S1: **threefty** /θri:ftɪ/

3 S2: [LAUGHS]

4 S1: no co ja się uczę po angielsku mówić
what? I'm learning to speak English

(4.38) [grade III; subject area: science; topic: space; context: Ls match pictures of objects in space with appropriate word cards]

1 S1: [MATCHES THE WORD CARD WITH A PICTURE OF A SPACE SHIP]

2 T: zobaczcie **space** i **ship** czyli razem statek kosmiczny
*look **space** and **ship** so together space ship*

3 S2: [ASIDE] **ship**. **sheep**. statek 'owcowy' [LAUGHS]
space sheep

Excerpt (4.37) comes from the recording of the already described everyday routine of changing the date and the weather symbol on a class calendar. In move 2 the learner makes a conscious attempt to make a word (*thirtieth*) relying on her knowledge of basic numerals and a self-created rule. Although the attempt is not successful it is still valuable as an example of hypothesis testing in a risk taking move. The learner's explanation of her own behaviour in move 4 is evident of her rather mature understanding of language learning as hypothesis testing. In the previous observation of this fixed point of the lesson the students focused their attention mainly on the weather, which was the first element frequently and directly referred to in classroom discussions. Once they had had enough practice in naming the days of the week, pupils started to be very active in changing this element of the calendar. The same process was observed in the case of names of the months. The last element that learners turned their attention to was the date, as ordinal numbers were the last to acquire in this routine. All the elements of the calendar were practiced and chorally repeated by the learners from the very beginning of English education but they chose to consciously participate in the process gradually with the enrichment of linguistic experience gained as a result.

Exchange (4.38) is an example of an interesting play with words. The teacher draws the learners' attention to the structure of the word in an attempt to increase their sensitivity to the meaningful elements of words. S2 takes the analysis one step further by substituting one of the words for a phonetically similar one he knows. This may suggest his emerging phonological awareness and a conscious decision to create a new word that would be funny in translation. It is also interesting to note that move 3 is an aside comment and it is not meant for other pupils to hear. S2 plays with the words for his own pleasure just as children do in their first language.

Most of the observed learner utterances contained code switches, many of which occurred for no specific reason other than sheer pleasure of using newly learned English words. It seems that pupils enjoy using the L2 words in otherwise Polish discourse as it makes their interactions unique and they take pleasure in creating and comprehending mixed utterances, as well as creative uses of English.

4.2.8. Results and discussion

The data collected in a group of 23 students that comprised 240 hours of observation does not claim to be representative. Nor does the analysis attempt to be exhaustive. However, certain tendencies are visible in what has been found in the course of this longitudinal study. The unique character of the observed context seems to rely on three elements: teacher-student relations, organisation of input and the character of classroom discourse.

The teacher, especially in the lower primary classroom is the central figure. Children spend most of their days with the teacher and the classroom is often the first environment they get to know outside home. It is, therefore, of utmost importance for all parties involved to create best possible relationship between the teacher and the students. In the first three years of primary education, learners are provided with a safe classroom environment with one teacher to ensure stability and holistic approach to teaching. These elements are essential for the learners' comfort in the classroom and willingness to participate in the educational processes. A study of primary school English language learners in Canada by Toohey (2000) found that affiliation with teachers, peers and common classroom practices enabled children to claim desirable classroom identities. In the context of the present longitudinal study all the elements are provided: there is only one teacher and she introduces elements of all required areas of education including English in the form of integrated topical units. As a result a specific form of discourse is developed and used in the observed context.

The above analysis allows for observing certain patterns and providing some of the possible answers to these questions at the same time posing new challenges in this field.

(1) As it follows from the analysis of the examples of linguistic data gathered during the observation and discussed in detail above, English is used on everyday basis. Some instances of its use, like the calendar routine or saying hello in the morning are predictable and they constitute fixed elements of every day. Others, such as instructions, discipline keeping procedures, classroom maintenance, etc. occur each day but their frequency varies considerably. There are also other elements of English that are pre-planned by the teacher as part of activities devoted to particular extralinguistic topics covered in a cross-curricular manner. Finally, there are instances of L2 use that are totally unpredictable both on the part of the teacher, who suddenly decides to switch codes in order to revise some language previously taught or emphasise some cultural similarity or difference, and the learners who insert elements of English into their utterances to practice them or use newly acquired linguistic elements in a creative way. Regardless of the variety of occasions on which English is used the total time of use and exposure is much longer than ninety minutes per week offered in the traditional model. As a result students seem to acquire some elements of L2 incidentally through constant exposure, much like the learners in a German-English formal bilingual context studied by Dalton-Puffer (2007) who quotes one of the interviewed teachers explaining the learners' vocabulary acquisition

> es laufen ihnen Wörter wie assume dauernd über den Weg und dann verwenden sie sie gazn selbstverständlich in ihren Englischaufsätzen *they just come across words like assume all the time and then they just go and use them in their English essays* (282).

(2) English is used in a variety of contexts and both English and Polish have been recorded as occurring in the same context interchangeably in the teacher's as well as the learners' utterances. The teacher seems more likely to use English in instructions. She also frequently switches to L2 in mathematical tasks where numbers are practiced. Other typical contexts for the use of English include storytelling, drama, songs, pre-planned tasks involving worksheets, routines, discipline

keeping, arts and crafts (especially materials distribution) and seasonal celebrations. The learners use English in otherwise L1 utterances whenever they can remember some of the words in L2 and the activity is conducted in English or the instruction or question is asked in L2. They switch codes not only while talking to the teacher but also during play or talk with their friends.

(3) and (4) As in any language classroom where the teacher is in control of the educational process, teacher-elicit exchanges dominate the discourse. Learners are asked questions and are expected to answer them. It seems that for the teacher it is equally important that her pupils understand the questions in L2 and answer them with as much English as they can. The questions are typically closed taking into consideration the expanded definition of closed questions assuming a limited range of possible answers. In the same way more display than referential questions are asked as the teacher asks for previously taught items or asks general knowledge questions. There is no significant difference in the ratio of the types of questions asked and the language in which they are asked or expected to be answered. Inform sequences are present both in teacher and learner utterances although the teacher definitely relies heavily on elicit exchanges often using Socratic questioning as a technique of building common understanding - a feature more characteristic of general lower primary educators than English teachers. Teacher-direct exchanges often take the form of instructions in L2. Interestingly, pupil-direct exchanges have been observed even though they are absent from the original IRF model.

(5) A variety of reasons for codeswitching were observed. Teacher initiated code switches are motivated by the function of the utterance (more frequent in questions and instructions) and context (more frequent when vocabulary is known and ready for revision and in culture related topics). Learner initiated code switches are motivated by communicative need and curiosity (frequent when pupils learn L2 names of new objects presented in Polish) and creative use of L2 (frequent when trying out a hypothesis or analysing the structure of a new word of phrase). Both learners and the teacher also tend to switch codes in response to the change of language of the interlocutor. As a result the classroom discourse is characterised by frequent codeswitching at both intersentential and intrasentential level. As a result of the above analysis the conclusions are contrary to the belief in a negative effect of code mixing on language attainment by the learners following the finding of Moll, Saez and Dworin (2001) study which showed that Spanish-English bilingual preschoolers engage in producing bilingual utterances even before they master conventions of alphabetic literacy in either language. While it may be true that in a traditional EFL teaching context especially at higher

levels and with older learners "L2 only" policy should be applied, in a partially bilingual L2 instruction in the studied context mixed discourses seem to have positive results. Rampton's (1995) study of language "crossing" in Britain showed that teenagers engage creatively in mixed language practices with peers in social contexts outside the classroom where Afro-Caribbeans use and learn Panjabi in their interactions.

All due care has been taken to minimize the limitations of the study. The samples were taken on different days of the week to ensure a wider range of subject areas and topics covered by the teacher. Each observation was accompanied by a video recording of whole activities regardless of whether elements of English were anticipated. Other, traditional EFL lessons at the same level of lower primary education were observed in order to notice some major differences in the discourse. Nevertheless, some variables of the studied context were beyond the researcher's control and certain limitations of the present longitudinal qualitative study have to be borne in mind.

First of all, due to its longitudinal character, within a period of three years only one group of learners was observed and the language behaviours recorded might prove endemic to this particular class. Similarly, only one teacher was observed and her personal characteristics rather than the specific processes of language teaching might have exerted influence on the observed linguistic behaviours. Secondly, the character of the teaching environment involved elements of English both planned ahead by the teacher (worksheets, cultural elements, realia, prompts, songs, stories, etc.) and others that occurred rather spontaneously during other activities and often inspired by learners' curiosity (vocabulary items requested by the learners, elements of instruction, elements of pupils' responses, etc.). This variability of L2 use made it impossible to predict or determine the amount of English used in the whole period of lower primary education, as well as its ratio in particular education areas (mathematical, science, social, etc.). Thirdly, the teacher was not always consistent with the context of her own L2 use, e.g. sometimes instructions or other procedural utterances were rendered in English and at other times in Polish. This may in fact be an advantage of this EFL context since the provision of both versions at different times makes the discourse truly bilingual, i.e. the learners were provided with the same content in both languages but not in immediate translation, so they learned to comprehend them in two codes. For the study context, however, such inconsistencies are less beneficial as they are difficult to measure and control. Finally, the character of the pedagogical innovation allowing the teacher to introduce English each day to varying degrees, creates a risk of not being able to document all possible contexts of its use due to time limitations.

Observations of similar EFL policies in different contexts could validate the present study. It would also be interesting to monitor further development of communicative patterns in the learners who left the lower primary context and their interactions with specialist EFL teachers in a traditional classroom. A comparative study of discourse patterns in interactions between the studied and native speakers of English at the same age versus control group could also produce interesting data. Further study of such partially bilingual education at lower primary level of education are highly desirable and may lead to a significant enhancement of communicative competence, language awareness and readiness for risk taking strategies in young learners of English. Such an improvement could, in turn, lead to a higher self-confidence and motivation of the learners to become proficient users of English in the future.

5. EXECUTIVE CONTROL IN INTEGRATED EFL AND SUBJECTS EDUCATION IN A LOWER PRIMARY CLASSROOM. A QUANTITATIVE STUDY

Executive functions is a collective term that refers to a set of skills which allows individuals to select an action that is proper in a particular situation, inhibit improper behaviour and concentrate or maintain attention in the presence of distractions. There seems to be no consensus over the exact composition of executive functions. Researchers tend to include a variety of cognitive skills into the set. Elliott (2003: 50), for instance, defines executive functions as "those involved in complex cognitions, such as solving novel problems, modifying behaviour in the light of new information, generating strategies or sequencing complex actions". Malloy, Cohen and Jenkins (1998: 574) believe that executive functions "include the following abilities: (1) Formulating goals with regard for long-term consequences; (2) Generating multiple response alternatives; (3) Choosing and initiating goal-directed behaviours; (4) Self-monitoring the adequacy and correctness of the behaviour; (5) Correcting and modifying behaviours when conditions change; (6.) Persisting in the face of distraction". Troyer, Graves and Cullum (1994:45) in turn, see executive functioning as involving "problem solving abilities such as abstraction, planning, strategic thinking, behavioural initiation and termination, and selfmonitoring".

Miyake et al. (2000: 54), on the other hand, propose a convenient model of three core components: (1) selective attention and *inhibition* of dominant or prepotent responses; (2) *shifting* between tasks or mental sets; and (3) *updating* and monitoring of working memory representations. Whatever elements of cognitive processing the definitions include, it seems certain that executive functions allow people to consciously plan and control their behaviour and involve an element of reflection upon their own thinking processes. This makes executive functions, by far, "the most complex of human behaviours being primarily concerned with planning and organization of purposeful behaviour" (Tuokko and Hadjistavropoulos, 1998: 143). The development of executive control is, thus, one of the most significant achievements in childhood.

5.1. THE NATURE OF EXECUTIVE CONTROL

Executive processes and problem solving skills are largely improved in the middle childhood. Owing to a growth spurt in the prefrontal cortex and development of connection between this region and other parts of the brain, the speed and efficacy of information processing is immensely improved after the age of seven (Luna et al., 2004). At the early primary stage children display a wide range of executive functions that allow them to effectively participate in the formal learning processes that were earlier beyond their reach as a result of cognitive immaturity. The range of basic cognitive improvements learners undergo in this period are summarized by Davis (2011):

– Ability to articulate a problem and generate ideas about what actions can be taken to solve it
– Knowing cognitive strategies that will help in problem solving (e.g. looking more closely at a picture will increase the chances of recalling its details on request)
– Knowing when to activate cognitive rules and strategies to solve problems (e.g. deciding what things to take into consideration before solving a problem)
– A more flexible approach to problem solving - being able "to discard inefficient solutions that are not working and to search systematically for better alternatives"
– Longer attention span, ability to resist distractions, and better control of anxiety (e.g. persisting to do a difficult task despite frustration)
– Ability to continuously monitor performance (paying attention to one's output and modifying it accordingly)
– Faith in her ability to think about problems (persisting to do the task despite initial failure)
– Awareness of shortcomings in thinking (searching for the best solutions) (357).

The newly developed skills require, however, effective coordination of the various subsystems involved in executive functioning. The process responsible for this management is referred to as *executive control*.

Exerting control over such complex executive functions as inhibition, monitoring, switching, processing speed, response speed and working memory (Salthouse, 2005) is effortful and requires voluntary attention. This effortful control refers to conscious attempts of a child to manage his feelings and continue a task despite interference or frustration (Kochanska, Murray and Harlan, 2000). Children at the early primary level of education are expected to be able to focus their attention voluntarily and deliberately. Mastering this skill is a sign of developing executive control. Clearly, this process is aided by general maturation of the brain resulting in developing conceptual thinking and increased speed of processing information.

The world of an early primary student is filled with stimuli that continuously attract his attention. It is virtually impossible to effectively analyse all incoming impulses. In response to this uncontrollable influx of information, young brain develops a mechanism of control that Desimone and Duncan (1995: 207) describe as an attentional bias, which allows to attend to relevant information while, at the same time, inhibiting irrelevant information. Mastery of this control seems to be a decisive factor in educational success as it allows children not only to pay selective attention to the elements presented by the teacher, but also to quickly shift this attention to another element. As such, it is of major interest for educators to maximize the opportunities for executive control development. In fact, a number of studies have shown improved executive functioning by systematic cognitive training in the area of updating, working memory and task switching.

A study by Dahlin et al. (2008) tested the effect of cognitive training on executive functions in the areas of mental speed, working memory, episodic memory, and reasoning. The results suggest that the ability to perform these operations can be modified throughout life span. However, transferability of these skills was noted only in the case of younger participants suggesting that children are able, through training, to use the newly acquired skills in novel tasks, thus, showing significant plasticity of executive functioning. Karbach (2009) showed that children at the age 8-10, typically characterized by deficits in task-set selection and maintenance, displayed an ability to transfer the benefits of the training to a novel activity. The author concludes that this finding has significant implications for educational contexts. Additionally, Klinberg's (2010) study, focusing on working memory enhancement, showed that training can improve performance in non-trained tasks relying on working memory and control of attention. The author recommends its application in contexts where remediating intervention is required in the case of students at risk of academic failure.

If systematic training leads to improved executive control and thus results in better performance in cognitive tasks, children who experience conditions where there is more opportunity for practice are therefore in a privileged position as compared to their peers. One of the environments promoting executive functions training is a bilingual context. Children raised with two languages where they experience frequent codeswitching receive more practice in attention switching and inhibition. The significant differences in executive control measurement are often referred to as *bilingual advantage*.

5.2. SELECTED STUDIES ON EXECUTIVE CONTROL IN BILINGUALS

Bilingual children need to possess an effective control mechanism that regulates the usage of the different codes in their linguistic production. Bialystok (1999) suggested that bilingual children might develop improved cognitive control systems compared to monolingual children as a result of switching and attentional control demands from early age. In this study she showed that bilingual children have the capacity to become exceptionally proficient at switching not only between languages but between different cognitive tasks as well as at ignoring distractive information. In fact, a number of research studies have shown bilingual advantage in executive functions, especially in the area of inhibiting irrelevant information (cf. Carlson and Meltzoff, 2008; Costa et al., 2008; Soveri et al., 2011). Additionally, bilinguals proved to excel monolinguals in working memory performance (Bialystok et al., 2004).

In another study, Bialystok (2001) proposes that the bilingual advantage is related to the attention control while information processing. Since users of two language codes need to constantly monitor their performance as to its appropriateness in terms of the choice of language items available in the bilingual mental lexicon, their executive control is constantly in use. Each time a bilingual forms an utterance, he needs to choose between competing lexemes and grammar rules of both languages. Effective production in this case relies on the ability to inhibit elements of the language that is not currently in use (cf. Moreno et al., 2008; Bialystok et al., 2009; Ye and Zhou, 2009). This cognitively difficult process must involve a complex mental mechanism. Rodrigues-Fornels et al. (2006) propose that "the prefrontal cortex probably mediates cognitive control in bilingual speakers through the interplay between a top-down selection-suppression mechanism and a local inhibitory mechanism in charge of changing the degree of selection-suppression of the different lexicons" (134).

Switching and mixing languages are frequent in many bilingual speakers, especially when the interlocutor is able to understand both languages for a variety of reasons described in Chapter One. Fluent bilinguals easily switch from one language to the other and can separate both languages completely without much effort. Nevertheless, code switching is frequent as bilinguals tend to embed single lexical items from one language into the matrix language of the current utterance. General switching proficiency and codeswitching depend on the degree of activation of both languages at the moment of speaking (Grosjean, 1997). The deliberate choice of one of the available languages should, therefore, activate the corresponding lexicon and set of rules. A number of research studies have shown, however, that in the production of a word in a particular language, the conceptual system of a bilingual activates the lexical representation of both languages (cf. de Bot, 1992; Poulisse, 1999). As a result, the speaker is constantly offered conflicting choices and needs to direct his attention to one of them while at the same time inhibiting the other. This simultaneous activation of both systems "requires a mechanism for keeping the languages separate so that fluent performance can be achieved without intrusions from the unwanted language" (Bialystok et al., 2004: 291). In ideal conditions, in the cases of so-called balanced bilinguals, the chances of the competing lexemes are more or less equal and thus attention paid consistently to the choice of one of the codes, as well as intentional shift are fluent and seemingly effortless. However, it is much more common that the lexicons in the bilingual mind consist of words that, through experience, are more readily available in one language than in the other. In the case of such unequal power relation between competing lexemes, the speaker can either give up and choose the dominant alternative or inhibit the word in order to access the less vivid vocabulary item. Such operation requires voluntary attention, effort and inhibition skills. This, in turn, will entail certain cost in terms of time and energy.

A study by Gollan and Ferreira (2009) showed that many bilinguals voluntarily mixed languages even if the switching was costly. They were recorded to switch between languages when nothing compelled the switch. Gollan and Ferreira observed that the freedom to mix languages voluntarily allows unbalanced bilinguals to produce utterances resembling those of more balanced bilinguals. Voluntary switch costs show a superior role for inhibitory control in bilingual language production and suggest a compulsory separation by language in bilingual lexical choice. As a result of facing a constant exercise in dealing with two languages and controlling their use, bilinguals develop a strong ability to solve response conflict in tasks that are not based on linguistic control. In such tasks, bilinguals present advantages in time and quality of information processing over monolinguals.

On the other hand, in tasks requiring vocabulary retrieval (in which bilinguals have to resolve the lexical conflict), bilinguals show significant fluency disadvantages as compared with monolinguals (e.g., Gollan and Acenas, 2004; Ivanova & Costa, 2008). However, when in the same vocabulary retrieval task bilinguals are offered a choice to name the objects in whichever language they can access more quickly, their fluency is improved. Kohnert, Hernandez and Bates (1998) for instance, studying balanced Spanish–English bilinguals found that they score significantly better on the Boston Naming Test (a test of naming pictures presented by the experimenter), when they were offered an opportunity to produce correct responses in either of their languages. Gollan and Silverberg (2001) found similar results in Hebrew-English bilinguals who were able to come up with the same number of low-frequency words as monolinguals.

Bialystok and Shapero's (2005) study results show that bilinguals are better than monolinguals in conflict tasks involving interference suppression. However, the authors claim that bilinguals not only differ from monolinguals in inhibitory control, but they also display better cognitive flexibility underlying task switching. Costa et al. (2009) suggested that the bilingual advantage in executive control may correlate with the degree to which bilinguals switch codes in everyday conversations. The research findings showed that bilinguals who mix codes throughout the day get more practice in controlling the selection of language and, as a result, display better executive performance than bilinguals coming from sociolinguistic contexts where languages are used separately. It was assumed that bilinguals who use different languages in different contexts and do not frequently switch between them, do not exhibit executive control advantage and have less practice in monitoring language use.

Since consistent use of one language in one context does not produce beneficial effects in executive functions development, it is perhaps not fully justified to separate the languages in the context of EFL formal education. The context of the present longitudinal study offering the opportunity to integrate elements of English into the early primary education practice may, to a very modest degree, allow for the development of executive control mechanisms similar to the ones described above. The switches observed in the course of this study were often motivated by voluntary choice of the non-dominant language item in contexts that did not necessarily call for the switch (cf. transcript 4.16), even though the cost of such switch is higher if the suppressed language is the dominant one.

5.3. EXECUTIVE CONTROL IN ENGLISH AND SUBJECTS INTEGRATED TEACHING CLASSROOM – STROOP TEST

The methodology of examining executive control in children is rich in variety of test batteries. Some of the most popular tools are listed in Table 6 but there are multiple varieties and adaptations of these tools available in literature on this subject.

Table 6. Executive control measurements

Test	Description	Measured feature
A-not-B	A test used with infants. An object is hidden in location A where the infant is allowed to find it. Then the object is hidden in location B but the infant will typically search for it in location A. The number of persistent errors in situation analysis is measured.	Switching skills
Children's Gambling Task	A test used with preschoolers. Two piles of card are presented to the participant. One pile consists of cards with sad faces and the other of smiley faces. The number of smiley faces gained marks the number of sweets won by the participant. The child is allowed 25 trials and the following 25 trials are measured.	Effective rule making
Day-Night Stroop	A test used with preschoolers and school children. The participants are shown line drawings of moon and stars but requested to say ‚day' on seeing the picture and a line drawing of sun on which cue they are asked to say ‚night'.	Inhibition skills
Delayed response	A test used with infants and children. The participants are shown an object hidden under one of two or more identical cups. The delay is created by hiding the stimuli behind an opaque screen. After the delay the screen is lifted and the child is asked to retrieve the object.	Working memory
Dimensional Change Card Sort (DCCS)	Children are shown cards presenting pairs of objects in two different colours. They are asked to sort them according to one dimension and them immediately to sort them according to the other dimension.	Switching skills
Flexible Item Selection Task (FIST)	Children are shown a set of 3 cards and asked to pick two that match according to one dimension and then to pick another pair according to another dimension.	Switching skills
Go-NoGo Task	Children are asked to display a motor response to one cue and ignore the other.	Inhibition skills
Handgame	Children imitate a pair of presented hand actions and then present the opposite action to the one presented by the experimenter	Inhibition skills
Object reversal	Children are presented with two objects and rewarded for reaching at one of them. After a few trials they are rewarded for reaching at the other object. The number of trials needed to adjust the rule is measured	Switching skills

Test	Description	Measured Feature
Self-Orde-red Pointing	Children are presented with pictures arranged in a matrix. At each trial they are asked to point at a different picture and each time the pictures are arranged differently. The number of errors is measured.	Switching skills
Stop-Signal Task	Children are shown two symbols X and O on a computer screen and are asked to press appropriate button on seeing the symbol unless they hear a stop sound in which case they should not press any button. Reaction time and number of errors are measured	Inhibition skills
Stroop Test	Participants are presented with names of colours printed in non-corresponding ink colour. Participants are asked to name the colour of the ink	Inhibition skills
Tower of Hanoi	Children are asked to place a number of disks varying in diame-ter on three wooden pegs to form a target shape. The number of trials is measured.	Problem solving skills
Tower of London	Based on Tower of Hanoi. Children are presented with target location of coloured balls on three pegs and an initial arrange-ment. They are asked to describe the sequence of moves that will lead to the target arrangement.	Problem solving skills
Wiscon-sin Card Sorting Test (WCST)	Children are presented with cards that vary on a number of dimensions. They are asked to sort the cards and each time they assign a card to a pile the experimenter tells them whether it's correct. After a number of correct trials the experimenter changes the dimension.	Effective rule making
Flanker task	Participants are presented with a number of arrows (or birds or fish etc.) pointing at one direction in congruent trials on a com-puter screen. In incongruent trials the middle arrow points at the opposite direction. The task is to recognise the direction of the middle arrow and press the correct button.	Selective attention

Source: Adapted from Zelazo and Müller (2011).

For the present study Stroop test has been chosen to measure the possible advantage of children from the observed group as opposed to control group with regard to executive control, especially in the area of inhibition skills.

Different versions of the Stroop test have been heavily used in research on a variety of cognitive phenomena, such as selective attention, conflict detection and monitoring, inhibition and executive control and lexical access (MacLeod, 1991). The paradigm has also been used in clinical tests for studying deficits in various areas (cf. Green et al., 2010 for studies on aphasia, Peckham et al., 2010 for studies on depression). In the research on bilingualism, Stroop test has typically been used to study interference and automaticity of lexical access to words within and across both languages. In the original version of the Stroop test (1935), participants were asked to name the colours of the words printed either in corresponding colours (congruent conditions) or different colour ink (incongruent conditions).

The Stroop effect is observed in incongruent conditions when the reaction time in completing the task is slower due to the competing stimuli requiring selective attention. The conflict between the word and the ink colour requires cognitive control to be resolved. This leads to a delay in response time in comparison to control conditions. In the basic conflict conditions, in monolingual within language test, the delay is due to two dimensions, of colour and word, competing for attention. In bilingual conditions the complexity of the task may further be modified by adding a third element in the form of the other language. As a result, the experimenter can induce interference not only between the name of the word and its colour in incongruent conditions but also by printing the word in a different language than the required response language (e.g. Rosselli et al., 2002 study on Spanish-English bilinguals). In extreme conditions, yet another distracter can be added in the form of the colour words written in a different alphabetic script than the required response language (e.g. Coderre et al., 2013 study on Arabic-Chinese-English trilinguals). The most common types of colour-word Stroop tests conditions are summarised in Table 7 below.

Table 7. Experimental conditions for the most common studies with the use of the basic version of Stroop test

Condition	Stimulus	Response
(1) congruent conditions for monolinguals	RED	/red/
(2) incongruent conditions for monolinguals	RED	/blu:/
(3) congruent within language conditions for bilinguals	RED and ROJO	/red/ and / rɒxɒ/
(4) congruent within language conditions for bilingual	RED and ROJO	/blu:/ and / aθul/
(5) congruent across language conditions for bilinguals	RED and ROJO	/rɒxɒ/ and / red/
(6) incongruent across language conditions for bilinguals	RED and ROJO	/aθul / and / blu:/
(7) incongruent across language conditions for bilinguals (different alphabetic scripts)	RED and 红	/blu:/ and /lʌn/

Source: own elaboration.

Bilingual advantage can manifest itself in better results in the Stroop task compared to monolinguals (e.g. Bialystok et al., 2008) possibly resulting from greater practice in sustaining the cognitive demands of managing two languages. Moreover, one language dominance and degree of proficiency in the languages have been shown to influence the Stroop test result (e.g. Rosselli et al., 2002; Zied et al., 2004; Gasquoine et al., 2007). The effect of complex incongruence conditions in terms of colour, language and alphabetic script as well as phonological overlap between the tested languages (Preston and Lambert, 1969; Roelofs, 2003) has also been identified in the Stroop task results. In general, unbalanced bilinguals (with one dominant language) show more significant interference effect on the Stroop task in their dominant language in within language conditions. They also experience a stronger interference when the distracter words are in the dominant language than in between language conditions. However, the across language condition also produces significant interference results, as MacLeod (1991: 187) notices "interference between the two languages of a bilingual, although not as great as that within either one of the languages is very robust".

A study by Fang et al. (1981) of Chinese-English, Japanese-English and Spanish-English bilinguals showed that interference was greater in within language than across language conditions. Goldfarb and Tzelgov (2007) refer to this consistent result as *within-language Stroop superiority effect* (WLSSE). The researchers studied Hebrew-English bilinguals performing the task showed more significant interference results in within language than across language conditions when the distracter was ink colour but not when it was a colour-associated word (grass, sky, tomato). They concluded that objects automatically activate items in the response set and lexical representations do not. In other words, if the distracter is a picture and the required response language is L1 or L2, the images are matched immediately with the correct lexicon. This could suggest that the studied participants had separate mental lexicons triggered by the experiment condition and followed consistently throughout the trial. The within versus across language Stroop result difference is ascribed to a greater conflict for response relevant than irrelevant words (Lavelda, 2012).

All the above-cited studies have been conducted in naturalistic conditions and the participants have acquired (or were acquiring at the moment of research) both (or more) of their languages in target language speaking environments. They represented balanced and unbalanced, early and late bilinguals but the languages they spoke were used in their everyday lives (if to unequal degrees). The participants in the present longitudinal study differ significantly from those described above in their exposition to L2 and level of competence. Early primary students learning

EFL in a country where the target language is not commonly used outside the classroom context can hardly be referred to as unbalanced bilinguals. Their functional command as well as metalinguistic knowledge is minimal as compared to their peers raised in naturally bilingual conditions. However, the specific structure of language instruction as described in the previous chapter provides the learners with an L2 input that differs in quantity and quality from what is offered in the traditional classroom. It would, therefore, be interesting to see whether this mode of instruction had any influence on the development of cognitive abilities of the learners. The following procedure describes a quantitative study conducted on the same group of participants as described in the previous chapter and a control group in quasi-experimental conditions.

5.3.1. Research questions

The present study aims to investigate the possible correlation between the form of language instruction and the results of Stroop test in study and control groups. Quantitative analysis of data gathered in this part of the longitudinal study aimed to address the following research questions:

(1) Will the study group results confirm the within-language superiority effect in L1?

(2) Will the study group results confirm the within-language superiority effect in L2?

(3) Will the study group results reflect the bilingual processing advantage over control group results in within-language L1 and L2 conditions?

(4) Will there be a difference in reaction times between the study and control group in across language condition?

5.3.2. Method and materials

The current study aims to examine the degree of the Stroop colour-word interference effect in three language conditions: (1) *incongruent L1 condition*, in which the names of Polish colours are printed in incompatible colours of ink and the participants are asked to name the colour of the ink in L1 suppressing the urge to read the word; (2) *incongruent L2 condition*, in which the names of English colours are printed in incompatible colours of ink and the participants are asked to name the colour of the ink in L2 suppressing the urge to read the word; and (3) *in-*

congruent bilingual condition, in which the names of English colours are printed in incompatible colours of ink and the participants are asked to name the colour of the ink in L1. In the first two trials, therefore, there is only one distracter in the form of the incongruent name of colour, while in last trial there are 2 distracters the name of the colour and the language code of this word.

The participants were tested individually during 40 minute-long sessions conducted in comfortable conditions in a separate classroom used for speech therapy. The room was small and quiet with good daytime lightning. Additionally, potential stress was minimized by the fact that the children knew the experimenter from the observation context so she was not a stranger. The study was conducted at the end of the first semester of the third grade after a two-and-a-half year period of EFL instruction. Children were informed that they are going to take part in a competition whose winner is the one who completes the tasks the fastest and most accurately. All participants were awarded sweets at the end of the test. None of the participants had any diagnosed impairments of learning difficulties. The participants' ability to recognise and name colours in both languages was tested before the first trial on the basis of a set of rectangles in the colours used in the proper task as presented in Figure 19. All participants completed this task successfully and without any problems or hesitations.

Figure 19. Colour recognition test

Source: own materials

Similarly, participants were tested on their ability to read the names of colours in both languages. They were presented with a list of words in black ink (as presented in Fig. 20) and asked to read them aloud. All participants completed the task successfully.

Subjects received verbal instructions in Polish prior to each task throughout the whole experiment.

The Stroop task material contained five A4 (297 x 210 mm) cards. Cards 1 and 2 presented 120 colour rectangles while cards 3, 4 and 5 presented 120

BRĄZOWY	**ZIELONY**	**CZERWONY**	**NIEBIESKI**
RED	**BLUE**	**GREEN**	**BROWN**

Figure 20. Word recognition test

Source: own materials

names of colours, arranged in 6 columns of 20 items each. Words were printed in Calibri capitals 14 point bold. The colours used in the test were: red, green, blue, and brown. Each colour was used five times in each column. The Polish names of colours were three syllables long (CZERWONY, ZIELONY, NIEBIESKI, BRĄZOWY) and the English names consisted of one syllable (RED, GREEN, BLUE, BROWN). The colour rectangles on cards 1 and 2 were arranged in different order to avoid habituation effect. Each colour was presented in each column 5 times and arranged in such a way that no colour was repeated one after the other either in line or in column to avoid interference. The names of colours in cards 3 and 4 were presented in quasi-random order so that no name was printed in its matching colour and no name or colour was repeated one after the other either in line or in column. To avoid habituation effect the arrangement of Polish and English colour words and colours was different.

The test was administered in 3 conditions, within which there were 5 trials with the use of the 5 cards. The response language in trials 1, 2 and 5 was Polish, while in trials 3 and 4 the learners were asked to provide the names of ink colour in English.

(1) *Incongruent L1 condition*

In the first condition, two trials were conducted. In trial I the participants were given card 1 and asked to name the colours of the rectangles in Polish. The times were measured by the experimenter with a stopwatch. In trial II participants were given card 3 in which the Polish colour words were written in non-corresponding colours. The participants were asked to name the colour of the font of each word as quickly and accurately as possible starting from the top left hand side corner and moving along rows from top to bottom. The experimenter with a stopwatch measured the times. The numerical data for reaction time analysis were calculated as a difference between trials II and I.

(2) *Incongruent L2 condition*

In the second condition, analogically, two trials were conducted. In trial III participants were given card 2 and asked to name the colours of the rectangles in English. The times were measured by the experimenter with a stopwatch. In trial IV participants were given card 4 in which the English colour words were written in non-corresponding colours. The participants were asked to name the colour of the font of each word as quickly and accurately as possible starting from the top left hand side corner and moving along rows from top to bottom. The times were measured by the experimenter with a stopwatch. The numerical data for reaction time analysis were calculated as a difference between trials IV and III.

(3) *Incongruent bilingual condition*

In the final condition one trial (V) was conducted. Participants were given card 5 in which the English colour words were written in non-corresponding colours in the same order as the Polish colour names on card 2. The distance between the two trials using this arrangement and the difference in language code assured avoidance of habituation effect. The participants were asked to name the colour of the font of each word in Polish as quickly and accurately as possible starting from the top left hand side corner and moving along rows from top to bottom. The times were measured by the experimenter with a stopwatch. The numerical data for reaction time analysis were calculated as a difference between trials II and I.

5.3.3. Data collection and quantitative analysis

The results gathered in all trials produced no significant data on the number of errors. All participants completed the trials with no or minimal errors that had a form or hesitations or immediate corrections. No mistakes were left without repair, which might have slightly influenced the reaction time calculated on the basis of the duration of trials but were not significant enough to merit analysis on their own. The small number of such instances in any individual trial and their even distribution among all participants allows for speculating that the minimal influence on time measurement in individual trials is insignificant for the present discussion. The general statistical analysis of results discussed below has been conducted with the use of Microsoft Excel 2007 to determine the mean, median and standard deviation for each individual test in each group and supplemented by a two-way analysis of variance (ANOVA) to present the interrelations between all the studied elements.

Mean and median scores of all the tests are presented in Table 8 below.

Table 8. Mean and median reaction times

	Within-language (Polish)			Within-language (English)			Across languages		
	study	control	difference	study	control	difference	study	control	difference
Mean	100	179.3	-79.3	101.3	107.5	-6.2	96.7	84	12.7
Median	92.5	193.6	-101.6	87.3	122.7	-35.4	91.7	80.5	11.2
SD	19.2	45.1	-26.1	38.4	59.5	-21.1	26.8	33.2	-6.4

Source: own elaboration.

The longer the reaction times, the grater the degree of interference. Negative results reflect study group advantage in the reaction time speed, i.e. lower degree of interference or faster switching. Although the analysis below often refers to the average scores (following the common practice in other studies in literature on the subject), it is important to remember that the more accurate results are represented in the median as they reflect consistency as opposed to incidental peaks. The above presented results will be discussed in two dimensions: within each group and between both groups.

Control group results

Table 9. Mean and median reaction times in control group

	Within-language (Polish)	Within-language (English)	Across languages
Mean	179.3	107.5	84
Median	193.6	122.7	80.5
SD	45.1	59.5	33.2

Source: own elaboration.

The results obtained by the control group are in line with the previously discussed findings of other studies indicating a significant interference effect in the within-language condition where the distracter words are in L1 and the response language is the same. Since the tendency is observable in both monolingual and bilingual Stroop task results, the control group data obtained in this study seems to support the general understanding of the phenomena. The significant values of standard deviation may result from low homogeneity of linguistic experience in L2 among the participants whose exposure to English outside school was beyond control of the experimenter in the current study.

The mean score of interference in across-language conditions constitutes 41% of within-language results (for L1 and 78% for L2), as compared to the approximate 75% found in numerous studies of bilingual Stroop effect (e.g. Dyer, 1971; MacLeod, 1991; Preston & Lambert, 1969). The difference in within-language and across-language Stroop effects is attributed to powerful activation of the response language, which results in greater conflict between the spoken and written representation of the same code. Bilinguals have also been found to be able to partially suppress the non-target language (Green, 1998), which results in less interference of the weaker written language with the response L1. In the control group results the significantly lower proportional relation of within-language L1 to across-language results may indicate very low interference of L2 in the test. This, in turn, may suggest minimal familiarity of the participants in the control group with the English names of colours which did not interfere with their L1 response significantly enough to mirror results obtained in similar conditions by bilinguals. In other words, the result may suggest that the participants do not display features characteristic of bilingual processing typically found in Stroop test.

The within-language test results where the language of both distraction and response was English (L2) produced predictably shorter median reaction times. Since it is more difficult to suppress the dominant language stimulus, the L2 written words did not require the same amount of inhibition as the more familiar words in L1. Additionally, in the context of the present study, the result may have been influenced by the fact that the control group participants had very basic skills of reading in L2. Although they could read the names of colours in English (which was tested at the beginning of the experiment) they did so with considerable difficulty and certain pronunciation problems, which may suggest that their familiarity with the written colour names in L2 was considerably limited. This reading disadvantage of the control group seems justified in the light of the observed traditional EFL classes where very little attention is devoted to the written forms of words. It is highly probable that the control group participants were much more frequently exposed to the names of colours in English in their spoken form, than to their written representations. As a result, control group participants found it much easier to ignore the script and focus on naming the colours, which resulted in less effort and time devoted to inhibition and, consequently, led to shorter reaction times.

Study group results

Table 10. Mean and median reaction times in study group

	Within-language (Polish)	Within-language (English)	Across languages
Mean	100	101.3	96.7
Median	92.5	87.3	91.7
SD	19.2	38.4	26.8

Source: own elaboration.

The results obtained by the study group presented in Table 10, are different from those of the control group (Table 9 above) in that the differences between reaction times in all three conditions are minimal. The considerably lower values of standard deviation than observed in the control group may result from higher homogeneity of linguistic experience in L2 among participants whose exposure to formal English instruction outside school was controlled, and practically eliminated, by the experimenter in the current study.

The mean score of interference in across-language conditions constitutes 97% of within-language results, as compared to the approximate 75% found in bilingual Stroop effect studies quoted above. In fact, very similar results were obtained in all three conditions. This similarity of results may be explained by the study group's familiarity with the tested terms. The command of English exhibited by the observed learners can by no means be even approximated to that of balanced bilinguals, but their exposure to and production of these particular names of colours was significant throughout the whole observation period. All tasks completed by the learners during the two-and-a-half year period of general early primary education that required working with colours (e.g. colouring pictures, creating colour cards, describing objects etc.), employed English as the medium of communication. The names of English colours were heavily used in recorded tasks (cf. 4.26), in students' responses (cf. 4.33) and by the teacher in giving instructions

(5.1) [grade I; arts and crafts; clothes; Ls are making traditional dresses in flat origami]
1 T: bierzemy karton **blue** i wycinamy z niego **one big circle**.
we take ***blue*** *cardboard and cut out*

The learners also showed sensitivity to colour naming:

(5.2) [grade II; subject area: arts and crafts; topic: grandparents' day; context: students choose colour paper presented by the teacher to make invitations]
1 T: Choose the colour. How many do you need?
2 S1: Four. Blue, purple and blue… ale to taki inny blue… jaki to blue?
3 T: navy blue
4 S1: navy blue and pink

It seems that colours for the study group participants are not merely terms in two languages but are closely linked to the extralinguistic concepts in L1, as well as in L2. Such a strong identification of colour words in L2 and the actual colours might not have developed in control group learners. While control group results clearly indicate high interference in L1 distracter – L1 response condition, suggesting a natural bond between the words and concepts, it is easier for these students to ignore the same connection in the case of L2. For the study group it is nearly just as difficult to inhibit the habitual urge to name the colour in within-language conditions regardless of the cue/response language involved.

In the final, across-language condition the test results are very similar to the other two. This may suggest that although the participants were able to partially suppress the interference of the weaker written language, the cost of this operation was similar to the one observed in the within-language conditions. Although L2 colour words were used as distracters, and the response language was the dominant L1, the participants still experienced significant interference. The observed distraction was twofold. It came both from the English written words and colour names in L2, which was observed in the form of immediately corrected errors where RED was named "blue" or "czerwony" as opposed to the correct response - "niebieski" /blue/. The median results show the commonly reported tendency of higher interference effect in the L1 within-language test than in the same conditions in L2. Although English names of colours are very familiar in the spoken, as well as written form to the study group, the effect of the weaker language inhibition is still visible.

Study vs. control group results

The results obtained by both groups in all three conditions were juxtaposed to reveal potential differences. Table 11 below summarizes the differences in reaction times between the scores of the study group as opposed to the control group. Negative results mark the advantage of the former (shorter reaction times). Positive results reflect the advantage of the control group (shorter reaction times). Figures 21, 22 and 23 illustrate the obtained results of reaction time for 23 participants of the respective groups. The vertical axis represents time in seconds, while the horizontal axis signifies the participants. The scores obtained in the study have been arranged in ascending order for both groups individually for a better visual representation of the tendency. Additionally, all graphs include a finer trend line for each of the groups in respective colours.

Table 11. Differences in mean and median reaction times between the study group and the control group

	Within-language (Polish)	Within-language (English)	Across languages
	Difference	Difference	Difference
Mean	-79.3	-6.2	12.7
Median	-101.6	-35.4	11.2
SD	-26.1	-21.1	-6.4

Source: own elaboration.

The most significant difference in the three tested conditions was recorded in the within-language test where the cue and response language was L1. Even though this is the condition where the interference is greatest (as noted in literature and reflected in the present study), it may be concluded that the study group displays an advantage over the control group in terms of shorter reaction times.

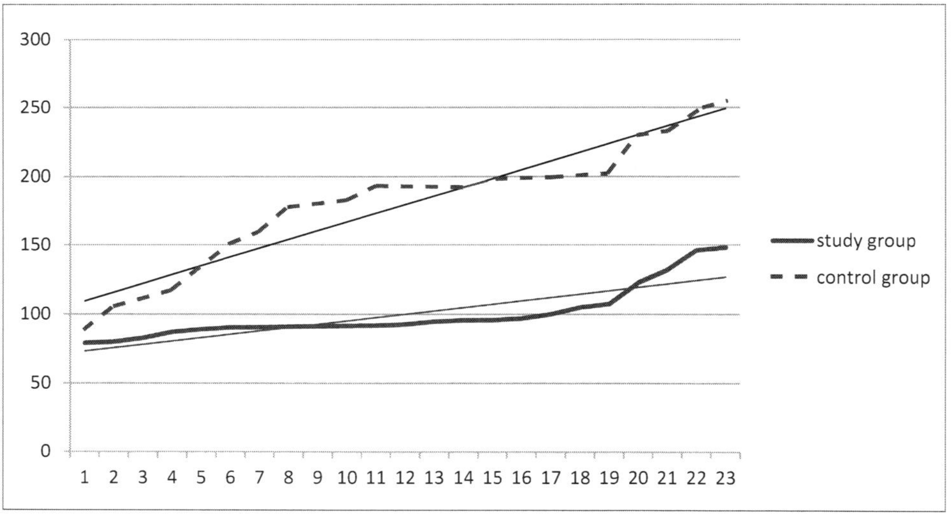

Figure 21. Within-language L1 test results (in seconds)

Source: own elaboration

The considerably faster reaction times in the study group may suggest an advantage in terms of inhibition of the written distracter. The learners in this group seem to be much better able to suppress the habitual reaction of reading the words instead of focusing on the ink colour. Although both trend lines go upward, the control group trend line ascends at a much higher rate, thus creating a broadening wedge formation that is likely to increase in volume as the breakout advances. It may, therefore, be concluded that in the within-language L1 test, the study group will consistently gain advantage over the control group in reaction time exhibiting better executive control.

The graphical representation of scores obtained by both groups in the test where both the cue and response language was English shows an interesting pattern. Although a few members of the control group were faster in their reaction to the stimuli, most of them took more time to do the test in this particular condition. The median difference (-35.4) is small as compared to the L1 condition (-101.6) but it still gives advantage to the control group. This is reflected in the intersecting trend lines in Figure 22.

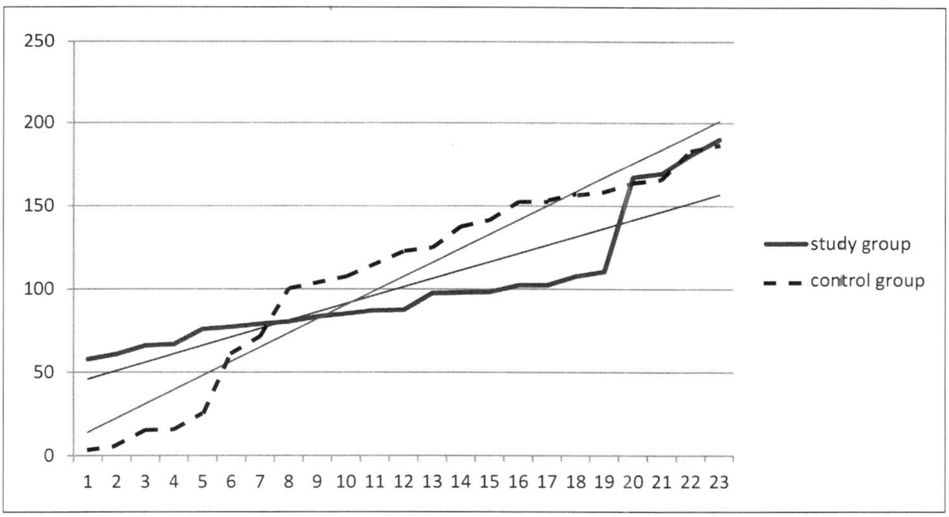

Figure 22. Within language L2 test results (in seconds)

Source: own elaboration

Although in some areas the results of both groups are nearly identical while in some the control group displays shorter reaction times than the study group, the trend foretells a growing discrepancy in the function of time giving advantage to the study group (in the form of lower reaction time values). The inconsistency of control group score values may result from lower homogeneity discussed before. While some participants of the group did exceptionally well on the test showing very low reaction times, most of the learners took longer to name the colours in this condition. The incidental low scores in the control group may reflect additional exposure to L2 outside school likening the performance abilities of these particular students to those from the study group (or even outdoing their performance). The less steep trend line of the control group signifies a weaker but also a more consistent trend, with only a few students whose reaction times are considerably high (at the level of control group participants).

In the final condition the reaction time results of the study and control groups are reversed. The control group completed the task faster than the study group participants, but the difference is much smaller than in the previous conditions (11.2 as opposed to -101.6 and 35.4). As depicted in Figure 23, the reaction times of the study group are slightly longer in the case of most participants than those of the control group.

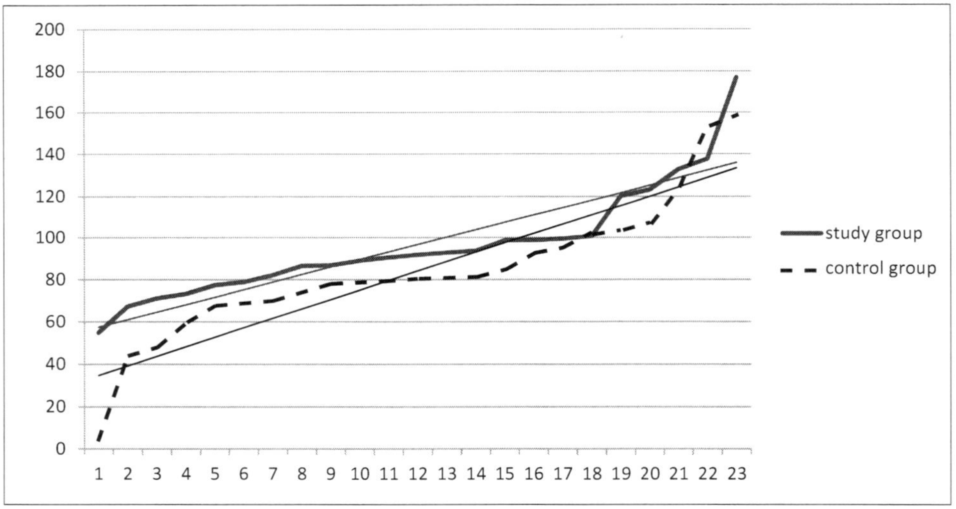

Figure 23. Across-language test results (in seconds)

Source: own elaboration

It seems that the cue words written in English distracted the study group more than the control group participants. As a result, they took longer to name the ink colour in Polish. Since the common practice for the study group is continuous code shifting and analysing which response language is preferred by the interlocutor in any particular conversation, the students are slightly confused as to which code to analyse and use in the third test condition. This hesitation is reflected in minimally longer reaction times than in the case of the control group. However, the narrowing wedge formation of the trend lines foretells a forthcoming intersection and a reversal of trend in the function of time. When the breakout advances after the intersection the study group may gain advantage also in this condition.

In addition to the descriptive statistical analysis, a more detailed two-way analysis of variance (ANOVA) was conducted with the use of SPSS 20. software to ensure reliability of results.

Descriptive statistics

Dependent variable: reaction time; independent variables: group, test

Table 12. Mean effects of the group and of the test

Group	Test	Mean	SD
Study	within language – Polish	99.9583	19.18092
	within language – English	101.2739	38.36990
	across languages	96.6596	26.76547
	Total	99.2972	28.82604
Control	within language – Polish	179.3435	45.09054
	within language – English	133.5889	35.42239
	across languages	87.6636	28.88532
	Total	134.2556	53.59716
Total	within language – Polish	139.6509	52.76711
	within language – English	115.4610	40.08261
	across languages	92.2616	27.87641
	Total	115.9819	45.80527

Source: own elaboration.

Marginal means for the main effect are $\bar{x} = 139.6509$ for the within-language - Polish test, $\bar{x} = 115.4610$ for the within-language - English test and $\bar{x} = 92.2616$ for across-language test. The results are expressed in seconds and signify the mean reaction time for the completion of each test. The analysis of total results shows that in general for both groups the within-language test in Polish generated the highest interference and thus required longest reaction time.

Figure 24 is a summative graphical representation of all reaction time means scored by both groups in the three experiment conditions. The graph clearly shows a significant difference in the distribution of results in both groups. While the study group results do not differ drastically across all tests, the control group scores are exceptionally high for the within-language test and show a falling trend towards the across-language test result which is even lower than that obtained by the study group.

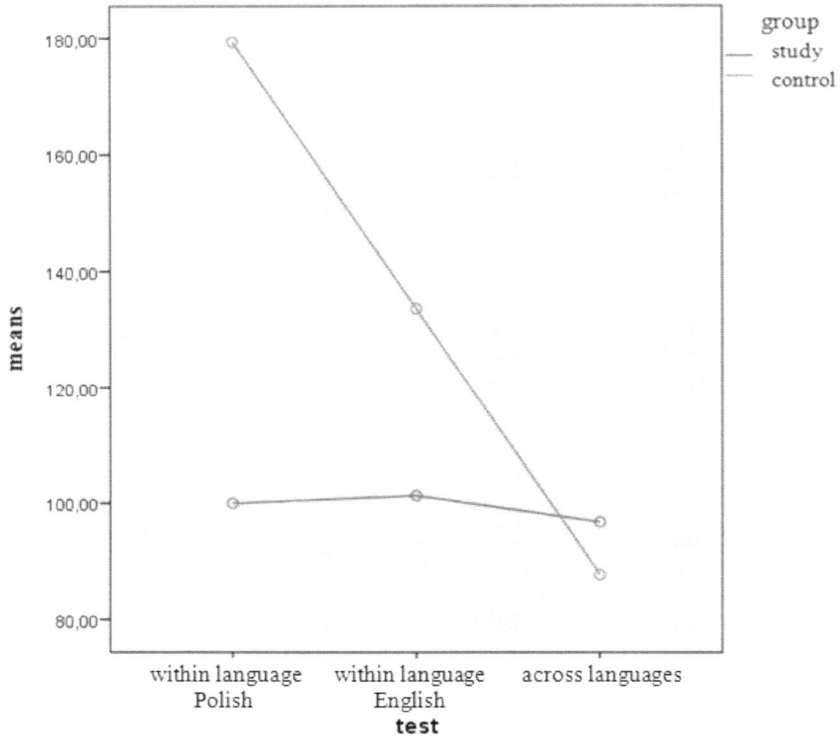

Figure 24. Summary of mean results for both groups in all test conditions

Source: Source: own elaboration

Effects analysis

The analysis showed that the marginal means of both groups are statistically significant and that they also significantly differ from each other. The analysis of variance additionally allows for checking whether the interaction means differs significantly between the groups.

Table 13. Effect analysis of interaction and marginal means

Dependent variable: Reaction time						
Source	Type III sum of squares	df	Mean Square	F	Significance	Partial Eta squared
Corrected model	135028.293	5	27005.659	24.335	.000	.491
Constant	1774623.695	1	1774623.695	1599.152	.000	.927
Group	38367.690	1	38367.690	34.574	.000	.215
Test	51331.786	2	25665.893	23.128	.000	.269
group * test	44489.608	2	22244.804	20.045	.000	.241
Error	139825.765	126	1109.728			
Total	2050491.621	132				
Total corrected	274854.057	131				

Source: own elaboration.

Main group effect is statistically significant, $F(1.126) = 34.574$, $p < 0.001$. This means that the mean results of the study and control groups are significantly different. Significantly lower mean was recorded in the study group (comparison of marginal means). Multiple comparisons have shown that main test effect is statistically significant, with $F(2.126) = 23.128$, $p < 0.001$. Three tests have been compared in all possible pairs (each with each). In order to indicate which pairs differ significantly, post-hoc Bonferroni test was conducted.

Table 14. Multiple comparisons post-hoc Bonferroni test

(I) test	(J) test	Mean diffe-rence (I-J)	SD	Significance
within language - Polish	within language - English	24.1899*	7.15479	.003
	across languages	47.3893*	6.98464	.000
within language - English	within language - Polish	-24.1899*	7.15479	.003
	across languages	23.1994*	7.19216	.005
across languages	within language - Polish	-47.3893*	6.98464	.000
	within language - English	-23.1994*	7.19216	.005
*. mean difference is significant at the value of < 0,05.				

Source: own elaboration.

The results in the particular tests differ significantly in all pairs even at the more restrictive significance value of $p < 0.01$. The highest result was obtained for within-language - Polish test and the lowest for the across-language test (comparison of marginal means).

Interaction (combined group and test impact)

A significant interaction was found, $F(2.126)=20.045$, $p<0.001$. The impact of one factor on the other differs on different levels of the other factor. The interpretation is made with the use of means graph. In the case of within-language tests lower means were obtained in the studied group, whereas in the across languages test the control group scored lower. Interaction is marked by the crossing lines in the graph. Comparison of means between the groups separately for each test is presented in Table 15 below.

Table 15. Pair comparison for group

Dependent variable: reaction Times					
Test	(I) group	(J) group	Means difference (I-J)	SD	Signifi-cance
within langu-age – Polish	study	control	-79.385*	9.823	.000
	control	study	79.385*	9.823	.000
within langu-age – English	study	control	-32.315*	10.483	.003
	control	study	32.315*	10.483	.003

Dependent variable: reaction Times					
Test	(I) group	(J) group	Means difference (I-J)	SD	Significance
across languages	study	control	8.996	9.934	.367
	control	study	-8.996	9.934	.367
Based on estimated marginal means. Statistical significance at the value of <0.05.					

Source: own elaboration.

The results in study and control group differ significantly ($p<0.01$) in the case of both within-language tests. In the case of across-language test the difference is statistically insignificant ($p=0.367>0.05$). Pair comparison for test is presented in Table 16 below.

Table16. Pair comparison for test

Dependent variable: Reaction time					
Group	(I) test	(J) test	Means difference (I-J)	SD	Significance
Study	within language - Polish	within language - English	-1.316	9.823	.894
		across languages	3.299	9.823	.738
	within language - English	within language - Polish	1.316	9.823	.894
		across languages	4.614	9.823	.639
	across languages	within language - Polish	-3.299	9.823	.738
		within language - English	-4.614	9.823	.639
Control	within language - Polish	within language - English	45.755*	10.483	.000
		across languages	91.680*	9.934	.000
	within language - English	within language - Polish	-45.755*	10.483	.000
		across languages	45.925*	10.587	.000
	across languages	within language - Polish	-91.680*	9.934	.000
		within language - English	-45.925*	10.587	.000
Based on estimated marginal means. Means difference is significant at the value of <0.05.					

Source: own elaboration.

In the control group the test results differ significantly in all pairs (each with each) ($p<0.001$). In case of the study group the differences between the tests are statistically insignificant for each pair ($p>0,05$).

5.3.4. Results and discussion

The aim of this part of the present study was to determine how formal instruction conditions influence the pattern of interference effects in unbalanced, L1-dominant young learners of L2. The participants came from the same background and were taught in the same way in all other subjects except English. The analysed factor was the influence of the mode of L2 instruction on the performance of executive control in within-language conditions (L1 and L2), as well as in across-language conditions (with L1 as response language).

The above analysis attempted to provide answers to the previously formulated research questions. The first question concerned the participants' performance in the first condition where the cue and response language was Polish as opposed to the third, across-language condition.

(1) *Will the study group results confirm the within-language superiority effect in L1?*

Table 17. Mean results of study group of within-language (L1) and across-language tests

	Within-language (Polish)	Across-languages
	Study	Study
Mean	100	96.7

Source: own elaboration.

Although the study group experienced greater interference in the within-language than in across-language condition, the difference in mean score is minimal with the across-language result of 97% of the within-language condition. Since the same ratio in the control group amounts to 41%, the findings seem to be in line with Costa et al. (2006) suggestion that the inhibition of the non-response language depends on the difference between the proficiency of participants in the two languages. The researchers conclude that the greater the difference, the weaker the interference effect. The study, however, was conducted on bilinguals who gain their command of the languages in naturalistic conditions. Okuniewska (2007) failed to show the same regularity in the case of English speakers who learned L2 in formal instruction. She ascribes the findings to the age of the participants and the type of bilingualism they represent, stating that "the benefiting influence of bilingualism on cognitive control was observed mainly in early, relatively balanced bilinguals" (Bialystok et.al., 2004; in Okuniewska, 2007: 60) The participants of the present study are much younger than those in Okuniewska's research but they still represent largely unbalanced, minimal bilingualism gained through formal instruction. If the results of the present study were to be confirmed by further research, it could indicate that the mode of EFL instruction in early primary education is a powerful factor in executive functions development, despite the non-naturalistic conditions of L2 acquisition.

The second question concerned the participants' performance in the second condition where the cue and response language was English, as opposed to the third, across-language condition.

(2) *Will the study group results confirm the within-language superiority effect in L2?*

Table 18. Mean results of study group in within-language (L2) and across-language tests

	Within-language (English)	Across languages
	study	Study
Mean	101.3	96.7

Source: own elaboration.

The mean results of the across-language test were lower than the within-language scores but the ratio of 95% is nearly as high as for within language in L1. It seems that the inhibition of the non-response factor (name of colour in conditions I and II and language in condition III) requires similar effort in all experiment conditions for the study group. This is contrary to the results obtained by the control group, which more closely resemble the findings of previous studies in the reviewed literature also for test in monolinguals. Perhaps the participants of the control group are only minimally influenced by the second language and it does not significantly interfere with the much more salient concept of colour.

(3) *Will the study group results reflect the bilingual processing advantage over control group results in within-language L1 and L2 conditions?*

Table 19. Comparison of within-language L1 results in both groups

	Within-language (Polish)		
	study	control	Difference
Median	92.5	193.6	-101.6

Source: own elaboration.

The bilingual processing advantage in the first and second experiment conditions where the cue and response language is the same, are better visible in the comparison of median scores. The results of the study in the first condition where the cue and response language was Polish, show the greatest discrepancy in the whole study. The study group participants completed the task in less than half of the time that was required by the control group. In this condition the interference effect is not influenced by the linguistic competence of the participants. The difference, thus, can be attributed to the bilingual processing advantage of the study group over the control group. This particular result is most valuable for the present study, as it reflects better executive control of the study group, which is believed to have developed as a result of the character of classroom discourse discussed in Chapter Four. The instruction mode in the process of EFL education characterised by considerable exposure to L2 and frequent codeswitching in the teacher's and the learners' discourse might have influenced executive functions of the learners leading to the presented test results. The control group, deprived of everyday contact with the foreign language or the natural contexts of its use, did not experience enough attention switches to develop a high level of executive control to be reflected in the within-language (L1) Stroop task scores. The interference of the distracter in the case of the control group participants is much greater than recorded in the study group. It may, thus, be assumed that the study group have developed better inhibition skills than the control group participants.

Table 20. Comparison of within-language L2 results in both groups

	Within-language (English)		
	study	control	Difference
Median	87.3	122.7	-35.4

Source: own elaboration.

Similarly to within-language condition where the cue and response code was L1, in the second condition the study group completed the task faster than the control group. The difference is not as significant as in the former case, but the median difference of 35.4 seconds is considerable. Again, it may be interpreted as a bilingual processing advantage of the study group. Although both groups exhibited expectedly shorter reaction times in the second condition, the tendency remained and the study group's scores are again lower than those of the control group suggesting better executive control in the studied participants.

(4) *Will there be a difference in reaction times between the study and control group in across-language condition?*

Table 21. Comparison of within-language L1 results in both groups

	Across languages		
	study	control	Difference
Median	91.7	80.5	11.2

Source: own elaboration.

The control group performed better (had shorter reaction times) only in the third, across-language condition where the cue language was English and the response language was L1. This result can be explained by a lower level of familiarity of the English names of colours in the written form in the control group, and higher level of hesitation in the choice of response language in the case of the study group. For the control group the natural language of response is Polish since they have experienced less codeswitching throughout the two-and-a-half year period of formal EFL education at school. The distracter in the form of English colour names was, thus, not strong enough to attract their attention. The postulated activation of both lexicons in conflict conditions discussed earlier might have been too weak to significantly influence the test result. In the case of the study group, the activation was not very much stronger and allowed the students to complete the task in a shorter time than the previous ones, but it was still more noticeable than in the case of the control group participants. In conclusion, the study group participants find it easier to inhibit L2 than L1 cues when the response language is Polish, but the interference of L2 cue is still stronger than in the control group.

5.3.5. Limitations and suggestions for further research

Although the research has reached its aims, there were some unavoidable limitations despite careful planning. Thus, for one thing, it was not possible to eliminate exposure to foreign language in the form of additional private classes and courses in the control group, which resulted in high levels of standard deviation in this group, as opposed to the study group where this factor was controlled. Interestingly, however, even though some of the students in the control group were attending additional English classes, it did not influence the overall average score of the group to the extent that would signify their advantage in executive control over the study group. This may suggest that the decisive factor is not the amount of exposure, or even the level of the language the learners are exposed to outside the classroom, but rather the mode of formal instruction. The frequent code switches in the study group discourse might be responsible for the shorter reaction times, especially in the first experiment condition. It is highly probable that the instruction pattern in the additional courses resembled more closely the control group formal EFL instruction at school rather than the one delivered to the study group. It may, thus, be suggested that the typical structure of EFL education of two 45-minute lessons a week in the early primary sector, even accompanied by one or two extra hours of private tuition, produces worse results in the development of executive control than systematic codeswitching characteristic of the study group discourse.

It is, however, not certain exactly which executive functions played a decisive role in the study group reaction times advantage. The foregoing discussion suggests that it is their ability to inhibit the competing stimulus that is responsible for the result. Learners of the study group had more experience in consciously ignoring the language that was not the response code in a particular context and, as a result, developed more effective inhibition mechanisms. However, inhibition might not be the only executive function involved in the process. Goswami (2011) offers a neat summary of the discussion on this issue.

The concept of inhibition may explain why an action is not executed or why interfering information is ignored, but it does not explain why the correct response is executed. For example, the construct of inhibition, by itself, fails to address how one decides what is to be inhibited. Hence, as a function, inhibition needs to interact with other functions, including problem representation and planning (584).

As demonstrated in Chapter Four, the study group do not only switch between the two language codes for typical reasons (e.g. cued by language used in the previous utterance or when a given item is characteristic of the language culture or context in which it was acquired), but also when the switch cannot be easily justified (cf. transcript 4.16). The English word islands appear in the Polish matrix sentences in places where Polish words would normally be expected. Since it is more costly to inhibit the dominant language, the occurrence of an L2 lexical item whose Polish counterpart is more easily available for the learners in their L1 may signify a conscious decision to inhibit the natural response in Polish. What is more, the recording shows that the learners inserting the L2 words in L1 sentence do so with no signs if hesitation and the whole utterance sounds as fluent as if it was structured wholly in the dominant language. The motivation for the use of L2 words seems to be utterly intrinsic as the response language is not indicated by the interlocutor, nor is there any chance of inaccessibility of the lexical items in Polish. It appears that the study group participants take pleasure in mixing the codes and still being understood by the other members of the interaction. There is also a common acceptance of the practice as no one ever protested against the use of an English word or phrase in a discourse. Therefore, the findings of this study seem to support Goswami's conclusion that inhibition mechanism does not fully explain how the participants decide which items to suppress. Therefore, inhibition may be a necessary but not sufficient factor to account for the development of executive functions and problem solving (Müller et al., 2006).

Some studies have reported that the changes in actual and functional capacity of working memory are also responsible for the development of executive functions (cf. Diamond, 2002; Morton and Munakata, 2003). Memory capacity increases with age, which implies better executive control in older participants. The present study, however, tested two groups of third-graders whose age was similar and this factor was marked as insignificant for the test results. If memory capacity is responsible for the differences in the scores, then this would suggest that the codeswitching practice in the study group classroom discourse influenced the participants' executive functions in this respect. Osaka et al. (2012) have shown that verbal to visual codeswitching improves working memory capacity in older adults. If the limited extent to which the study group participants experienced codeswitching between L1 and L2 produced similar results, then working memory should also be considered responsible for the bilingual advantage in the within-language (L1) Stroop test results.

The design of the teaching practice in the two and a half years of the observation was not under strict control of the researcher since she was not teacher of the class. The specific character of the discourse which was very often modified by the learners' needs was virtually impossible to plan ahead. Some instances of L2 discourse stretches were fixed elements of daily routine (e.g. classroom calendar; saying hello), while others were imposed by the teacher's plan to run some activities in English. Yet another group were elements of instructions accompanying other subjects-related tasks that were observed to transform gradually from L1 with one element of English in the first grade to fully L2 instructions in grade three. However, the teacher was not always consistent with this practice providing a variety of combinations of both languages in her instructions throughout the study. The final and most interesting group of instances of L2 use were those inspired by the learners themselves when they demanded to know the English version of the material taught within another subject area. Although this unpredictability of the amount and contexts of L2 use may be treated as a limitation to the study, it seems to constitute the strength of the teaching process in developing executive control in the learners (as reflected in the test results). Perhaps it is this flexibility and student partial control over L2 teaching process that created the advantage. The participants of the study group also seem more language aware and ready to take risks in their use of L2.

The outcomes of the quantitative analysis of the results obtained in this part of the present research suggest that the study group participants might have benefited from the mode of L2 instruction they had been provided with. The control group, on the other hand, did not exhibit significant signs of L2 interference in the task. It would be interesting to see if the control group across-language results would mirror the ones obtained by another group of third-graders consisting of L1-only speakers. If the results are similar, it could suggest that traditional EFL teaching does not provide enough language experience to enhance the learners' executive control (cf. Roselli et al., 2000). This, however, would be very difficult to test as foreign language learning is obligatory in all early primary education settings. The only other context that could be used for this purpose is the third grade in a school where the foreign language is not English. The control group could also be tested in the same way as in the present study but with a different (unknown to the learners) language cue words in the second and third conditions. If the results were similar to the ones obtained in this study it could suggest that the typical EFL instruction did not increase the learners' familiarity of the L2.

Finally, this short experimental test does not, by any means, claim to be conclusive. Further research in the field of EFL teaching mode correlations with the executive control development in early primary learners of English is necessary to confirm the findings. The tendency found in this study may indicate the direction of necessary changes in EFL teaching practice in this sector. The findings suggest a desirable shift in the stakeholders' focus from the expected increase in linguistic competence of young learners to a broader issue of their cognitive development. Should these finding be confirmed by further study, the teaching practice adopted by the study group teacher should be popularised and introduced as a widely accepted policy of teaching foreign languages in early primary education on a wider scale.

CONCLUSIONS AND IMPLICATIONS

The main aim of the present work has been to explore the discourse structure in an English classroom where the foreign language is taught as an integral element of early elementary curriculum rather than a separate subject. The preliminary theoretical considerations included in Chapter One provided a relevant and current state of the art background for the understanding of maturational processes involved in the development of an early primary student. Chapter Two discussed the multiple perspectives on the notion of bilingualism in an attempt to place the context observed in the present study along the continuum of the phenomenon. Special attention was paid to codeswitching as a characteristic feature of any bilingual discourse with a view to observing similar patterns of linguistic behaviour in the studied environment. Theoretical issues of pedagogy and education constituted the core of Chapter Three, where separate space was devoted to forms of bilingual education and their applications in Polish schools. The presentation and discussion of the theoretical, experimental and pedagogical contexts of early development and formal education served as an introduction to the two empirical chapters (Four and Five), which provided an account and analysis of both qualitative and quantitative character. The discussion that ensued was based on a longitudinal ethnographic study of a group that was taught English as an element of integrated subjects. The examples quoted in this part of the dissertation were recorded during 240 hours of non-participant observations conducted in the school. The quantitative part of the study involved a Stroop test for executive control measurement, administered in quasi-experimental conditions in the study and control group in the same school.

The discussion concerning the linguistic behaviour of the learners led to a conclusion that the patterns of discourse recorded during the study resemble bilingual contexts in that they are rich in code switches that are difficult to justify by merely linguistic reasons. It has been found that the learners change the codes not only in the presence of the teacher but also in interactions with their peers, and they take pleasure in practicing newly acquired language. They also show risk taking strategies with multiple examples of applying the learned language to new contexts. The pupils' lexicons have been found to be partially motivated by their own initiative to learn the English counterparts of the Polish words and concepts they were learning in other subject areas. This resulted in their vocabulary being enriched with lexical items that would never be taught at this level and that is more likely to be found in a core curriculum for learning English as L1 in naturalistic contexts. The pupils were also found to play with English words and create new meanings. The teaching practices in the observed classroom constantly encouraged the children to make sense of unknown words and phrases form the context, as immediate translations were not used by the teacher. As a result, the learners had a chance to develop early language awareness that will be helpful in their future L2 education and real life.

The results of a Stroop test measuring executive control through reaction times in conflict conditions showed that the learners of the observed group have better developed cognitive skills in the area of inhibition. The obtained measures suggest that the study group students display similar patterns in the test completion to more advanced bilingual speakers, thus displaying a bilingual advantage. The discussion following the statistical analysis of the results led to a conclusion that, over time, the study group students have developed a cognitive flexibility and inhibition control by constant voluntary codeswitching displaying conscious control over the selective inhibition of competing lexemes.

The ultimate goal of the present study was to investigate the possible consequences of an EFL teaching mode that integrated L2 with content instruction at the early primary education level. The obtained results of the observation and findings of the Stroop test show that the described pattern of teaching foreign languages to young learners, as well as the observed classroom practices, indicate the right direction of the changes that should be implemented in other contexts.

A foreign language became an obligatory subject in the first grade of primary education in 2008 as a result of a large-scale educational reform in Poland. In consequence of the same legislative regulation, the age of children starting formal instruction has been lowered from seven to six. This has been a gradual process, which will finish in September 2014 with all pupils in the first grade at the age of six. Although lowering the age of starting primary education together with an earlier onset of foreign language instruction is a popular tendency in many European Union countries (Key Data on Teaching Languages in Europe, 2012), it seems reasonable to consider the possible effects of the reform on everyday teaching practice. Children who start primary education earlier than before require the teachers to adjust their methods of instruction to the less developed cognitive abilities of their learners. Although the lower age should not significantly hamper academic progress of the students, the specificity of younger learners' developmental abilities and constraints must be well-understood by the teachers.

A number of research studies have indicated a strong positive correlation between executive control and academic skills (cf. Blair & Razza, 2007; Duncan et al., 2007). This perspective, however, is often reported to have little impact on curriculum development and teaching practices (e.g. Bierman et al., 2008; Diamond, 2010). It seems crucial that curriculum development processes be informed by research findings in the field of developmental sciences and that dialogue be maintained between all stakeholders in the early primary education sector in order to provide the best conditions for nurturing competent learners.

Control over executive functions allows children to voluntarily direct their attention to one stimulus while ignoring other, competing distractions. This makes executive control an essential ability for successful participation in educational processes at school. In order to successfully take part in everyday early primary activities like shared reading or information exchange, children need to have a good grasp of conscious attention and inhibitory control, sometimes referred to as effortful control (cf. Liew, 2012). Academic achievement is determined by a number of executive functions, the most important of which are presented in Figure 25.

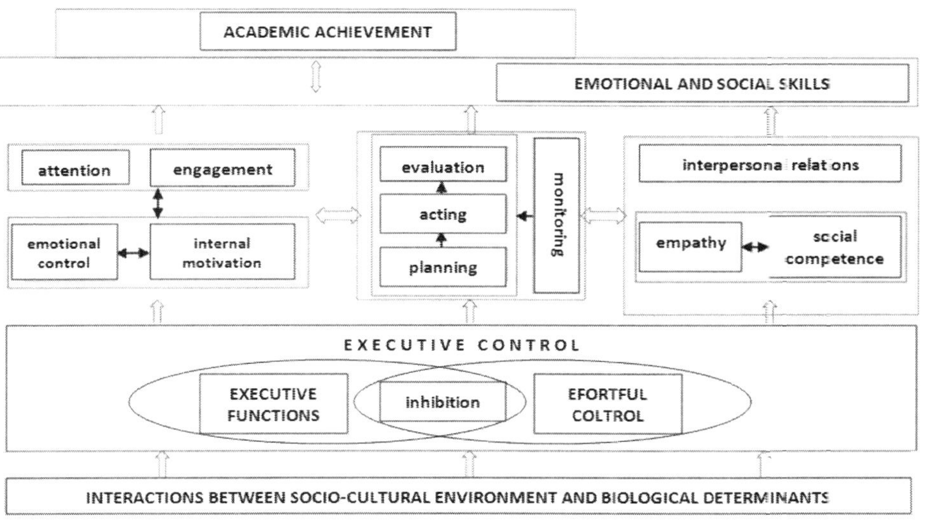

Figure 25. Executive control determining academic achievement

Source: Adapted from Brzezińska and Nowotnik, 2012: 71

As the diagram shows, there is a complex network of interrelated processes in which a child continuously participates in an educational context. Since the level of executive control predicts school success or failure, it would be highly beneficial to implement the classroom practices that support executive control development. With time, the formal learning context gradually becomes more structured and pupils who are not good at paying attention or controlling themselves are likely to face not only academic failure, but also conflicts with peers and teachers (Denham et al., 2003; Rimm-Kaufman et al., 2005). Those who are skilled at effortful control, on the other hand, tend to have higher social competences and display fewer problem behaviours.

Executive functions display considerable flexibility and react to training applied as early as at the age of four of five (Diamond et al., 2007). Well-developed executive control is a desired and highly valued skill in all formal education contexts, but it seems most wanted in early primary eduaction, which marks the onset of socialisation processes and major academic achievements such as gaining basic literacy and numeracy skills. This is the time when substantial cognitive work load is paired with behavioural demands on childern who have just entered the context of formal instruction. Young learners struggle not only with the new requirements and content material but also, or perhaps primarily, with their own cognitive capacities to internalise them. Teachers, constrained by the rich curriculum, tend to focus on knowledge transfer and development of literacy and numeracy outcomes, rather than the underlying processes that govern and the effectiveness of their work.

It would of course be highly unjustified to assume that the results of the present study constitute sufficient grounds for the formulation of far-fetched pedagogical recommendation, and there surely exists the need to explore the issue much further. However, some directions and suggestions seem admissible. It appears legitimate to advocate integration of foreign language teaching with all other subject areas to offer ample opportunities for language exposure and use. The type of instruction described in the present study may not be replicable in all contexts, as there might be a shortage of teachers qualified for delivering both early primary and foreign language instruction. However, it seems justified to promote such professional development. In contexts where instruction is necessarily shared between two teachers, close cooperation between the instructiors should be strongly encouraged in order to provide the learners with coherent units of knowledge in all subject areas, including English. In the light of the present study, codeswitching and the use of both langugaes by the teacher in partially unpredictable patterns appear to be beneficial, contrary to what is advocated by some researchers who promote a clear-cut separation of the codes of instruction. Magdalena Szpotowicz, for instance, instructs early primary teachers who also teach English to young learners to definitely indicate the beginning and end of an English lesson.

Early primary teacher should assign a strict time in a day for a language lesson. Such lessons may be conducted twice or three times a week or even every day for a few minutes. The teacher has to clearly mark the boundaries of the lesson using for instance a puppet or a hat (I'm putting on my English hat), it can also be a song. It's important to signal that from now on the tecaher will speak English (2011: 8).

The classroom procedure proposed by the author in question does not differ from a typical L2 teaching practice, with the exception of the same person acting as the early primary instructor and English teacher. Additionally, such a solution seems rather artificial, as the teacher with whom the learners spend all day, suddenly pretends to be unable to communicate in the language in which the whole day teaching practice was conducted. The idea seems to stem from the OPOL (one person, one language) principle in bilingual families. However, as it has been discussed in Chapter 2, the rule is inconsistent even in naturalistic conditions, as parents themselves do not always use their own mother tongue in communicating with their children, while language mixing and switching is a common phenomenon. By adopting the practice suggested by Szpotowicz (2011), teachers deprive learners of the experience of codeswitching, which was shown to be beneficial in the present study in terms of their cognitive development. More studies are needed in order to establish whether the form of foreign language instruction that was subject to the present study has in any way influenced the learners development of L2 competence, but even if the benefits do not include exceptional foreign language progress, the significant advantage in the area of executive control is vital in the light of its decisive role in general academic achievement.

It seems that early primary teachers may not display the highest proficiency level of English, but they have a better understanding of developmental processes of young learners and a closer relationship with their learners. They also create more opportunities for the natural occurrence of the foreign language. Repetitive nature of daily routines allows them to revise functional structures many times. In other words, they are working in a context that provides conditions for foreign language introduction and use that are beyond access of a specialist English teacher, who sees a given group twice a week, for organizational as well as socio-emotional reasons. Since most of the foreign language instruction to date is delivered by English teachers, it seems reasonable that their teaching practices are revisited and adjusted to provide optimal conditions for children's development. Foreign language lessons should always be closely connected with the topics covered in all other subject areas on a given day to abide by the principle of holistic teaching. The content of the classes should be flexible enough to offer the learners an opportunity to expand their lexicon in the areas they are truly interested in. Teaching individual items of vocabulary should be replaced by phrases and functional chunks that give the pupils a feeling of being communicative. Encouraged should be exposure to repetitive instructions in the target language, instead of immediate translations to foster language awareness. The ultimate goal of the teacher should not be to equip young learners with impressive lexicons filled with words that cannot be put in any structures or contexts, but rather to give them tools for very basic communication, develop awareness and foster general cognitive development. But most importantly of all, students should be allowed to take pleasure in learning a new language and express themselves in ways they find suitable even if it requires multiple code switches.

It is the hope of the author that the implementation of the recommendations outlined above will make English instruction more effective and conducive to the attainment of executive control, which, in turn, will improve academic performance in their future education. At the same time, it is essential to adjust the teaching practices discussed in this study to the specific teaching contexts, including the availability of resources and patterns of cooperation among all the stakeholders.

REFERENCES

Akbari, R. (2008), Post-method discourse and practice. *TESOL Quaterly*, 42(4) 641–652.

Alcón, E. and Safont Jordà, M. (2008), Pragmatic awareness in second language acquisition. In: Cenoz, J. and Hornberger, N. (eds.), *Encyclopedia of language and education*. Vol. 6: *Knowledge about language*. New York: Springer Science.

Alexander, R. (2004), Still no pedagogy? Principle, pragmatism and compliance in primary education, *Cambridge Journal of Education*, 34 (1): 7–33.

Allhusen, V. (2002), Stages of development. In: Salkind, N. (ed.), *Child development*. New York: Macmillan Reference USA.

Allwright, D. and Hanks, J. (2009), The developing language learner. An introduction to exploratory practice. Houndmills: Palgrave Macmillan.

Allwright, R. L. (1991), *The death of the method*. Working Papers 10. The exploratory practice centre. University of Lancaster.

Allwright, R. L. (2003), Exploratory practice: rethinking practitioner research in language teaching. *Language Teaching Research*, 7: 113–141.

Allwright, R. L. and Bailey, K. M. (1991), *Focus on the language classroom*. Cambridge: Cambridge University Press.

Anglin, J. (1993), *Vocabulary development: a morphological analysis. Monographs of the Society for Research in Child Development*: 581–165.

Aristotle (1998), *The metaphysics. Book lambda*. Translated by Lawson-Tancred, H. London: Penguin Books.

Austin, J. (1962), *How to do things with words*. London: OUP.

Baetens Beardsmore, H. (ed.) (1981), *Elements of bilingual theory*. Brussels, Belgium: Vrije Universiteit te Brussel: 28–47.

Baetens Beardsmore, H. (1986), *Bilingualism: basic principles*. Clevedon: Multilingual Matters.

Baetens Beardsmore, H. (1999), Language policy and bilingual education in Brunei Darussalam. *Bulletin des séances* (Académie Royale Des Sciences D'Outre-Mer) 45 (4): 507–523.

Baetens Beardsmore, H. (2003), Who is afraid of bilingualism? In: Dewaele, J-M. and Housen, A. (eds.), *Bilingualism: beyond basic principles*. Clevedon: Multilingual Matters: 10–28.

Baker, C. (2001), *Foundations of bilingual education and bilingualism*. Clevedon: Multilingual Matters Ltd.

Bandura, A. (1989), Social cognitive theory. In: R. Vasta (ed.), *Annals of child development*. Vol. 6: *Six theories of child development*. Greenwich: JAI Press: 1–60.

Barnes, D. (1969) Language in the secondary classroom. In: Barnes, D., Britton, J. and Rosen, H. (eds.), *Language, the learner and the school*. Harmondsworth: Penguin.

Barnes, D., Britton, J. and Rosen, H. (eds.) (1990), *Language, the learner and the school*, Harmondsworth: Penguin.

Barron, A. (2003), *Acquisition of Interlanguage Pragmatics*. Amsterdam: John Benjamins.

Bentahila, A. (1983), *Language attitudes among Arabic-French bilinguals in Morocco*. Clevedon, UK: Multilingual Matters.

Berk, L. (2001), *Awakening children's minds. How parents and teachers can make a difference*. Oxford: OUP.

Berry, J. W. (1980) Acculturation as varieties of adaptation. In: Padilla, A. (ed.), *Acculturation: theory, models and findings*. Boulder: Westview: 9–25.

Bialystok, E. (1999), Cognitive complexity and attentional control in the bilingual mind. *Child Development*, 70: 636–644.

Bialystok, E. (2001), *Bilingualism in Development: Language, Literacy and Cognition*, New York: CUP.

Bialystok, E., Craik, F., Klein, E. and Viswanathan, M. (2004), Bilingual aging and cognitive control: Evidence from the Simon task. *Psychology and Aging* 19 (2): 290–303.

Bialystok, E., Craik, F.I.M., and Luk, G. (2008), Cognitive control and lexical access in younger and older bilinguals. *Journal of Experimental Psychology: Learning, Memory, and Cognition*, 34(4): 859–873.

Bialystok, E., Craik, F.I.M., Green, D.W. and Gollan, T.H. (2009) Bilingual minds. *Psychology, Science and Public Interest*, 10: 89–129.

Bialystok, E., and Shapero, D. (2005), Ambiguous benefits: the effect of bilingualism on reversing ambiguous figures. *Developmental Science*, 8: 595–604.

Bierman, K., Nix, R., Greenberg, M., Blair, C., and Domitrovich, C. (2008), Executive functions and school readiness intervention: Impact, moderation, and mediation in the Head Start REDI program. *Development and Psychopathology*, 20: 821–843.

Bjorklund, D. and Bering, J. (2002) Milestones of development. In: Salkind, N. (ed.) (2002), *Child Development*. New York: Macmillan Reference USA.

Blair, C., and Razza, R. (2007), Relating effortful control, executive function, and false belief understanding to emerging math and literacy ability in kindergarten. *Child Development*, 78: 647–663.

Blommaert, J. and Bulcaen, C. (2000), Critical discourse analysis, *Annual Review of Anthropology*, 29: 447–466.

Bloomfield, L. (1927), Literate and illiterate speech. *American Speech*, 2: 432–439.

Bloomfield, L. (1933), *Language*. London: Allen and Unwin.

Bowkett, S. (2005), *100 ideas for teaching creativity*. London: Continuum

Brainerd, C. and Reyna, V. (1990), Gist is the grist: Fuzzy-trace theory and the new intuitionism. *Developmental Review*, 10: 3–47.

Bredekamp, S. and Copple, C., eds. (1997), *Developmentally appropriate practice in early childhood programs*. Washington: National Association for the Education of Young Children.

Breen, M.P., Hird, B., Milton, M., Oliver, R., and Thwaite, A. (2001), Making sense of language teaching: Teachers' principles and classroom practices. *Applied Linguistics*, 22: 470–501.

Brinton, D.M., Snow, M.A. and Wesche, M.B. (1989), *Content-based second language instruction*. Boston: Heinle and Heinle Publishers.

Brock, C. (1986), The effect of referential questions on ESL classroom discourse. *TESOL Quarterly*, 20: 47–59.

Brooks, G. and Brooks, M. (1993), In search of understanding: the case for constructivist classrooms. Alexandria: ASCD.

Brown, D. (2008), English language teaching in the "post-method" era: toward better diagnosis, treatment and assessment. In: Richards, J. and Renandya, W. (eds.), *Methodology in language teaching: an anthology of current practice*. Cambridge: C UP.

Brown, H. D. (1994), Teaching by principles: an interactive approach to language pedagogy. Englewood Cliffs: Prentice Hall Regents.

Brown, H. D. (2011), Exchange structure in the modern classroom: 'Jamie's dream school'. In: *Innervate. Leading undergraduate work in English studies*. Vol. 3, Nottingham: University of Nottingham.

Brunson, L. (2002), Development. In: Salkind, N. (ed.), *Child development*. New York: Macmillan Reference USA.

Brzezińska, A. (ed.) (2000), *Wygotski i z Wygotskim w tle*. Toruń: Wydawnictwo Uniwersytetu Mikołaja Kopernika.

Brzezińska, A. (2000a), *Społeczna psychologia rozwoju*. Warszawa: Wydawnictwo Naukowe Scholar.

Brzezińska, A and Nowotnik, A. (2012), Funkcje wykonawcze a funkcjonowanie dziecka w środowisku przedszkolnym i szkolnym. *Edukacja*, 1(117): 61–74.

Brzostek, J. (1994), *Teacher talk: evidence from Polish classrooms*. Unpublished MA thesis. Institute of English Studies, University of Łódź.

Brzózka, J., Glinka, K., Harmak, K., Izbińska, K., Jasiocha, A. and Went, W. (2010), *Razem w szkole*. Warszawa: WSiP.

Burton, D. (1981), Analysing spoken discourse. In: Coulthard, M. and Montgomery (eds.), *Studies in discourse analysis*. London: Routledge&Kegan Paul Ltd.

Butler, Y. and Hakuta, K. (2006), Bilingualism and second language acquisition. In: Bhatia, T. and Ritchie, W. (eds.), *The handbook of bilingualism*. Oxford: Blackwell Publishing: 114–145.

Campos, J., Frankel, C., and Camras, L. (2004), On the nature of emotion regulation. *Child Development*, 75: 377–394.

Caprara, G and Cervone, D. (2000), *Personality. Determinants, dynamics and potentials*. Cambridge: CUP.

Card, N., Isaacs, J. and Hodges, E. (2002), Social development. In: Salkind, N. (ed.), *Child development*. New York: Macmillan Reference USA.

Carlson S. M., Meltzoff A. N. (2008), Bilingual experience and executive functioning in young children. *Developmental Science*, 11: 282–298.

Carr, D. (2003), *Making sense of education: an introduction to the philosophy and theory of education*. London: Routledge Falmer.

Cattell, H.E. (1996), The original big five: A historical perspective. *European Review of Applied Psychology*, 46: 5–14.

Cazden, C. and Beck, S. (2003), Classroom discourse. In: Graesser, A, Gernsbacher, M. and Goldman, S. (eds.), *Handbook of discourse processes*. Mahwah: Lawrence Erlbaum: 165–197.

Celce-Murcia, M. (2007), Rethinking the role of communicative competence in language teaching. In: Soler, E. and Safont Jordà, M. (eds.), *Intercultural language use and language learning*. Dordrecht: Springer: 41–57.

Cenoz, J. and Hornberger, N. (eds.), (2008), *Encyclopedia of language and education.2nd edition volume 6: knowledge about language*. New York: Springer Science: 193–204.

Chess, S. and Thomas, A. (1977), Temperamental individuality from childhood to adolescence. *Journal of Child Psychiatry*, 16: 218–226.

Chomsky, N. (1971), The case against B.F. Skinner. *The New York Review of Books*, December 27: 18–24.

Clark, E. (1995), Language acquisition: the lexicon and syntax. In: Milne, J. and Eimas, P. (eds.), *Speech, Language and Communication*. San Diego: Academic Press: 303–337.

Coderre, E. Van Heuven, W. and Conklin, K. (2013), The timing and magnitude of Stroop interference and facilitation in monolinguals and bilinguals. *Bilingualism*, 16(2): 420–441.

Collins, J. (2004), Foreword In: Rogers, R. (ed.), *An introduction to critical discourse analysis in education*, Mahwah: Lawrence Erlbaum Associates: xxi-xxv.

Costa, A., Hernández, M. and Sebastián-Gallés, N. (2008), Bilingualism aids conflict resolution: evidence from the ANT task. *Cognition*, 106: 59–86.

Costa A., Hernández M., Costa-Faidella J. and Sebastián-Gallés N. (2009), On the bilingual advantage in conflict processing: now you see it, now you do not. *Cognition*, 113: 135–149.

Coulthard, M. and Montgomery, M. (eds.) (1981), *Studies in discourse analysis*. London: Routledge&Kegan Paul Ltd.

Coyle, D. (2007), Content and language integrated learning: Towards a connected research agenda for CLIL pedagogies. *The International Journal of Bilingual Education and Bilingualism*, 10: 543–562.

Cummins, J. (1984), *Bilingualism and special education: issues in assessment and pedagogy*. Clevedon: Multilingual Matters.

Cummins, J. (2000), *Language, power and pedagogy: bilingual children in the crossfire*. Clevedon, UK: Multilingual Matters.

Dahlin, E., Nyberg, L., Bäckman, L. and Neely, A.S. (2008), Plasticity of executive functioning in young and older adults: immediate training gains, transfer, and long-term maintenance. *Psychology of Aging*, 23: 720–730.

Dalton-Puffer, C. (2007), *Discourse in content and language integrated learning (CLIL) classrooms*. Amsterdam: Benjamins.

Dalton-Puffer, C. (2008), Outcomes and processes in content and language integrated learning (CLIL): current research from Europe. In: Delanoy, W., Volkmann, L., *Future perspectives for English language teaching*. Heidelberg: Carl Winteer.

Dalton-Puffer, C. and Nikula, T. (2006), *Current research on CLIL: special issue of VIEWZ*, 15 (3).

Damon, W. and Lerner R. (eds.) (2008), *Child and adolescent development. An advanced course*. Hoboken NJ: John Wiley & Sons, Inc.

Dalton-Puffer, C. and Smit, U. (eds.) (2007), *Empirical perspectives on CLIL Classroom Discourse*. Frankfurt: Peter Lang.

Davis, D. (2011), *Child development. A practitioner's guide*. London: Guilford Press.

De Bot, K. (1992), A bilingual production model: Levelt's "speaking" model adapted. *Applied Linguistics*, 13: 1–24.

de Cock, S., Granger, S., Leech, G. and McEnery, T. (1998), An automated approach to the phrasicon of EFL learners. In: Granger, S. (ed.), *Learner English on computer*. Harlow: Longman.

de Graaff, R., Koopman, G.J., Anikina, Y., and Westhoff, G. (2007), An observation tool for effective L2 pedagogy in content and language integrated learning (CLIL). *The International Journal of Bilingual Education and Bilingualism*, 10: 603–624.

Delanoy, W., Volkmann, L. (2008), *Future perspectives for English language teaching*. Heidelberg: Carl Winteer.

Dempster, F. N. (1981), Memory span: sources of individual and developmental differences. *Psychological Bulletin*, 89: 63–100.

Denham, S.A., Blair, K.A., DeMulder, E., Levitas, J., Sawyer, K. and Auerbach-Major, S. (2003), Preschool emotional competence: pathways to social competence? *Child Development*, 74: 238–256.

DePalma, R. (2010), *Language use in the two-way classroom. Lessons from a Spanish-English bilingual kindergarten*. Bristol: Multilingual Matters.

Desforges, Ch. (2004), Learning. In: Moon, B.; Ben-Peretz, M. and Brown, S.(eds.), *Routledge international companion to education*. London: Routledge: 65–82.

Desimone, R. and Duncan, J. (1995), Neural mechanisms of selective visual attention. *Annual review of neuroscience*, 18: 193–222.

Dewaele, J., Housen, A. and Li Wei (eds.) (2003), *Bilingualism: beyond basic principles*. Clevedon: Multilingual Matters.

Dewey, J-M. (1958), *Experience and nature*, La Salle: Open Court.

Di Pietro, R. (1977), Code-switching as a verbal strategy among bilinguals. In: F. Eckerman (ed.), *Current themes in linguistics*. Washington: Hemisphere Publishing: 3–13.

Diamond, A. (2002), Normal development of prefrontal cortex from birth to young adulthood: Cognitive functions, anatomy and biochemistry. In: Stuss, D. and Knight, R. (eds.), *Principles of frontal lobe function*. London: Oxford University Press: 466–503.

Diamond, A. (2010), The evidence base for improving school outcomes by addressing the whole child and by addressing skills and attitudes, not just content. *Early Education and Development*, 21: 780–793.

Diamond, A., Barnett, W., Thomas, J., Munro, S. (2007), Preschool program improves cognitive control. *Science*, 30: 1387–1388.

Diebold, Jr. A.R. (1961), Incipient bilingualism. *Language* 37: 97–112.

Diesendruck, G. (2007), Mechanisms of word learning. In: Hoff, E. and Shatz, M. (eds.), *Blackwell handbook of language development*. Oxford: Blackwell Publishing.

Dolson, D and Meyer, J. (1992), Longitudinal study of three program models for language-minority students: A critical examination of reported findings. *Bilingual Research Journal*, 16(1, 2): 105–157.

Doodley, J. and Evans, V. (2009), *Fairyland 1*. Newbury: Express Publishing.

Duff, P. (2008), Language socialisation, participation and identity: ethnographic approaches. In: Martin-Jones, M., de Mejía, A., Hornberger, N. (eds.) (2008), *Encyclopaedia of langugae education*. Vol. 3: *Discourse and education*. New York: Springer Science: 107–119.

Duncan, G., Dowsett, C., Claessens, A., Magnuson, K., Huston, A. and Klebanov, P. (2007), School readiness and later achievement. *Developmental Psychology*, 43: 1428–1446.

Dyer, F. (1971), Colour-naming interference in monolinguals and bilinguals. *Journal of Verbal Learning and Verbal Behaviour*, 10(3): 297–302.

Edge, J. (ed.) (2001), *Action research*. Washington: TESO.

Edwards, J. (1985), *Language, society and identity*. Oxford: Blackwell.

Edwards, J. (2006), Foundations of bilingualism. In: Bhatia, T. and Ritchie, W. (eds.), *The Handbook of Bilingualism*. Oxford: Blackwell Publishing: 7–31.

Ek, L. (2008), Social Bilingualism. In: Gonzalez, J. (ed.), *Encyclopedia of bilingual education* Thousand Oaks: SAGE Publications Inc.: 749–752.

Elliott, R. (2003), Executive functions and their disorders. *British Medical Bulletin*, 65: 49–59.

Ellis, B. and Bjorklund, D. (eds.) (2005), *Origins of the social mind. Evolutionary psychology and child development*. London: Guildford Press.

Ellis, R. (1997), *Second language acquisition*. Oxford: OUPress.

Ellis, R., (1997), *SLA research and language teaching*. Oxford: Oxford University P.

Erikson, E.H. (1950), *Childhood and society*. New York: Norton.

Eurydice 2009 – *Key data on education in Europe*. Brussels: European Commission.

Falk, M. (2001), *SPRINT – Hot eller möjlighet?* Stockholm: Skolverket, Liber Distribution.

Fang S.P., Tzeng O.J.L., & Alva L. (1981), Intralanguage vs. interlanguage Stroop effects in two types of writing systems. *Memory & Cognition*, 9(6): 609–617.

Farrell, T., and Jacobs, G. (2010), *Essentials for successful English language teaching*. London: Continuum International Publishing Group.

Fasold, R. (1984), *The sociolinguistics of society*. Oxford: Blackwell.

Ferguson, C.A. (1972 [1959]) Diglossia. In: Giglio, P. (ed.), *Language in social context*. Harmondsworth: Penguin: 325–340.

Fishman, J.A. (1971), The sociology of language. In: Fishman, J. (ed.), *Advances in the sociology of language*. Vol.1. The Hague: Mouton.

Fishman, J.A. (1976), *Bilingual education. An international sociological perspective*. Rowley, MA: Newbury House.

Fishman, J.A., Cooper, R.L. and Ma, R. (1971), *Bilingualism in the Barrio*. Bloomington: Indiana University Language Sciences Series.

Fishman, J. A. (1980), Bilingualism and biculturalism as individual and as societal phenomena. *Journal of Multilingual and Multicultural Development*, 1: 3–15.

Fitouri, C. (1983), *Biculturalisme, bilinguisme et education*. Paris: Delachaux & Niestle.

Flavell, J. and Hartman, B. (2004), What children know about mental experiences. *Young Children*, 59: 102–109.

Fodor, J.A. (1975), *The language of thought*. New York: Crowell.

Fodor, J. A., and Pylyshyn, Z. W. (1988), Connectionism and cognitive architecture: A critical analysis. In: S. Pinker and J. Mehler (eds.), *Connections and symbols*. 3–71. Cambridge MA: MIT Press / Bradford Books.

Flowerdew, J. (2013), *Discourse in English language education*. Abingdon: Routledge.

Fox, E. J. (2008), Contextualistic perspectives. In: Spector, J., Merrill, M., van Merriënboer, J. and Driscoll, M. (eds.), *Handbook of research on educational communications and technology*. Mahwah: Lawrence Erlbaum Associates: 55–66.

Freud, S. (1905), Three essays on the theory of sexuality. *Standard Edition*, 7: 130–243.

García, A. (2008), Classroom bilingualism at an early age: towards a more natural EFL context. In: Pérez-Vidal, C., Juan-Garau, M., and Bel, A. *A portrait of the young in the new multilingual Spain*. Clevedon: Multilingual Matters: 185–199.

Gardner, N. (2000), *Basque in education in the Basque autonomous community*. Vitoria-Gasteiz: Euskal Autonomi Erkidegoko Administrazioa.

Garrett, P. (2008), Researching language socialisation. In: King, K. and Hornberger, (eds.), *Encyclopedia of language and education*. Vol. 10: *Research methods in language and education*, New York: Springer Science: 189–201.

Garrett, P. and Bequedaño-López, P. (2002), Language socialization: continuity, transformation and change. *Annual Review of Anthropology*, 31: 339–361.

Gasquoine, P.G., Croyle, K.L., Cavazos-Gonzalez, C. and Sandoval, O. (2007), Language of administration and neuropsychological test performance in neurologically intact Hispanic American bilingual adults. *Clinical Neuropsychology*, 22: 991–1001.

Gassner, D. and Millat, D. (2006), Spoken competence in CLIL: a pragmatic take on recent Swiss data. In: Dalton-Puffer, C. and Nikula, T., *Current research on CLIL: special issue of VIEWZ*, 15(3): 15–22.

Gee, J. (2011), *An introduction to discourse analysis. Theory and method.* Abingdon: Routledge.

Genesee, F. (1987), *Learning through two languages: Studies of immersion and bilingual education.* Cambridge: Newbury House.

Gentner, D., and Boroditsky, L. (2001), Individuation, relational relativity and early word learning. In: Bowerman M. and Levinson S. (eds.), *Language acquisition and conceptual development.* Cambridge: Cambridge University Press: 215–256.

Gilligan, C. (1982), *In a different voice: psychological theory and women's development.* Cambridge MA: Harvard University Press.

Goldfarb L. and Tzelgov J. (2007), The cause of the within-language Stroop superiority effect and its implications. *Quarterly Journal of Experimental Psychology*, 60: 179–185.

Goldhaber, D. (2002), Theories of development. In: Salkind, N. (ed.), *Child development.* Macmillan Reference USA: New York.

Goldstein, T. (2004), Performed ethnography for critical language teacher education. In: Norton, B. and Toohey, K. (eds.), *Critical pedagogies and language learning*, Cambridge: Cambridge University Press: 311–326.

Golinkoff, R.M., Mervis, C.B., and Hirsh-Pasek, K. (1994), Early object labels: The case for a developmental lexical principles framework. *Journal of Child Language*, 21: 125–156.

Gollan, T. and Acenas, L. (2004), What is a TOT? Cognate and translation effects on tip-of-the-tongue states in Spanish-English and Tagalog-English bilinguals. *Journal of Experimental Psychology: Learning, Memory, and Cognition*, 30: 246–269.

Gollan, T. and Silverberg, N. (2001), Tip-of-the-tongue states in Hebrew-English bilinguals. *Bilingualism: Language and Cognition*, 4: 63–83.

Gollan, T. and Ferreira, V. (2009), Should I stay or should I switch? A cost-benefit analysis of voluntary switching in young and aging bilinguals. *Experimental Psychology: Learning, Memory, Cognition*, 35(3): 640–665.

González, J. (ed.) (2008), *Encyclopedia of bilingual education.* Thousand Oaks: SAGE Publications .

González, J. (2008), Views of bilingual education. In: González, J. (ed.), *Encyclopedia of Bilingual Education*: 887–892.

Goswami, U. (2011), *Blackwell handbook of childhood cognitive development.* Malden: Blackwell Publishers Ltd.

Graesser, A., Gernsbacher, M. and Goldman, S. (eds.) (2003), *Handbook of discourse processes*. Mahwah: Lawrence Erlbaum.

Grant, R. and Wong, S. (2003), Barriers to literacy for language-minority learners: An argument for change in the literacy and education profession. *Journal of Adolescent and Adult Literacy* 46: 386–394.

Green, D.W. (1998), Mental control of the bilingual lexico-semantic system. *Bilingualism: Language and Cognition*, 1: 67–81.

Green, D. W., Grogan, A., Crinion, J., Ali, N., Sutton, C. and Price, C. J. (2010). Language control and parallel recovery of language in individuals with aphasia. *Aphasiology*, 24: 188–209.

Greenspan, S. (1997), *The growth of the mind and the endangered origins of intelligence*. New York: Addison-Wesley.

Grin, F. (2005), *Added value of CLIL*. Paper presented at the changing European classroom - the potential of plurilingual education conference, Luxembourg.

Gumperz, J. J. (1982), *Discourse strategies*. Cambridge: Cambridge University Press.

Gutiérrez, K., Baquedaño-López, P. and Asato, J. (2001), English for the children: The new literacy of the old world order, *Bilingual Review Journal*, 24: 87–112.

Guz, S. (ed.) (2005), *Rozwój i edukacja dziecka: szanse i zagrożenia*. Lublin: Wydawnictwo Uniwersytetu Marii Curie-Skłodowskiej.

Halford, G. S. (1993), *Children's understanding: The development of mental models*. Hillsdale: Erlbaum.

Halford, G. and Andrews, G. (2006), Reasoning and problem solving. In: Kuhn, D. and Siegler, R. (eds.), *Child psychology*. Vol. 2: *Cognition, perception and language*. New Jersey: Wiley & Sons Inc.

Hamer, H. (1994), *Klucz do efektywności nauczania*. Warszawa: Veda.

Hamers, J. (1981), Psychological approaches to the development of bilinguality. In: Baetens Beardsmore, H. (ed.), *Elements of bilingual theory*. Brussels, Belgium: Vrije Universiteit Brussel: 28–47.

Hamers J. and Blanc, M. (2000), *Bilinguality and bilingualism*. Cambridge: Cambridge University Press.

Haney, C., Banks, C., and Zimbardo, P. (1973), A study of prisoners and guards in a simulated prison. *Naval Research Reviews*, 9: 1–17.

Hansegard, N. E. (1972), *Tvåspråkighet eller halvspråkighet?* Stockholm: Aldus Series: 253.

Harding-Esch, E. and Riley, P. (2003), *The bilingual family. A handbook for parents*. Cambridge: CU P.

Hardman, F., Smith, F. and Wall, K. (2003), 'Interactive whole class teaching' in the national literacy strategy. *Cambridge Journal of Education*, 33 (2): 197–215.

Harmer, J. (1995), *The practice of English language teaching*. Harlow: Longman.

Haugen, E. (1953), *The Norwegian language in America: a study in bilingual behaviour*. Philadelphia: University of Pennsylvania Press.

Hawkins, M. (2004), Researching English language and literacy development in schools, *Educational Researcher* 33 (3): 14–25.

Heller, M. (1992), The politics of codeswitching and language choice. *Journal of Multilingual And Multicultural Development*, 13(1–2): 123–142.

Herrera, M., Pinkley, D. (2009), *Backpack Gold 1*. Harlow: Pearson Longman.

Hinchman, K. and Young, J. (2001), Speaking but not being heard: Two adolescents negotiate classroom talk about text. *Journal of Literacy Research*, 33 (2): 243–268.

Hinde, R.A. (1987), *Individuals, relationships and culture*. Cambridge: CUP.

Hirsh-Pasek, K and Golinkoff, R. (2002), Language development. In: Salkind, N. (ed.), *Child development*. New York: Macmillan Reference USA: 228–232.

Hoare, P., & Kong, S. (2008), Late immersion in Hong Kong: Still stressed or making progress? In: T. W. Fortune and D. J. Tedick (eds.), *Pathways to multilingualism: evolving perspectives on immersion education*. Clevedon: Multilingual Matters: 242–266.

Hockett, C. (1958), *A course in modern linguistics*. New York: Macmillan.

Hoff, E and Shatz, M. (2007), *Child development*. Oxford: Blackwell Publishing.

Holm, J. (1988), *Pidgins and Creoles. volume 1: theory and structure*. Cambridge: CUP.

Housen, A. and Baetens Beardsmore, H. (1987), Curricular & extra-curricular factors in multilingual education. *Studies in Second Language Acquisition*, 9: 83–102.

Hughes, C. (2002), Executive functions and development: Why the interest. *Infant and Child Development*, 11: 69–71.

Iluk, J. (2000), *Nauczanie bilingwalne: modele, koncepcje, założenia metodyczne*. Katowice: Wydawnictwo Uniwersytetu Śląskiego.

Iluk, J. (2011), Stan i perspektywy nauczania dwujęzycznego w sekcjach niemieckojęzycznych w Polsce. In: Kątny, A. and Lukas, K. *Sprach- und Kulturkontakte in interkultureller Sicht*. Gdańsk: Wyd. Uniwersytetu Gdańskiego: 229–242.

Inhelder, B. and Piaget, J. (1964), *The early growth of logic in the child, classification and seriation*. New York: Harper & Row.

Ivanova I, Costa A. (2008), Does bilingualism hamper lexical access in speech production? *Acta Psychologica*, 127: 277–288.

Jäppinen, A.K. (2005), Thinking and content learning of mathematics and science as cognitional development in content and language integrated learning (CLIL): Teaching through a foreign language in Finland. *Language and Education*, 19: 148–169.

Jeffrey, B. and Woods, P. (2003), *The creative school*. London: Routledge.

Johnson, R and Swain, M. (1997), *Immersion education: international perspectives*. Cambridge: CUP.

Kagan, J. (1984), *The nature of a child*. New York: Basic Books.

Kagan, J. and Lamb, S. (eds.), (1987), *The emergence of morality in young children*, Chicago: University of Chicago Press.

Kamińska, K. (2005), Edukacja dwujęzyczna a zasób leksykalny dzieci w wieku przedszkolnym. In: Guz, S. (ed.), *Rozwój i edukacja dziecka: szanse i zagrożenia*. Lublin: Wydawnictwo Uniwersytetu Marii Curie-Skłodowskiej: 245–252.

Kamwangamalu, N.M. (2006), Bi-/Multilingualism in Southern Africa. In:Bhatia, T. and Ritchie, W. (eds.), *The handbook of bilingualism*. Oxford: Blackwell Publishing: 725–741.

Karbach J., Kray J. (2009), How useful is executive control training? Age differences in near and far transfer of task-switching training. *Developmental Science*, 12: 978–990.

Kasper, G. and Rose, K. (2001), Pragmatics in language teaching. In: Rose, K. and Kasper, G. (eds.), *Pragmatics in language teaching*. Cambridge: CUP: 1–12.

Kątny, A. and Lukas, K. *Sprach- und Kulturkontakte in interkultureller Sicht*. Gdańsk: Wyd. Uniwersytetu Gdańskiego.

Kegan, J. and Lamb, S. (1987), *The emergence of morality in young children*. Chicago: University of Chicago Press.

Kennedy, T. (2006), Language learning and its impact on the Brain: connecting language learning with the mind through content-based instruction. *Foreign Language Annals*, 39 (3): 471–486.

Kholberg, L. (1984), *Essays on moral development*. Vol 2: *The psychology of moral development*. San Francisco: Harper & Row.

King, K. and Hornberger, N. (eds.) (2008), *Encyclopedia of language and education*. Vol. 10: *Research methods in language and education*. New York: Springer Science.

Kleifgen, J. (2008), Discourse analysis. In: González, J. (ed.), *Encyclopedia of bilingual education*. London: Sage: 226–229.

Klieme, E. (2006), *Zusammenfassung zentraler Ergebnisse der DESI Studie*. Frankfurt am Main: Deutsches Institut für Internationale Pädagogische Forschung.

Klingberg T. (2010), Training and plasticity of working memory. *Trends in Cognitive Science*, 14: 317–324.

Kochanska, G., Murray, K. and Harlan, E. (2000), Effortful control in early childhood: continuity and change, antecedents, and implications for social development. *Developmental Psychology*, 36: 220–232.

Kohnert, K., Hernandez, A., Bates, E. (1998), Bilingual performance on the Boston Naming Test: preliminary norms in Spanish and English. *Brain and Language*, 65: 422–440.

Kolers, P.1963, Interlingual word association. *Journal of Verbal Learning and Verbal Behaviour*, 2: 291–300.

Kong, K. (2009), Content-based instruction: what can we learn from content-trained teachers' and language-trained teachers' pedagogies? *Canadian Modern Language Review*, 66: 233–267.

Krapp, K. (ed.) (2005), *Psychologists and their theories for students*. Farmington Hills: Thomson Gale.

Krauss, Michael E. (1995), *Inuit, Nunait, Nunangit, Yuget, Unangan Tanangin*. Fairbanks: Alaska Native Language Center, University of Alaska.

Kroll, J.F. and Dussias, P.E. (2006), The comprehension of words and sentences in two languages. In: Bhatia, T. and Ritchie, W. (eds.), *The handbook of bilingualism*. Oxford: Blackwell Publishing: 169–200.

Kuhn, D. and Siegler, R. (eds.), (2006), *Child psychology.* Vol. 2: *Cognition, perception and language*. New Jersey: Wiley & Sons Inc.

Kulick, D. (1992), Language shift and cultural reproduction: socialization, self, and syncretism in a Papua New Guinean village. Cambridge: Cambridge University Press.

Kumaravadivelu, B. (1992), Macrostrategies for the second/foreign language teacher. *Modern Language Journal*, 76 (1): 41–49.

Kumaravadivelu, B. (2001), Toward a postmethod pedagogy. *TESOL Quarterly*, 35: 537–560.

Kumaravadivelu, B. (2003), *Beyond methods: Macrostrategies for language teaching.* New Haven: Yale University Press.

Kumaravadivelu, B. (2006), *Understanding language teaching. From method to postmethod.* Mahwah: Lawrence Erlbaum Associates, Inc.

Lambert, W. (1977), The effects of bilingualism on the individual: Cognitive and sociocultural consequences. In: Hornby, P. (ed.), *Bilingualism: psychological, social, and educational Implications*. New York: Academic Press: 15–27.

Landry, R. and Allard, R. (1992), Subtractive bilingualism: The case of Franco-Americans in Maine's St John Valley. *Journal of Multilingual and Multicultural Development*, 13(6): 515–544.

Langford, P. (2005), *Vygotsky's developmental and educational psychology*. New York: Psychology Press.

Lavelda, J., Stanley, E. and Wicha, N. (2012), Cognitive and electrophysiological correlates of the bilingual Stroop Effect. *Frontiers in Cognition*, 3: 81–121.

Lazaraton, A. (2008), Utilizing qualitative methods for assessment. In: King, K. and Hornberger, N. (eds.), *Encyclopedia of language and education*, 2nd edition, vol. 10: *research methods in language and education*, New York: Springer Science: 197–209.

Lehto, J., Juujarvi, P., Kooistra, L. and Pulkkinen, L. Dimensions of executive functioning: Evidence from children (2003), *British Journal of Developmental Psychology*, 21: 59–70.

Leopold, W.F. (1954), *Speech development of a bilingual child: a linguist's record.* 4 Volumes. Evanston, Ill.: Northwestern University Press.

Lerner, R. (2002), *Concepts and theories of human development*. Mahwah: Lawrence Erlbaum Associates.

Liew,J. (2012), Effortful control, executive functions, and education: bringing self-regulatory and social-emotional competencies to the table. *Child Development Perspectives*, 6: 105–111.

Li Wei (2005), *The bilingualism reader*. London: Routledge.

Lickona, T. (1993), The Return of Character Education. *Educational Leadership*, 51: 6–11.

Lieberson, S. (1969), How can we describe and measure the incidence and distribution of bilingualism. In: Kelly L.G. (ed.), *Description and measurement of bilingualism.* Toronto: University of Toronto Press: 231–254.

Liew, J. and McTigue, E. M. (2010), Educating the whole child: the role of social and emotional development in achievement and school success. In: Kattington, L. (ed.), *Handbook of curriculum development*. Hauppauge: Nova Sciences: 455–478.

Long, M. and Sato, C. (1983), Classroom foreigner talk discourse: forms and functions of teachers' questions. In: Seliger, H. and Long, M. (eds.), *Classroom oriented research in second language acquisition*. Rowley: Newbury House: 268–286.

Lüdi, G. (2003), Code-switching and unbalanced bilingualism. In: Dewaele, J.-M. and Housen, A. (eds.), *Bilingualism: beyond basic principles*. Clevedon: Multilingual Matters: 174–188.

Luk, J. (2008), Classroom discourse and the construction of learner and teacher identities. In: King, K. and Hornberger, N. (eds.), *Encyclopedia of language and education*. Vol. 10: *Research methods in language and education*, New York: Springer Science: 211–134.

Łukasik, S., Petkowicz, H., Folejewska, R., Walczak-Sarao, M., Kręcisz, D., Lewandowska, B. (2010), *Wesoła szkoła i przyjaciele*. Warsaw: WSiP.

Luna, B., Garver, K., Urban, T., Lazar, N. and Sweeney, A. (2004), Maturation of cognitive processes from late childhood to adulthood. *Child Development*, 75: 1357–1372.

Mac Eoin, G., Alhqvist, A. and hAodha, C. (eds.) (1997), *Third international conference on minority languages*. Clevedon: Multilingual Matters.

Mackey, W. (1968), The description of bilingualism, In: Fishman, J. (ed.). *Readings in the sociology of language*. The Hague: Mouton: 554–584.

Mackey, W. (2005), The description of bilingualism, In: Li Wei (ed.), *Bilingualism reader*. London: Routledge: 22–50.

MacLeod, C. M. (1991), Half a century of research on the Stroop effect: an integrative review. *Psychology Bulletin*, 109: 163–203.

MacLure, M. and French, P. (1981), A comparison of talk at home and at school. In: Wells, G. *Learning through interaction: the study of language development*. Cambridge: CUP.

Maher, J. (1997), Linguistic minorities and education in Japan. *Educational Review* 49 (2): 115–127.

Majer, J. (1998), Analysis of classroom communication: implications for teacher training. In: Lewandowska-Tomaszczyk, B. (ed.), *Perspectives on foreign language teaching*. Piotrków Trybunalski: Kielce Pedagogical University Affiliated College at Piotrków Trybunalski Press: 73–101.

Majer, J. (2003), *Interactive discourse in the foreign language classroom*. Łódź: Wyd. Uniwersytetu Łódzkiego.

Malherbe, E. (1969), Comments on 'how and when do persons become bilingual?' In: Kelly L.G. (ed.), *Description and measurement of bilingualism*. Toronto: University of Toronto Press: 325–327.

Malloy, P., Cohen, R., and Jenkins, M. (1998), Frontal lobe function and dysfunction. In: Snyder, P. and Nussbaum. P. (eds.), *Clinical neuropsychology. A pocket handbook for assessment*. Washington: American Psychological Association: 573–590.

Marsh, D., Zając, M., Gołębiowska, H., Czura, A., Gapińska, A., Papaja, K., Roda, M., Urbaniak, M. (2008), *Profile report bilingual education (English) in Poland – overview of practice in selected schools*, Warszawa: CODN, British Council Poland, University of Jyväskylä.

Marsh, D., Zając, M., Gozdawa-Gołębiowska, H., Czura, A., Gapińska, A., Majewska, R., Papaja, K., Roda, M., Urbaniak, M. and Wróblewska, E. (2008), *Raport ewaluacyjny. Edukacja dwujęzyczna w Polsce (język angielski)*, Warszawa: CODN.

Martin, D. (1997), Towards a new multilingual language policy in South Africa. *Educational Review*, 49(2): 129–139.

Martin, P. (2003), Bilingual encounters in the classroom. In: Dewaele, J-M., Housen, A. and Li Wei (eds.), *Bilingualism: beyond basic principles*. Clevedon: Multilingual Matters.

Martin-Jones, M., de Mejía, A. and Hornberger, N. (eds.) (2008), *Encyclopaedia of language education*. Vol. 3: *Discourse and education*. New York: Springer Science.

McConvell, P. (1988), Nasal Cluster Dissimilation and constraints on phonological variables in Gurindji and related languages. *Aboriginal Linguistics*, 1: 135–164.

McCrae, R., and Costa P. (1986), Clinical assessment can benefit from recent advances in personality psychology. *American Psychologist*, 41: 1001–1003.

McLaughlin, B. (1985), *Second-language acquisition in childhood*. Vol. 1: *Preschool children*. Hillsdale: Lawrence Erlbaum.

Mehan, H. (1985), The structure of classroom discourse. In: van Dijk, T. (ed.), *Handbook of discourse analysis*. Vol. 3: *Discourse and dialogue*. London: Academic Press: 120–132.

Mehan, H. (1979), *Learning lessons: social organization in the classroom*. Cambridge MA: Harvard University Press.

Met, M. (1999, January), Content-based instruction: defining terms, making decisions. *NFLC reports*. Washington: The National Foreign Language Center.

Mey, J. (2001), *Pragmatics. An introduction*. Oxford: Blackwell.

Miller, J. J. (1998), Making connections through holistic learning. *Educational Leadership*, 56(4): 46–48.

Miyake, A., Friedman, N., Emerson, M., Witzki, A., Howerter, A. and Wager T. (2000), The unity and diversity of executive functions and their contributions to complex, 'frontal lobe' tasks: A latent variable analysis. *Cognitive Psychology*, 41: 49–100.

Mobidic (2004), *Nauczanie dwujęzyczne w Polsce*. http://www.mobidic.org/home-PL/index.html (accessed 12.09.2012).

Moje, E. (1997), Exploring discourse, subjectivity, and knowledge in chemistry class, *Journal of Classroom Interaction*, 32(2): 35–44.

Moll, L., Saez, R. and Dworin, J. (2001), Exploring biliteracy: two student case examples of writing as a social practice, *Elementary School Journal*, 101(4): 435–449.

Moon, B., Ben-Peretz, M. and Brown, S. (eds.) (2004), *Routledge international companion to education*. London: Routledge

Moreno, E., Rodriguez-Fornells, A. and Laine, M. (2008), Event-related potentials (ERPs) in the study of bilingual language processing. *Journal of Neurolinguistics*, 21: 477–508.

Morton, J. and Munakata, Y. (2002), Active vs. latent representations: a neural network model of perseveration, dissociation, and décalage. *Developmental Psychobiology*, 40: 255–265.

Müller, U., Dick, A., Gela, K., Overton, W. and Zelazo, P. (2006), The role of negative priming in preschoolers' flexible rule use on the Dimensional Change Card Sort Task. *Child Development*, 77: 395–412.

Myers-Scotton, C. (2002), *Contact linguistics. Bilingual encounters and grammatical outcomes*. New York: Oxford University Press.

Myers-Scotton, C. and Bolonyai, A. (2001), Calculating speakers: codeswitching in a rational choice model. *Language in Society*, 30: 1–28.

Myers-Scotton, C. and Ury, W. (1977), Bilingual strategies: the social functions of codeswitching. *Journal of Linguistics*, 193: 5–20.

National Reading Panel (2000, April 13), National reading panel reports combination of teaching phonics, word sounds, giving feedback on oral reading most effective way to teach reading. Available: http://www.nationalreadingpanel.org/Press/press_rel_4_13_00_htm.

Navés, T. (2009), Effective content and language integrated learning (CLIL) programmes In: Zarobe, Y. and Catalán, R. *Content and language integrated learning evidence from research in Europe*. Clevedon: Multilingual Matters: 22–40.

Nelde, P. (1987), Language contact means language conflict. In: Mac Eoin, G., Alhqvist, A. and hAodha, C. (eds.), *Third international conference on minority languages*. Clevedon: Multilingual Matters: 33–42.

Nelson, Ch. III, Thomas, K. and Haan, M. (2008), Neural bases of cognitive development. In: Damon, W. and Lerner R. (eds.), *Child and adolescent development. An advanced course*. Hoboken: John Wiley & Sons, Inc.: 19–49.

Nelson, K. (2005), Evolution and development of human memory systems. In: Ellis, B. and Bjorklund, D. (eds.), *Origins of the social mind. Evolutionary psychology and child development*. London: Guildford Press: 354–382.

Nikula, T. (2007), The IRF pattern and space for interaction: Observations on EFL and CLIL classrooms. In: Dalton-Puffer, C. and Smit, U. (eds.), *Empirical perspectives on CLIL classroom discourse*. Frankfurt: Peter Lang: 179–204.

Nunan, D. (1990), The language teacher as decision maker. A case study. In: Brindley, D. (ed.), *The second language curriculum in action*. Sydney: NCELTR: 9–35.

Ochs, E. and Schieffelin, B. (2011), *The handbook of language socialisation*. Oxford: Blackwell Publishing Ltd.

Okuniewska, H. (2007), Impact of second language proficiency on the bilingual Polish-English Stroop task. *Psychology of Language And Communication*, 11(2): 49–63.

Oller, D (1980), The emergence of sounds of speech in infancy. In: Yeni-Komshian, G., Kavanagh, J., Ferguson, A. (eds.), *Child phonology*. New York: Academic Press

Oller, D (2000), *The emergence of speech capacity*. Mahwah: Lawrence Erlbaum.

Osaka, M., Otsuka, Y. and Osaka, N. (2012), Verbal to visual codeswitching improves working memory in older adults: an fMRI study. *Frontiers in Human Neuroscience*, 6: 24–41.

Padilla, A. (ed.), *Acculturation: theory, models and findings*. Boulder: Westview: 9–25.

Papaja, K. (2007), Exploring the use of L1 in CLIL. In: Skowronek, B. (ed.), *Glottodidactica XXXIII*. Poznań: UAM: 129–137.

Parke, R and Burial, R. (2008), Socialization in the family: ethnic and ecological perspectives. In: Damon, W. and Lerner R. (eds.), *Child and adolescent development. An advanced course*. Hoboken NJ: John Wiley & Sons, Inc.: 95–128

Pawlak, M. (2010), Zintegrowane kształcenie przedmiotowo-językowe: założenia, praktyka, perspektywy In: Otwinowska-Kasztelanic, A. and Woynarowska-Sołdan, M. (eds.), *CLIL w polskich szkołach. Od teorii do praktyki*. Warszawa: ORE: 13–25.

Payton, J., Weissberg, R., Durlak, J., Dymnicki, A., Taylor, R., Schellinger, K. and Pachan, M. (2008), *The positive impact of social and emotional learning for kindergarten to eighth-grade students: Findings from three scientific reviews*. Chicago: Collaborative for Academic, Social, and Emotional Learning.

Peal, E. and Lambert, W. (1962), The relation of bilingualism to intelligence. *Psychological Monographs*, 76, 1–23. (Reprinted in R. Gardner and W. Lambert, *Attitudes and motivation in second-language learning*. Rowley, MA: Newbury House).

Peckham, A.D., McHugh, R.K. and Otto, M.W. (2010), A meta-analysis of the magnitude of biased attention in depression. *Depression and anxiety*, 27: 1135–1142.

Pepper, S. C. (1942), *World hypotheses: a study in evidence*. Berkeley: University of California Press.

Pérez-Vidal, C., Juan-Garau, M. and Bel, A. (2008), *A portrait of the young in the new multilingual Spain*. Clevedon: Multilingual Matters.

Pessoa, S., Hendry, H., Donato, R., Tucker, G. R., and Lee, H. (2007), Content-based instruction in the foreign language classroom: A discourse perspective. *Foreign Language Annals*, 40: 102–121.

Piaget, J. and Inhelder, B. (1969), *The psychology of the child*. New York: Basic Books.

Piller, I. and Pavlenko, A. (2006), Bilingualism and gender In: Bhatia, T. and Ritchie, W. (eds.), *The handbook of bilingualism*. Oxford: Blackwell Publishing: 489–511.

Pinker, S. (1994), The language instinct. How the mind creates language. New York: Harper Parennial.

Pinker, S. (2007), *The stuff of thought: language as a window to human nature*. New York: Viking Penguin.

Piotrowski, S. (2011), On the authenticity of communication in foreign language classroom. In: Pawlak, M., Waniek-Klimczak, E. and Majer, J. (eds.), *Speaking and instructed foreign language acquisition*. Bristol: Multilingual Matters: 215–229.

Pishghadam, R. and Mirzaee, A. (2008), English language teaching in postmodern era. *TELL*, 2(7): 89–109.

Platt, J. (1977), A model for polyglossia and multilingualism with special reference to Singapore and Malaysia. *Language in Society*, 6: 361–78.

Plomin, R. (1994), *Genetics and experience: the developmental interplay between nature and nurture*. Newbury Park, CA: Sage.

Podstawa programowa z komentarzami. T.3. *Języki obce w szkole podstawowej, gimnazjum i liceum*. (2009) Warszawa: Ministerstwo Edukacji Narodowej.

Poulin-Dubois, D. and Graham, S. (2007), Cognitive processes in early word learning. In: Hoff, E. and Shatz, M. (eds.), *Blackwell handbook of language development*. Oxford: Blackwell Publishing: 191–211.

Poulisse, N. (1999), *Slips of the tongue: speech errors in first and second language production*. Amsterdam: Benjamins.

Pressley, M (2001), Effective beginning reading instruction: executive summary and paper commissioned by the National Reading Conference. Chicago: National Reading Conference.

Preston M. S. and Lambert W. E. (1969), Interlingual interference in a bilingual version of the Stroop colour-word task. *Journal of Verbal Learning and Verbal Behaviour*, 8: 295–301.

Prodromou, L. (2007), Bumping into creative idiomaticity. *English Today*, 23: 4–25.

Quartz, S.R, & Sejnowski, T.J. (1997), The neural basis of cognitive development: A constructivist manifesto. *Behavioural & Brain Sciences*, 20: 537–596.

Rampton, B. (1995), *Crossing: language and ethnicity among adolescents*. London: Longman.

Richards, J. (2006), *Communicative Language Teaching Today*. Cambridge: CUP.

Rimm-Kaufman, S., LaParo, K., Downer, J. and Pianta, R. (2005), The contribution of classroom setting and quality of instruction to children's behaviour in the kindergarten classroom. *Elementary School Journal*, 105: 377–394.

Roberts, G.1994, Nurse/patient communication within a bilingual health care setting. *British Journal of Nursing*, 3 (2): 60–67.

Roda-Sroka, M. (2010), Analiza refleksji uczniów klas dwujęzycznych na temat nauczania dwujęzycznego. Wnioski z badania przeprowadzonego w grupie licealistów. *Języki Obce w Szkole* 6: 108–110.

Rodriguez-Fornells, A., De Diego Balaguer, R. and Münte, T. F. (2006),, Executive control in bilingual language processing. *Language Learning*, 56: 133–190.

Roelofs, A. (2003), Goal-referenced selection of verbal action: modeling attentional control in the Stroop task. *Psychological Review*, 110 (1): 88–125.

Rogers, T. (2000), Methodology in the new millennium. *English Teaching Forum online*, 28(2) http://exchanges.state.gov/englishteaching/forum/archives.html (accessed 20.08.2012).

Rogers, R. (2002), A critical discourse analysis of special education process. *Anthropology and Education Quarterly* 33 (2): 213–237.

Rogers, R. (ed.) (2004), *An introduction to critical discourse analysis in education*, Mahwah: Lawrence Erlbaum Essociates, xxi-xxv.
Rogers, R. (2008), Critical discourse analysis in education. In: Martin-Jones, M., de Mejía, A., Hornberger, N. (eds.) (2008), *Encyclopaedia of langugae education*. Vol. 3: *Discourse and education* New York: Springer Science: 53–68.
Romaine, S. (1995), *Bilingualism*. Oxford: Blackwell Publishers Ltd.
Rosselli, M., Ardila, A., Santisi, M. N., Arecco Mdel, R., Salvatierra, J., Conde, A. and Lenis, B. (2002), Stroop effect in Spanish-English bilinguals. *Journal of the International Neuropsychological Society*, 8: 819–827.
Rotter, J. (1966), Generalized expectancies for internal versus external control of reinforcement. *Psychological Monographs: General and Applied*, vol. 80 (1): 1–28.
Rubin, K., Bukowski, W., Parker, J. and Bowker, J. (2008), Peer interactions, relationships, and groups. In: Damon, W. and Lerner R. (eds.), *Child and adolescent development. An advanced course*. Hoboken: John Wiley & Sons, Inc.: 141–180.
Ryan, E and Giles, H. (eds.) (1982), *Attitudes towards language variation: social and applied contexts*. London: Edward Arnold.
Rzewuski, E. (2010), Disce puer/puella linguam bantam… reforma językowej polityki oświatowej w Mozambiku. In: Rzewuski, E. (ed.), *Języki, kultury i społeczeństwa Afryki w procesie przemian*. Warszawa: Katedra Języków i Kultur Afryki: 38–109.
Salkind, N. (ed.) (2002), *Child development*. New York: Macmillan Reference USA.
Salthouse, T. (2005), Relations between cognitive abilities and measures of executive functioning. *Neuropsychology*, 19 (4): 532–545.
Savage, J. (2011), *Cross-curricular teaching and learning in the secondary school*. Abingdon: Routledge.
Schneider, W. (2002), Memory development in childhood. In: U. Goswami (ed.), *Blackwell handbook of childhood cognitive development*. London: Blackwell: 236–256.
Schneider, W., Gruber, H., Gold, A., and Opwis, K. (1993), Chess expertise and memory for chess positions in children and adults. *Journal of Experimental Child Psychology*, 56: 328–349.
Schoenfeld, A. (2010), A theory of teaching. In: Preiss, D. and Sternberg, J. (eds.), *Innovations in educational psychology: perspectives on learning, teaching, and human development*. New York: Springer Publishing Company: 241–268.
Schuman, J. (1978), *The pidginization process: a model of second language acquisition*. Rowley: Newbury House.
Seliger, H. and Long, M. (eds.) (1983), *Classroom oriented research in second language acquisition*. Rowley: Newbury House.
Seligman, M.E.P. and Maier, S.F. (1967), Failure to escape traumatic shock. *Journal of Experimental Psychology*, 74: 1–9.
Serra, C. (2007), Assessing CLIL at primary school: a longitudinal study. *International Journal of Bilingual Education and Bilingualism*, 10: 582–602.
Shin, S. (2005), *Developing in two languages*. Clevedon: Multilingual Matters.

Shin, S. and Milroy, L. (2000), Conversational codeswitching among Korean-English bilingual children. *International Journal of Bilingualism*, 4(3): 351–383.
Shmoossi, N. (2004), The effect of teachers' questioning behaviour on EFL classroom interaction: a classroom research study. *The Reading Matrix*, 4 (2): 96–103.
Shultz, T.R. (2007), Connectionist learning and education: applications and challenges. In: McNamara, D. and Trafton, G. (eds.), *Proceedings of the twenty-ninth annual conference of the cognitive science society*. Mahwah, NJ: Lawrence Erlbaum: 1497–1502.
Sidhu, B i Mills, R. (2002), Teachers speak out. In: Mills, R. and Mills, J. (eds.), *Bilingualism in the primary school. A handbook for teachers*. London: Routledge: 129–143.
Sinclair, J. and Coulthard, M. (1975), *Towards an analysis of discourse: the English used by teachers and pupils*. Oxford: Oxford University Press.
Skinner, B. F. (1952), *Science and human behaviour*. London: Collier-Macmillan Ltd.
Skutnabb-Kangas, T. (1981), *Bilingualism or not: the education of minorities*. Clevedon: Multilingual Matters.
Smith, H. (2008), Biculturalism. In: González, J. (ed.), *Encyclopedia of bilingual education*. Thousand Oaks: SAGE Publications Inc.: 65–67.
Smykowski, B. (2000), Podejście rozwojowe do badania form zachowania. In: Brzezińska, A. (ed.), *Wygotski i z Wygotskim w tle*. Toruń: Wydawnictwo Uniwersytetu Mikołaja Kopernika: 137–152.
Soler, E. and Safont Jordà, M. (eds.) (2007), *Intercultural language use and language learning*. Dordrecht: Springer.
Sonuga-Barke, E., Dalen L and Remington B. (2003), Do executive deficits and delay aversion make independent contributions to preschool attention-deficit/hyperactivity disorder symptoms? *Journal of the American Academy of Child & Adolescent Psychiatry*, 42(11): 1335–1342.
Soveri A., Laine M., Hämäläinen H. and Hugdahl K. (2011), Bilingual advantage in focused attention: evidence from the forced-attention dichotic listening paradigm. *Bilingualism: Language and Cognition*, 14: 371–378.
Stern, H. (1992), *Issues and options in language teaching*. Oxford: OUP.
Stiles, J. (1998), The effects of early focal brain injury on lateralization of cognitive function. *Current directions in Psychological Science*, 7: 21–28.
Strauss, S. (2004), Theories of cognitive development and learning and their implications for curriculum development and teaching. In: Moon, B.; Ben-Peretz, M. and Brown, S. (eds.), *Routledge international companion to education*. Routledge: London: 33–50.
Stroop J. R. (1935), Studies of interference in serial verbal reactions. *Journal of Experimental Psychology*, 18: 643–662.
Stubbs, M. (1983), *Language, schools and classrooms*. 2nd ed. London: Methuen.
Stuss, D. and Knight, R. (eds.) (2002), *Principles of frontal lobe function*. London: Oxford University Press.

Sumiya, H. and Healy, A.F. (2004), Phonology in the bilingual Stroop effect. *Memory and Cognition* 32: 752–758.

Swain, M. (1981), Time and timing in bilingual education. *Language Learning*, 31: 1–15.

Swain, M. and R. Johnson (1997), Immersion education: a category within bilingual education. In: Johnson, R. and Swain, M. (eds.), *Immersion education: international perspectives*. Cambridge: CUP: 1–16.

Szpotowicz, M. (2011), Lekcja języka obcego w nauczaniu wczesnoszkolnym. *Języki Obce w Szkole*, 1: 4–11.

Szymańska, M., Stępień, B. and Szreder, M. (2009), *Nowe już w szkole 1*. Warszawa: Nowa Era.

Tatoj, C. (2008), *Raport ewaluacyjny – sekcje dwujęzyczne z językiem hiszpańskim w Polsce*. CODN: Warszawa.

Taubman, D. (1999), Critical pedagogy and the professional development of the NQT'. In: Cole, M. (ed.), *Professional issues for teachers and student teachers*. London: David Fulton.

Taylor, G. and MacKenney, L. (2008), *Improving human learning in the classroom*. Plymouth: Rowman & Littlefield Education.

Tedick, D. and Cammarata, L. (2012), Content and language integration in K-12 contexts: student outcomes, teacher practices, stakeholder perspectives. *Foreign Language Annals*. Summer: 28–53.

Thomas, W.P. and Collier, V.P. (2002), *A national study of school effectiveness for language minority students' long-term academic achievement*. Santa Cruz: Center for Research on Education, Diversity and Excellence.

Thornbury, S. (2002), Training in instructional conversation. In: Trappes-Lomax, H. and Ferguson, G. (eds.), *Language in language teacher education*. Amsterdam: John Benjamins: 95+106.

Thornbury, S., Slade, D. (2007), *Conversation: from description to pedagogy*. Cambridge: CUP.

Tomasello, M. (2008), Acquiring linguistic constructions. In: Damon, W. and Lerner R. (eds.), *Child and adolescent development. An advanced course*. Hoboken: John Wiley & Sons, Inc.: 255–298.

Toohey, K. (2000), *Learning English at school: identity, social relations and classroom practice*. Clevedon: Multilingual Matters.

Toohey, K. (2008), Ethnography and language education. In: King, K. and Hornberger (eds.), *Encyclopedia of language and education*, 2nd edition, vol. 10*: Research methods in language and education*, New York: Springer Science: 177–188.

Tosi, A. (1982), Mother-tongue teaching for the children of migrant. In: Harding-Esch, E. and Riley, P. (2003), *The bilingual family. A handbook for parents*. Cambridge: CUP.

Troyer, A., Graves, R., and Cullum, K. (1994), Executive functioning as a mediator of the relationship between age and episodic memory in healthy aging. *Aging and Cognition*, 1: 45–53.

Tuokko, H., and Hadjistavropoulos, T. (1998), *An assessment guide to geriatric neuropsychology*. Mahwah: Erlbaum.

Turnbull, M., Lapkin, S., and Hart, D. (2001), Grade 3 immersion students' performance in literacy and mathematics: province-wide results from Ontario (1998–99). *Canadian Modern Language Review*, 58: 9–26.

Valdés, G. (1998), The world outside and inside school: language and immigrant children. *Educational Researcher*, 27 (6): 4–18.

Valdés, G. and Figueroa, R.A. (1994), *Bilingualism and testing: a special case of bias*. Norwood: Ablex Publishing.

Valdés-Fallis, G. (1976), Social interaction and code-switching patterns: a case study of Spanish/English alternation. In: Keller G. et al. (eds.), *Bilingualism in the bicentennial and beyond*. New York: Bilingual Press: 209–229.

van Dijk, T. (ed.), (1985), *Handbook of discourse analysis*. Vol. 3: *Discourse and dialogue*. London: Academic Press.

van Dijk, T. (2001), Critical discourse studies. In: Wodak, R., Meyer, M. (eds.), *Methods of critical discourse analysis*. London: Sage: 121–138.

Várkuti, A. (2010), Linguistic benefits of the CLIL approach. *International CLIL Research Journal*, 1: 83–92.

Vázquez, G. (2007), Models of CLIL: an evaluation of its status drawing on the German experience. A critical report on the limits of reality and perspectives. *Revista Española de Lingüística Aplicada*, 1: 95–111.

Walsh, S. (2006), *Investigating Classroom Discourse*. New York: Routledge.

Watson, M. (2002), *Theories of human development*. Chantilly: The Teaching Company.

Watson-Gegeo, K. A. (1997), Classroom ethnography. In: Hornberger N. and Corson D. (eds.), *Encyclopedia of language and education*. Vol. 8: *Research methods in language and education*. Dordrecht: Kluwer: 135–144.

Weinreich, U. (1953), *Languages in contact*. The Hague: Mouton.

Wells, G. (1999), *Dialogic inquiry: towards a sociocultural practice and theory of education*. Cambridge: CUP.

Whittaker, R., Llinares, A., & McCabe, A. (2011), Written discourse development in CLIL at secondary school. *Language Teaching Research*, 15: 343–362.

Wieczorek, A. (2009), *New bingo 1 plus*. Warsaw: PWN.

Wiley, T. (2008), Bilingual education as language policy. In: *Encyclopedia of bilingual education*. Thousand Oaks: SAGE Publications Inc.: 70–74.

Willcutt, E., Doyle, A., Nigg, J., Faraone, S. and Pennington, B. (2005), Validity of the executive function theory of attention-deficit/hyperactivity disorder: A meta-analytic review. *Biological Psychiatry*, 57: 1336–1346.

Winer, G.A. (1980), Class-inclusion reasoning in children: a review of the empirical literature. *Child Development*, 51: 309–328.

Woollard, J. (2010), *Psychology for the classroom: behaviourism*. Abingdon: Routledge.

Wortham, S. (2006), *Early childhood curriculum. Developmental bases for learning and teaching*. Columbus: Pearson Education Ltd.

Wray, A. (1999), Formulaic language in learners and native speakers. *Language Teaching*, 32(4): 213–231.

Wray, A. (2002), *Formulaic language and the lexicon*. Cambridge: CUP.

Ye, Z. and Zhou, X. (2009), Executive control in language processing. *Neuroscientific Biobehaviour Review*, 33: 1168–1177.

Yeni-Komshian, G., Kavanagh, J., Ferguson, A. (eds.) (1980), *Child phonology*. New York: Academic Press.

Young, J. (2000), Boy talk: critical literacy and masculinities. *Reading Research Quarterly*, 35 (3): 312–337.

Zelazo, P. D. and Müller, U. (2011), Executive function in typical and atypical development. In: Goswami, U., *Blackwell handbook of childhood cognitive development*. Malden: Blackwell Publishers Ltd: 574–603.

LIST OF FIGURES

LIST OF TABLES

REVIEWER
Sebastian Piotrowski

EDITOR OF ŁÓDŹ UNIVERSITY PRESS
Elżbieta Marciszewska-Kowalczyk

TYPESETTING
AGENT PR

COVER DESIGN
Łukasz Orzechowski

COVER IMAGE
© *Depositphotos.com/agsandrew*

PRINT AND SETTING
Quick Druk

This publication has been partially financed by the Research Grant for Young Scholars
no. B1411300000519.02